LIVE
DEAD

LIVE DEAD

STUDIES IN THE GRATEFUL DEAD
Nicholas G. Meriwether, series editor

THE
GRATEFUL DEAD,
LIVE RECORDINGS,
and the IDEOLOGY
of LIVENESS

John Brackett

DUKE UNIVERSITY PRESS
Durham & London   2023

Cover design by Matt Tauch
Text design by Courtney Leigh Richardson
Project Editor: Jessica Ryan
Typeset in Warnock Pro and Queens Compressed
by Westchester Publishing Services

Library of Congress Cataloging-in-Publication Data
Names: Brackett, John Lowell, author.
Title: Live Dead : the Grateful Dead, live recordings, and the
ideology of liveness / John L. Brackett.
Other titles: Studies in the Grateful Dead (Duke University Press)
Description: Durham : Duke University Press, 2024. |
Series: Studies in the Grateful Dead | Includes bibliographical
references and index.
Identifiers: LCCN 2023004962 (print)
LCCN 2023004963 (ebook)
ISBN 9781478025481 (paperback)
ISBN 9781478020707 (hardcover)
ISBN 9781478027614 (ebook)
Subjects: LCSH: Grateful Dead (Musical group)—Performances. |
Live sound recordings. | Rock concerts—United States—
History—20th century. | Sound recordings—Pirated editions. |
Rock music—United States—History and criticism. | BISAC:
MUSIC / Genres & Styles / Rock
Classification: LCC ML421.G72 B65 2024 (print) | LCC ML421.
G72 (ebook) | DDC 782.42166092/2—dc23/eng/20230914
LC record available at https://lccn.loc.gov/2023004962
LC ebook record available at https://lccn.loc.gov/2023004963

Cover art: Photo © Jay Blakesberg

For Krisi, Zach, and Noah

In memory of Biggie

Dean, sandwich in hand, stood bowed and jumping before the big phonograph, listening to a wild bop record I had just bought called "The Hunt," with Dexter Gordon and Wardell Gray blowing their tops before a screaming audience that gave the record fantastic frenzied volume.
—Jack Kerouac, *On the Road* (1957)

He listened with fascination to the Victrola and played the same record over and over, whatever it happened to be, as if to test the endurance of a duplicated event.—E. L. Doctorow, *Ragtime* (1975)

Contents

Illustrations

Acknowledgments

Many people have offered suggestions, resources, and, at times, some much-needed perspective as I researched and wrote this book. First, I wish to thank the many anonymous reviewers who read parts (or all) of the manuscript and who provided invaluable comments, pointed criticisms, and insightful questions. Writing about the Grateful Dead can easily spin off in any number of directions, and throughout the review process, I was fortunate to receive valuable feedback, including when to delve deeper and when to pull back. I am especially grateful to Dean Smith and Jessica Ryan at Duke University Press for their support over the past few years as the manuscript continued to take shape. Writing about the Dead can also be very intimidating. There is a vast body of academic, critical, and popular scholarship devoted to the Dead that extends back decades and encompasses a variety of media and formats. As I examined and consulted various print publications, recordings, blogs, and podcasts, I was constantly reminded of (and humbled by) the amount of truly exceptional historical work that has been, and continues to be, carried out by fans of the band. (For just a few examples, I encourage readers to visit and explore sites such as deadsources.blogspot.com and lostlivedead.blogspot.com.) Having worked in and around the discipline of academic musicology for over two decades, I found the dedication and commitment exhibited by the many historians of the Dead truly inspiring.

I am grateful to all the friends and colleagues with whom I have had many spirited conversations and debates throughout the years on all things Dead. I would especially like to acknowledge Bruce Quaglia, who got me thinking (seriously) about the band during my time in Utah so many years ago. I also recall listening to Andy Flory, Shaugn O'Donnell, and Heather Laurel talk about concerts they had attended, noteworthy live recordings, and favorite eras as we walked around the Lower East Side nearly twenty years ago. In 2011, Shaugn and Heather accompanied me to my first Dark Star Orchestra show at Irving Plaza. (It was the fortieth anniversary of the Dead's final concert at the Fillmore East, and DSO were re-creating the setlist from the Dead's performance in 1971. I remember listening to Charlie Miller's tape of the original concert on archive.org in the days leading up to the show.) More recently, while exploring the French Quarter in New Orleans in 2019, Andy Flory encouraged me to visit the Dead Archive in Santa Cruz. Having read his own recent scholarship on the Dead and liveness, I sensed that there was much more to say on the topic, and I made my first research trip to the University of California, Santa Cruz a few months later. I would also like to thank Chris Reali for reading and commenting on early drafts of many chapters. I look forward to regrouping with Chris and Allison Portnow Lathrop as we celebrate the tenth anniversary of the release of our debut album!

My sincere thanks to Barry Barnes for providing me with a copy of Alan Trist's "A Balanced Objective" in preparation for our session at the Popular Culture Association conference in 2021. Along with Barry and Jeff Aulgur, I enjoyed speaking with many other presenters and attendees throughout the conference, including Rebecca Adams. I had communicated with Rebecca via email, and this was the first time we had met "face-to-face" (albeit via Zoom). I would especially like to thank Barry and Rebecca for their dedication and support in encouraging younger generations of fans to study and think about the Dead. I would also like to express my thanks to Eric Mlyn for inviting me to his class on the Grateful Dead at Duke University. I was inspired by the many discussions and interactions I had with students during my visits; I hope more students have the opportunity to take Eric's class.

I enjoyed speaking with Les Kippel about the early tape trading scene in New York City and his interactions with various members of the Dead organization in the 1970s. In the early stages of my research, Theo Cateforis graciously provided me with multiple issues of *Crawdaddy* from his personal library of original rock publications. Jonathan Hiam and Seth Coluzzi provided some welcome (and much-needed) diversions along the way—thanks for the hospitality and fun times!

I also wish to extend my thanks to Nicholas Meriwether. I enjoyed our many conversations over drinks and dinner in Santa Cruz and Davenport. I also want to thank Laura McClanathan Meriwether. I now recognize that Laura's casual reference to Sherry Turkle's book *Evocative Objects* came at an opportune time as I was just beginning to consider the complex meaning(s) of the Dead's live recordings.

I am especially grateful to the archivists and librarians at the Special Collections and Archives at the University of California, Santa Cruz. In particular, Luisa Haddad was incredibly helpful (and remarkably patient) in responding to all my emails and requests during my research visits to the Grateful Dead Archive. I would also like to thank Toni and Caroline (and Cleo) for sharing their homes with me during my trips to Santa Cruz.

Finally, I would like to thank Krisi, Zach, and Noah for their inspiration, support, humor, and (above all) indulgence. While researching and writing the book, I have experienced a tremendous amount of pride as Noah graduated from high school and set off for college (and became a *serious* shredder), Zach graduated from college and entered graduate school (and became a master of shuffle grooves), and my wife completed her PhD coursework and began work on her dissertation. Having devoted so much attention to thinking and writing about the Dead over the past three years, I look forward to spending some quality time among the living.

Introduction

BECOMING LIVE

In 2011, a recording of a live performance by the rock band the Grateful Dead was added to the National Recording Registry, a popular catalog maintained by the Library of Congress of recordings deemed "culturally, historically or aesthetically significant."[1] The recording documents the Dead's concert at Barton Hall on the campus of Cornell University in Ithaca, New York, on May 8, 1977. The concert was recorded by Betty Cantor-Jackson, an engineer and producer who had worked on some of the band's most acclaimed commercial releases, including *Live/Dead* (a live album released in 1969) and *Workingman's Dead* (a studio recording released in 1970). Although Cantor-Jackson is not identified, the press release announcing the recording's selection to the registry noted that her "soundboard recording of this show has achieved almost mythic status among 'Deadhead' tape traders because of its excellent sound quality and early accessibility, as well as its musical performances."[2]

To be sure, members of the Grateful Dead's touring crew (like Cantor-Jackson) had been recording the band's concerts since the late 1960s. At the same time, continuing a tradition that can be traced back to the early 1970s, some fans in the audience also taped the concert on equipment that had been smuggled into Barton Hall. While some of these amateur tapers made recordings for their own use and enjoyment, others were eager to share their tapes. Within weeks, recordings of the band's concert at Cornell were being duplicated and traded among a growing community of Deadhead tape collectors throughout the country and around the world.

Cantor-Jackson's recording is one of thousands of concert recordings that were produced by the Grateful Dead and their fans—the "Deadheads"—over the course of the band's thirty-year career. From 1965 until the death of founding member Jerry Garcia in 1995, the Grateful Dead (composed of different lineups) played more than twenty-three hundred concerts. A large percentage of those concerts were recorded by the band and/or their fans on a variety of audio and video formats. Presently, thousands of noncommercial recordings of the Grateful Dead can be accessed online at archive.org, including multiple recordings of the band's concert from May 8, 1977.[3]

Fans who wish to learn more about the concert at Cornell can also consult John Dwork's review in the second volume of the *Deadhead's Taping Compendium*, a massive three-volume set chronicling numerous live recordings of the Grateful Dead.[4] In his review, Dwork acknowledges that the band played exceptionally well on May 8, a fact that is documented by the recordings. Employing a lingo and a rhetoric that would be familiar to seasoned Deadheads, Dwork suggests, however, that "despite the lofty pinnacles reached throughout the evening, 5/8/77 simply does not compare *as a whole show* with other 'quintessential' performances such as 2/13/70."[5]

The tone of the review shifts as Dwork begins to wax philosophical about (in quick succession) the social, cerebral, spiritual, technological, erotic, narcotic, and transcendental qualities of the Dead's live recordings. He admits that "listening to the tapes of this show [5/8/77] got me thinking about the act of listening to recorded music." Specifically, Dwork recognizes how:

> For many Deadheads, tapes are much more than social lubricant [*sic*]. They are repositories of information that, because of our spiritual and intellectual link to this form, have the power to alter consciousness. As this information plays through our stereos, it acts as a moving thread upon which our emotional focus travels. When we hear the music of 5/8/77—particularly the second set—we recognize it, by comparison to other performances, as being unusually inspirational. During the exultant climax of this show's "Morning Dew," when Jerry [Garcia] strums harder and longer than on any other "Dew" in circulation, we Deadheads are often lifted to an emotional height higher, or as high, as any we have achieved while listening to recorded music. It is a remarkable synergist, a vehicle for attaining deep joy. How lucky we are to have such catalysts in our lives.[6]

In his examination of the "music, the myth, and the magnificence" of *Cornell '77*, Peter Conners observes how live recordings of May 8 contributed to an even more expansive mythology of the concert as being, perhaps, one of the

Dead's best live shows. Conners notes how "within the Deadhead community" live concert recordings were "traded, debated, celebrated, and, in the case of the Grateful Dead's show at Cornell University on May 8, 1977, consecrated." "If it wasn't for tapers and tape trading networks," Conners declares, "it is unlikely that [the Cornell concert] would have risen to the top of the twenty-three-hundred-plus shows the Grateful Dead performed [and] to be inducted, thirty-six years later, into the Library of Congress National Recording Registry."[7]

The tapes produced by fans and members of the Dead's crew constitute an enormous archive of live concert recordings, many of which are still "traded, debated, celebrated, and . . . consecrated." The band has also produced numerous commercial live concert recordings, many of which figure prominently in the history and the mythology of the Grateful Dead. Without a doubt, much of the popular, scholarly, and critical discourse devoted to the Dead has been shaped and influenced by the sounds documented on a variety of live recordings. But how did live recordings come to assume such a privileged position in the historiography of the Dead? Why do live recordings of the Grateful Dead mean so much to so many people? Why do live recordings even matter at all?

In what follows, I consider live recordings within (what I will refer to as) an ideology of musical liveness. As the critical and historical foundation for the chapters that follow, I will begin by considering how live recordings have commonly been critiqued and evaluated by critics, fans, and scholars. Much of this introduction is devoted to excavating and uncovering the roots of an ideology of musical liveness that emerged in the United States in the late 1920s. As I will suggest, it was during this time that a rhetorical discourse was being cultivated that served to elevate the experience of music made in the presence of "living musicians" over that of recorded, or "canned," music. More specifically, I describe how this discourse of liveness was developed in response to the economic and professional hardships that confronted many musicians following the rise of recorded sound and, in particular, the introduction of synchronized sound in theaters.

Finally, I will consider how the emergence of the live record as a marketable commodity beginning in the 1950s served to reassert the primacy of live performance in the imagination of consumers. By the middle of the 1960s, commercial live recordings offered musicians and record companies the opportunity to make a real profit on the perceived value and the imagined worth of "liveness," an idea that was now being packaged and sold to a new generation of record buyers and audiences at the dawn of the rock era.

On Live Records

Although we may cringe at his undeniably insensitive metaphor, many readers will understand what acclaimed pianist and essayist Alfred Brendel intended when he referred to live recordings as a "stepchild." Making "A Case for Live Recordings," Brendel observed that "standing between the two officially canonized sources of musical experience, concert performance and studio recording, the recorded concert has had less than its due."[8] Although Brendel considers performances and recordings associated with the tradition of "classical music," his observations on the perceived status of live recordings apply to a host of other musical styles and traditions. Indeed, among critics, fans, and scholars of rock music, live records are often debated and evaluated according to two ("officially canonized") ways of experiencing music: (1) the experience of the live performance event (i.e., the concert), and (2) the experience of listening to the performer's (often more familiar) studio records. When considered in relation to either or both of these experiences, live rock records typically come up short.

In his book *Rhythm and Noise*, Theodore Gracyk examines many of the peculiar ontologies and conceptual paradoxes represented by live records. Surveying the recorded history of rock music beginning in the mid-1960s, Gracyk notes that "live recordings are the one place where recorded rock has a significant documentary function."[9] However, he explains, as material objects that purportedly serve to document prior live musical events, most commercial "live recordings do not sound much like the originating event."[10] As he acknowledges, live records create an idealized listening experience that "does not belong to any particular seat in the [original] concert space."[11] Furthermore, the idealized listening location suggested by many live recordings (a location imagined, perhaps, somewhere onstage with the musicians or alongside the mixing engineer at the soundboard) is, in most cases, the product of numerous editing decisions made in postproduction. Overdubbing, panning, equalization, and the addition of effects such as reverb and compression enable producers, engineers, and performers to create an audio image of the music that is heard "not as it sounds coming from the speakers in the concert hall or arena" but, instead, "as if one is wearing special headphones whose sound is carefully mixed for clarity and balance."[12] Given the various technological and perspectival changes that have taken place in the transformation from live concert event to reproducible live concert recording, it may not be entirely clear exactly what (if anything) is being documented on live records.

Regarding the status of live recordings in comparison to an artist's studio records, Gracyk wonders if "given a choice between any band's best studio work and their live recordings, how often would we choose the live recording over the studio? Would anyone choose *The Beatles at the Hollywood Bowl* (1977) over any of their studio albums? Would any Led Zeppelin fan choose *The Song Remains the Same* (1976) over any of their first five studio albums?"[13] Of course, Gracyk is not *really* asking his readers (à la a sort of *Desert Island Discs* scenario) to "choose" among records. Instead, the rhetorical structure of Gracyk's thought experiment and the tone of feigned incredulity assumes that readers share his belief that studio recordings constitute rock's "primary documents." "In rock," he argues, "the musical work is less typically a song than an arrangement of recorded sounds."[14] In Gracyk's opinion, the authentic "musical work" in the rock tradition is represented by a performer's or group's studio recordings, recordings on which, as he describes, "every sound is now treated as deliberate and therefore relevant."[15] Of course, Gracyk's rock aesthetic adapts many of the well-worn ideals of the "musical artwork" as developed by nineteenth-century critics, composers, and philosophers of the German Idealist tradition.[16] It is against the background of a Romantic philosophy of art and an associated set of musical values (originally developed, it should be remembered, in relation to the "classical tradition") that Gracyk can confidently assert that, "apart from *Frampton Comes Alive!* (1976) and *Cheap Trick at Budokan* (1979), one is hard-pressed to think of a rock musician whose live recordings are better received by fans and critics than their studio confections."[17]

Gracyk notes that, because the "Grateful Dead are the exception that proves the rule," they deserve special comment, and that he will "turn to them in a moment." To be sure, I will return to what he has to say about the Dead and "record consciousness" in chapter 1. For now, however, I would argue that, far from being the "rule," Gracyk's aesthetic ideology is exceptional among the many discursive frameworks that have developed around live rock records.[18] Consider, for example, Lester Bangs's well-known review of *Get Yer Ya-Ya's Out*, a live album by the Rolling Stones that was released in 1970.[19] Recognized as one of the most colorful and iconoclastic music critics of the era, Bangs concludes his review by explaining that, while "it's still too soon to tell," he is "beginning to think [that] *Ya-Ya's* just might be the best album [the Rolling Stones] ever made. I have no doubt that it's the best rock concert ever put on record."

Thumbing his nose at Gracyk's aesthetic, Bangs even prefers the live versions of songs featured on *Get Yer Ya-Ya's Out* over the band's studio recordings. As Bangs explains, "I don't think there's a song on *Ya-Ya's* where the Stones didn't cut their original studio jobs." The live version of "Jumpin' Jack

Flash" has "a certain fierce precision which the studio single lacked and which makes the latter sound almost plodding by comparison." Similarly, the live version of "Sympathy for the Devil" "beats the rather cut-and-dried rendition on [the studio album] *Beggar's Banquet* all hollow." Bangs also suggests that the band's live performances of cover songs are better than the versions as performed and recorded by the original artists! Regarding the live version of "Little Queenie," for example, he admits, "I even think that this is one of those rare instances . . . where they cut Chuck Berry with one of his own songs."

Bangs certainly understands the distinction between a live recording conceived *as* a document and a live recording that stands for, or *constructs*, an experience of liveness. The live performances featured on *Get Yer Ya's Out* were recorded at various concerts in late 1969 during the band's tour of the United States. Like most commercially produced live albums of the era, many of the vocal performances and instrumental tracks were overdubbed in postproduction. Still, Bangs notes that, as the representation of an *idealized* live event, the record is "[more] than just the soundtrack for a Rolling Stones concert, it's a truly inspired session, [and] as intimate an experience as sitting in while the Stones jam for sheer joy in the basement."

At the same time, Bangs inverts the documentary perspective and considers how *Get Yer Ya's Out* might offer a better, perhaps even a more authentic, representation of the original concert experience. Bangs recalls what it was like to be in the audience at that time and thinking, "There they were in the flesh, the *Rolling Stones*, [the] ultimate personification of all our notions and fantasies and hopes for rock and roll, and we were enthralled." However, he continues:

> the nagging question that remained was whether the show we had seen was really that brilliant, or if we had not been to some degree set up, [P]avlov'd by years of absence and rock scribes and 45 minute delays into a kind of injection delirium in which a show which was perfectly ordinary in terms of what the Stones might have been capable of would seem like some ultimate rock apocalypse. Sure, the Stones put on what was almost undoubtedly the best show of the year, but did that say more about their own involvement or about the almost uniform lameness of the competition?

As to the last question, Bangs remarks that "some folks never did decide." Bangs, however, *did* decide, and in his opinion, *Get Yer Ya's Out* authenticates and verifies the many "notions and fantasies and hopes" that were indelibly linked to his (and other people's) experiences and expectations.

Even outside of the rock tradition, early reviews reveal how critics struggled with the various ontological and phenomenological complexities presented by recordings that were marketed and promoted as "live." Released on Columbia Records in 1950, Benny Goodman's *The Famous 1938 Carnegie Hall Jazz Concert* can arguably be considered the first critically and commercially successful live album to be released by a major label. In his glowing review in *Metronome,* Barry Ulanov, who also attended the original concert, considers Goodman's recording from a documentary perspective, noting how "one of the delightful sections of the bill, as we remember and the records confirm, was the 20-year survey of jazz," a segment of the concert that chronicled the development of jazz beginning with Dixieland up to the modern swing bands of the late 1930s.[20] Ulanov also notes that "one of the few weak moments of the evening as we remember and the records confirm, was the *Honeysuckle Rose* Jam Session, which, in spite of some fine moments by Lester Young, Johnny Hodges, and Benny, doesn't do much but rehearse some all too familiar Swing inanities."

Whereas in both of these instances the live recordings "confirm" his memories of the event, Ulanov also acknowledges the ability of *The Famous 1938 Carnegie Hall Jazz Concert* to influence his recollection of specific performances. Recalling Bangs (if only in substance and not necessarily style), the recordings convince Ulanov that the "high spot of the evening was clearly [pianist] Jess Stacy's five-chorus solo on the last scheduled number on the program, 'Sing, Sing, Sing,' though those of us who were there that night didn't realize it." "In recorded retrospect," Ulanov observes, "those delicate measures stand way out, as Jess makes his simple, developed way through as lovely a piece of construction as Swing ever offered."

Rapidly changing tastes in popular music in the years following World War II meant that, when the album was released in 1950, the sounds that appeared on *The Famous 1938 Carnegie Hall Jazz Concert* were heard as if they were emanating from another era. As the sounds of the big bands began to fade away, Ulanov considers Goodman's record to be the "most meaningful memento possible" of the swing era. He imagines that "one can return in spirit to the memorable evenings of Swing, and in such records as these, in the flesh." Writing in the *American Record Guide,* Enzo Archetti describes Goodman's record as "one of the authentic documents in American musical history, a verbatim report, in the accents of those who were present on 'The Night of January 16, 1938.'" "Columbia deserves an Oscar," Archetti continues, "for having made available this memorable history-making concert."[21]

For other contemporary reviewers—better described, perhaps, as "modernists," in contrast to the musically conservative "moldy figs"—Goodman's live record was a document that represented both the crass commercialism and the artistic, racial, and financial inequities of the swing era.[22] In his review in *Downbeat*, Michael Levin admits that, "as a historical index, this album is a valuable possession." "But by and large," he continues, "its freneticisms [sic] have a valid part only in the frame of reference in which they were created: the big-money aping of the great middle-30's Negro swing bands by Goodman, [Artie] Shaw, [Glenn] Miller, and all the rest."[23]

Catherine Tackley has described how, on its release in 1950, Goodman's record and the original 1938 concert were "implicitly canonized within the interlinked dimensions of the 'jazz tradition,' a developmental lineage of jazz and the history of jazz recording."[24] Rereleases of Goodman's record reaffirm the significance of both the original concert in the historiography of jazz and the live recording as a historical document. To commemorate the fortieth anniversary of the concert, Columbia rereleased *The Famous 1938 Carnegie Hall Jazz Concert* in 1977 under a different title: *Benny Goodman Live at Carnegie Hall*. On the one hand, the new title may have reflected the opinion of some Columbia executives and most jazz aficionados that the original title was, at that point in the history of jazz, redundant. On the other hand, Tackley recognizes that the name change also serves to foreground a quality of "'liveness' as a defining feature of the recording," a feature that, in her words, "could now be understood in the context of a longer history of live recording."[25]

Tackley's reference to a quality of "liveness" is noteworthy for, as I detail in the next section, a general ideology of musical liveness already existed when Goodman's album was released in 1950. In what follows, I examine how the ideology of liveness that was promoted throughout the United States and North America beginning in the late 1920s emphasized the artistic, aesthetic, and cultural value of musical performances experienced live ("in the flesh") over recordings ("canned music"). More than just an aesthetic theory of live performance, the nascent ideology of musical liveness that emerged at the dawn of the Great Depression reflected the fears and anxieties that many professional musicians were experiencing during a time of rapid technological development, economic uncertainty, and cultural transformation.

Of Robots, Records, and Revenue: The Formation of an Ideology of Musical Liveness

In his article "Liveness and the Grateful Dead," musicologist Andrew Flory considers "liveness" as an "*attitude* toward artistic expression," as a "*lens* through which to understand the scene that the Dead helped to pioneer," and as a "*manner* of expressing rock music during and after psychedelia that relied more on live performance practice than [on] studio-oriented approaches."[26] Variously described as an "attitude," a "lens," and a "manner" of musical expression, "liveness" functions as a malleable critical heuristic that Flory invokes while considering various facets of the music and culture of the Grateful Dead.

Flory recognizes how a vaguely defined sense of liveness has shaped the history and reputation of the band. The Dead, he explains, "have always been known as a band [to experience] in the flesh, a group to see in a live environment."[27] Having acknowledged what is, arguably, the foundational myth of the Grateful Dead, Flory's article rehearses an idea (and an ideal) that has been associated with the band for over half a century. Like much of the popular, critical, and scholarly discourse devoted to the band, Flory's article assumes that the concepts of "live" and/or "liveness" are already meaningful within the community, culture, and historiography of the Grateful Dead. But how did this happen? How and why did a body of conventional wisdom, a discourse of liveness, develop around the Grateful Dead? On a more fundamental level, why does the concept of "liveness" even matter at all?

As John Durham Peters has remarked, before the invention of the phonograph in 1877, "all sounds died."[28] One might infer, therefore, that prior to the invention of recording and reproduction technologies, all music created by performers and heard by audiences was experienced live. While such an observation is seemingly obvious, it is not trivial. It is important to remember that, even before such technologies were introduced, nobody would have used the word "live" to describe a musical performance featuring "living" musicians playing in the presence of a "living" audience. And why would they? "Live" compared to—what?

But while technologies such as Edison's phonograph provided the material conditions necessary for an ontology of "live" to form, the experience of "musical liveness" describes a critical self-awareness of one's relation to recorded sound. Clearly, recordings offered audiences a new way of experiencing music, one that was not bound by traditional performance spaces and that did not even require the presence of performers. Philip Auslander has identified three characteristics associated with an early conception of liveness (what he calls "classic" liveness): (1) the "physical co-presence of performers and audience," (2) the "temporal simultaneity of production and reception," and (3) the ability to create a shared "experience in the moment" for both performers and audience.[29] By the early decades of the twentieth century, audiences would have certainly recognized the ontological distinctions between, on the one hand, the experience of music as reproduced on recordings and, on the other hand, the experience of music as performed live. The vague outlines of a sense of liveness would begin to take shape, therefore, as audiences became cognizant of (and adapted to) the contrasting spatiotemporal characteristics and experiential qualities offered by traditional forms of musicking (i.e., live performances) and those offered by recordings.

It was not until the 1930s, however, that the term "live" first appeared in print to refer to musical performances that were experienced "in the flesh."[30] As the term gradually entered the popular lexicon, Sarah Thornton has examined how, in an effort to counteract dwindling job opportunities for professional musicians after World War II, the Musicians' Union in Britain developed a public relations campaign to promote the cultural value and aesthetic worth of "live music."[31] As she has observed, the newly developed phrase "live music" "gave positive valuation to and became generic for performed music."[32] Thornton explains how, as part of the union's campaign to "convince the community of the essential human value of live performance," live music was promoted as the "truth of music, the seeds of genuine culture."[33] Furthermore, she considers how the term "live" was wielded to affirm that musical "performance was not obsolete or exhausted, but full of energy and potential."[34] In contrast to live music, recorded music was depicted as "dead, a decapitated 'music without musicians'" and as "false prophets of pseudo-culture."[35] As described by Thornton, it was during this time that the outlines of an ideology of liveness began to emerge as the term "live" "accumulated connotations which took it beyond the denotative meaning of performance" and had, in her words, "soaked up the aesthetic and ethical connotations of life-versus-death, human-versus-mechanical, creative-versus-imitative."[36]

The seeds of the ideology of liveness that Thornton locates in Britain at midcentury were planted a few decades earlier in the United States. By the end of the 1920s, the rise of "talkies" contributed to massive job losses for the many musicians who worked in theaters throughout the country. On October 28, 1929, an alarming headline on the front page of *Film Daily* announced that approximately "7,000 of 25,000 theater musicians" were "jobless."[37] These unemployment figures were provided by Joseph N. Weber, the president of the American Federation of Musicians (AFM), the largest union of professional musicians in North America. Weber acknowledged that, following the introduction of synchronized sound technologies in motion pictures, AFM musicians would continue to lose jobs as "talkies" became more popular with audiences and theater owners.[38]

But just as Weber decried the professional and personal indignities that musicians faced in the age of mechanical reproduction, he also noted that a "great cultural calamity awaits the United States if its citizens allow one industry to force it into the acceptance of flat, savorless, mechanical music."[39] In an effort to rally support for professional musicians, Weber announced the launch of a public relations campaign that, in his words, was designed to "sell the public the value of manual music as contrasted with mechanical music."[40]

The same day that Weber was quoted in *Film Daily*, an advertisement titled "The Robot as an Entertainer" appeared in newspapers throughout the United States (figure I.1). Featuring a vivid illustration of a mechanical man struggling to play a harp, the ad details the methodical "dehumanizing of the theatre." Echoing Weber's remarks, the ad warns of an impending "cultural calamity" as audiences who had ever known and experienced "Real Music" created by living performers grew accustomed to the "monotony of Mechanical Music." Despite the remarkable technological and economic advantages offered by synchronized sound, and "however perfect reproduced music may be made," the text asserts that "canned music" would "always fall short of establishing a spiritual contact between performer and listener."[41]

Any sympathy that the advertisement may have elicited among the general public was probably forgotten by the next day as news of yet another major loss on Wall Street spread across the nation. Despite being upstaged by the events of "Black Tuesday," Weber and the AFM remained committed to their campaign, and over the next year and a half, the federation spent over a million dollars for advertising space in more than eight hundred newspapers and many popular magazines.[42] Between 1929 and 1931, the AFM produced numerous ads that implored readers to support "Real Music" performed by "flesh and blood artists" while warning of the myriad deleterious effects of canned music on the aesthetic sensibilities of American audiences and the emerging cultural prestige of the nation. Alongside the dramatic texts and the dynamic graphic illustrations by the Mexican American artist Leon Helguera, the AFM's ads extolled readers to join the "Music Defense League." By clipping out a portion of the ad and mailing it to the AFM's offices in New York City, audiences were encouraged to express their opposition "to the elimination of Living Music from the Theatre."

Although it is doubtful that any jobs were saved, the AFM's ad campaign did succeed in promoting and popularizing many modern ideas regarding the inherent value and intrinsic worth of live musical performance. Moreover, the symbolic associations and discursive meanings that Thornton identifies with the "aesthetic and ethical" connotations of liveness were promoted as part of the AFM's campaign to "sell the public the value of manual music." In what follows, I consider how the distinctive images and (melo)dramatic

texts of the AFM's ads promoted an idealized understanding of live musical performance according to the set of oppositions identified by Thornton, beginning with "human-versus-mechanical."

Contemporary audiences were almost certainly familiar with phrases such as "mechanical music" or "canned music" as pejorative descriptions of musical recordings. In 1906, John Philip Sousa, the renowned composer and conductor, helped to popularize the phrases in his essay "The Menace of Mechanical Music," a spirited defense of composers' rights and a vigorous critique of contemporary copyright laws.[43] The image of the robot was of a more recent vintage, having been introduced to theater audiences by the Czechoslovakian playwright Karel Čapek in 1921 in his play, *R.U.R. (Rossum's Universal Robots). R.U.R.* recounts how an army of mechanical laborers (the titular "robots," a neologism coined by Čapek and his brother) assume control over their masters and, after wiping out most of humankind, take over the world. Garnering widespread media attention following successful runs of *R.U.R.* in New York, Chicago, and Los Angeles in 1923, the nefarious image of the robot quickly entered the popular imagination.

Between 1929 and 1931, the robot, once a familiar foe from the theater, now represented a threat to a vital element of the theatrical experience: the music. As represented in Helguera's illustrations for the AFM's ads, the robot came to symbolize both the artistic limitations of recorded music and the threat to labor posed by the introduction of synchronized sound in theaters. Throughout the ad campaign, musical recordings are variously derided as "canned music," a mechanical form of music that is reflected in the figure of the robot as a type of "mechanical man." As part of the "human-versus-mechanical" dualism that was promoted by the ads, audiences were learning to appreciate the essential humanity of performances made by "living musicians" over the lifeless, mechanized reproductions of canned music. By linking recorded music with robots, the ads encouraged readers to consider recordings as inherently inferior to "real music" made by "flesh-and-blood" musicians.

In an ad titled "The Serenade Mechanistic," an illustration of a troubadour singing and playing a guitar is counterpointed against the image of a robot (also wearing a cowboy hat and poncho) emitting strained vocal tones and beating a spoon against a frying pan (the phrase "Canned Music in Theatres" appears on the pan). The superiority of "living music" is made clear in the text, where readers are told that the "troubadour had a great advantage over the Robot, for the Robot can't be gay any more than he could be sad or sentimental." "And where there is no feeling, no emotional capacity," the text continues, "there can be no music."[44] Similarly, the ad "The Robot Sings of Love" (reproduced in figure I.2) asserts that music "is an emotional art" by which *"feeling* may be translated into all tongues." "The Robot," the ad continues, "having no capacity for feeling cannot produce music in a true sense."[45]

The connotations that were accruing around the concepts of the "human" and the "mechanical" were intertwined with another dichotomy that Sarah Thornton has identified with the ideology of liveness, that of the "creative"

versus the "imitative." Many of the symbolic meanings that were developing around these notions are represented in the text and imagery of the ad titled "My Next Imita-a-ashun" (figure I.3).[46] The stylized spelling of the title suggests the sound of a record skipping, a negative assessment of the manufacturing quality of contemporary recordings and a reminder of the mechanical limitations of canned music. In Helguera's accompanying illustration, the specter of "Canned Music in Theatres" is once again represented by a robot, now attempting to play a violin. The robot is controlled by the figure of the theater owner, who acts as a ventriloquist. (The caption "Very Good, Eddy!" is most likely a reference to the well-known ventriloquist Edgar Bergen.) While controlling canned music with one hand, the theater owner uses the other to

FIGURE I.3. AFM advertisement, "My Next Imita-a-ashun" (*Austin Statesman*, October 13, 1930, 3)

push aside the figure of the Muse.[47] The implication is clear: the "Living Art of Music" (as represented by the Muse) is in peril as theater owners continue to replace performing musicians with cheap, inferior imitations offered by canned music.

Of course, the image of the theater owner—with his "healthy" physique, tailored suit (including a vest emblazoned with dollar signs), and impeccable grooming (note the "English" handlebar mustache and heavily greased hair parted down the middle)—was understood then, as now, as a graphic caricature associated with the figure of the "greedy boss," the "businessman," or, more generally, "management." The many textual and symbolic associations in the ad serve as powerful reminders that the ideology of musical liveness promoted by the AFM was motivated by massive unemployment and the very real labor concerns facing tens of thousands of musicians. As part of the creative-versus-imitative binary that was being developed around live and canned music, the AFM's ad campaign stressed the forms of labor (i.e., the *work*) that was required in the creation and performance of music in the age of synchronized sound. In an ad titled "Is Art to Have a Tyrant?," for instance, readers are reminded that, although the "Robot can make no music of himself, he can and does arrest the efforts of those who can. Manners mean nothing to this monstrous offspring of modern industrialism, as IT crowds Living Music out of the theatre spotlight."[48]

Alongside the pervasive antimodernist rhetoric of the ads, the ideology of musical liveness that was being promoted by the AFM's campaign emphasized the "aesthetic and ethical connotations of life-versus-death" as described by Thornton. Beginning with "The Robot as an Entertainer," the ads stress that "Real Music" (also characterized as "Good Music") is a form of "living music" created by "flesh and blood" artists. As described in the text of "The Robot as an Entertainer" (see figure I.1), machines were not artists and, while they were useful in saving "Men and Women from ignoble and soulless labor," were unable to perform "tasks that are only well done by the hands and hearts of gifted humans." By its very nature, therefore, mechanical music "must always fall short of establishing a spiritual contact between performer and listener."[49]

As with most of the AFM's ads, the text to "The Robot as an Entertainer" sentimentalizes the manner by which audiences experienced music before the invention of the phonograph. The text accompanying the ad "Music? A Picture No *Robot* Can Paint!" proclaims that the "intelligent theatre goer enjoys the thrill of the artist's presence, and the feeling that his presence, too, is felt."[50] In the presence of living performers, the audience is a "participant in the event—a critic of the performance, empowered to reward excellence and reprove fault." In contrast to the mindless repetition offered by mechanical music, "Living Music" manifests a sense of "drama in the artist's struggle to please and in the emotional response of the audience." According to the ideology that was being promoted in the ads, it is the shared emotional (and physical) experience among musicians and audiences that distinguishes "Living Music" from its mechanical imposter. "Life-glamour-excitement are fundamental requirements of the theatre," the ad states. Formerly, "music supplied this life, this human contact for the motion picture theatre until the coming of canned music."

As with "life," the image of "death" assumed a variety of symbolic meanings in the AFM's campaign. Of course, all the ads underscore the threat that recorded music posed to the livelihoods of professional musicians. At the same

"O Fairest Flower!
No Sooner Blown but Blasted!"

GOOD MUSIC in our country has grown to a glorious blossoming. American orchestras, American musicians now rank with the finest in the world. Shall we *continue* to nurture and cherish this beautiful flower, or shall we let it dwindle and die under blighting **Canned** Music poured out by mechanical Robots?

Which do *you* prefer for the money you pay at the theatre box office? The stirring performance of *Living* Music played and felt by flesh-and-blood musicians, or a strident din from the throat of a heartless piece of machinery? Shall it be glamor or clamor?

Millions of men and women who love *real* music are demanding that it shall *not* be blighted . . . demanding that they shall *not* be deprived of enjoy-

ment to which they're entitled. These millions are giving force to their demands by enrolling in the Music Defense League. **You** can swell this chorus of protest by mailing this coupon today. Do it!

AMERICAN FEDERATION OF MUSICIANS
1440 Broadway, New York, N. Y.

Gentlemen: Without further obligation on my part, please enroll my name in the Music Defense League as one who is opposed to the elimination of Living Music from the Theatre.

Name ....

Address ....

City.. State.................

THE AMERICAN
FEDERATION OF MUSICIANS
(Comprising 140,000 professional musicians in the United States and Canada)
JOSEPH N. WEBER, President, 1440 Broadway, New York, N. Y.

time, the campaign also suggested that the rise of recorded sound in theaters would lead to the death of musical culture in the United States. The ad "O Fairest Flower! No Sooner Blown but Blasted!" vividly details the uncertain future of "living music" in the United States (figure I.4).[51] Appearing almost a year after the collapse of the national economy, the ad appeals to the financial concerns faced by many Americans. "Which do *you* prefer for the money you pay at the theatre box office?" the text asks. "The stirring performance of *Living* Music played and felt by flesh-and-blood musicians, or a strident din from the throat of a heartless piece of machinery?" As emphasized in the text and the accompanying illustration, "canned music in theatres" (represented by a ruralized robot wearing overalls and a straw hat) threatens the survival of "American Musical Culture." "Good music in our country has grown to a glorious blossoming," the text boasts. In fact, "American orchestras" and "American musicians now rank with the finest in the world. Shall we *continue* to nurture and cherish this beautiful flower, or shall we let it dwindle and die under blighting *Canned* Music poured out by mechanical Robots?"[52]

Along with saving "American Musical Culture," the AFM was committed to preserving a modicum of the prestige that performing musicians had enjoyed within what Richard Middleton has described as the "bourgeois concert form." The introduction of canned music in theaters threatened to overturn the power dynamics of the traditional concert experience, an experience that, as Middleton has explained, had evolved to "act as a means of *limiting* music, in time and space" and of "*framing* sound stimuli in a clear producer-consumer spatial hierarchy and an equally clear transmitter-receiver communicative chain."[53] To be sure, the text and images of the AFM's advertisements emphasize the familiar "transmitter-receiver" relationship that had previously existed among musicians and an audience, a relationship, the ads argued, that established a "communicative chain" which, in turn, enabled a form of "spiritual contact." Following the rise of canned music, however, the role of performing musicians within this "producer-consumer spatial hierarchy" was upended as recordings freed audiences from the temporal and spatial boundaries that had traditionally been associated with the (live) experience of music.

According to the ideology of musical liveness that was being promoted by the AFM's campaign, "living music" was imagined as a fundamentally human form of artistic communication whereby emotions and feelings could be shared among performers and an audience. In the absence of living performers, "canned music," it was argued, was unable to facilitate this type of "spiritual contact" and was depicted as an inferior musical experience that threatened the professional livelihoods of living musicians, the future of American musical culture, and the bourgeois conventions of the concert hall.

In an effort to elevate the status of "living music" (and ultimately preserve jobs for performing musicians), the AFM's ad campaign posited a metaphysical element of the live performance experience that resembles what Walter Benjamin would later describe as the "aura" of a work of art. Much like Benjamin's formulation of the aura, the notion of "spiritual contact" serves to authenticate "living music" as "True Music" and, therefore, as a form of "true art"; "spiritual contact" accords value and meaning to the "uniqueness"—the authenticity—of a live musical performance. As part of the AFM's campaign, "living music" was imagined as the authentic manner of experiencing music; recordings, by contrast, offered an ersatz musical experience and were only capable, as Benjamin recognized, of extracting "sameness even from what is unique."[54]

Just as the invention of sound recording and reproduction technologies laid the foundation for an ideology of liveness to develop, those same technologies also precipitated new ways of conceiving of the "work of art." Jonathan Sterne has reminded us that, much like the formulation of "spiritual contact," the "very construct of [Benjamin's] aura is, by and large, retroactive, something that is an artifact of reproducibility, rather than a side effect or an inherent quality of self-presence." "Aura," Sterne notes, "is the object of a nostalgia that accompanies reproduction."[55] Similarly, "spiritual contact" evinces a sense of nostalgia for a traditional, more "authentic," manner of experiencing music prior to the invention of recorded sound. To be certain, though, appeals to vague concepts such as "spiritual contact" and/or "aura" tell us less about contemporary theories of art and more about the collective anxieties that performers and audiences were experiencing when confronted with the dramatic and far-reaching effects of technological change and innovation.

As the AFM's advertising campaign was beginning to wind down, Weber made a final dramatic plea on behalf of performing musicians. In an essay published in 1930 with the provocative title "Canned Music—Is It Taking the Romance from Our Lives?," Weber explained that "people are becoming satiated with mechanics" and that "they want surcease from it." He observed that "romance has almost passed out of existence along with living music" and that "romance must have a background, a setting." "If living music is to be also gone," he explained, "a mechanical substitute cannot take its place."[56] "Unless music is restored to life," Weber warned, "romance will to a great extent perish."[57]

Weber's remarks on the effects of mechanical music on the "mood" of the nation appear alongside familiar talking points regarding the plight of performing musicians following the rise of "talkies" and the uncertain future of music in the United States. In contrast to the repetition and monotony offered by canned music, Weber dramatizes the "uniqueness" of the theater experience and the palpable sense of energy that often accompanies music making "in the flesh." Weber notes that "when one listens to a living artist sing or play an instrument, anything might happen." Weber imagines how:

> A singer, on one certain night, might sing an aria in an altogether unforgettable way. An obscure artist might, in one evening, achieve the heights. Or a pianist or violinist might, unexpectedly, one day play as

he had never before, play in such a glorious fashion that he would bring the whole house to its feet with excited cries of "Bravo! Bravo!" Thus every concert, every opera or operetta, every theater performance, every musical entertainment of any kind in which living music has a place, may prove to be an epoch-making occasion. A music lover, holding a ticket of admission, thrills with the anticipation as he enters the place of entertainment.[58]

Despite the many assaults on what he calls a "cherished" tradition of "live music," Weber sees a "few bright rays on the dark horizon of our culture." He continues, "I have observed recently that people are tiring of dead music in the theater. They are weary of the soul-less quality of the machine."[59] Drawing on the "live/dead" duality that was being promoted in the AFM's advertisements at the time, Weber is "not surprised that millions of Americans have put themselves on record as demanding the revival of living music, the kind that will vitalize us, and quicken our stagnant blood, which now runs cold to the mechanical kind."[60]

Becoming "Live" and Selling Liveness

By the time the AFM's ad campaign ended in 1931, approximately three million people had pledged their support for living music by joining the "Music Defense League." Despite the best efforts of the AFM and its supporters, broadcasting technologies continued to displace thousands of performing musicians. Throughout the 1930s, the expanding use of recorded music on radio and the increased reliance on jukeboxes in hotels and nightclubs contributed to the professional and psychological hardships facing many Depression-era musicians. Even as the country began to emerge from the Depression by the late 1930s, the spread of "wired music" in hotels (best represented by the Muzak Corporation) and the rising popularity of television meant even fewer job prospects for union musicians.

As employment opportunities continued to shrink throughout the 1930s and into the 1940s, AFM leaders recognized that the fight to preserve jobs would require more than a public relations campaign. Following the election of James Petrillo as union president in 1940, the AFM adopted a more aggressive strategy by initiating numerous strikes against radio stations and theaters throughout the country. In a move that was designed to impact almost every aspect of the entertainment industry, Petrillo announced a "recording ban" prohibiting union musicians from performing on all commercial records and transcription discs. The ban went into effect in August 1942 and would remain in place for approximately two years.[61]

Even as the country's involvement in the war came to dominate headlines in the early 1940s, people throughout North America were becoming familiar with the AFM, James Petrillo, and the ideological debates and economic issues involving the recording ban. It was also at this time that, in the United States, the term "live" was starting to be used in its modern sense to refer to a performance that was experienced "in the flesh." In October 1942, a short piece titled "Mr. Petrillo's Hopeless War" appeared in *The Nation*. The author, Charles Williams, was no fan of Petrillo, describing the AFM president as a "cocky Chicago labor politician with a great disdain for public opinion."[62] While Williams was sympathetic to the plight of performing musicians, he described the strike as a "desperate but probably futile effort to stave off the effects of technological advance."[63] Moreover, Williams predicted that the public "will continue to choose first-rate recordings in preference to second or third-rate 'live' music."[64]

Later that year, Bernard B. Smith acknowledged that, throughout the entertainment industry, "the trend has been increasingly away from 'live' music" in favor of recordings.[65] In Smith's opinion, the "problem of canned music vs. 'live' music is one in which the public interest is profoundly involved" as it forces audiences to consider some difficult questions.[66] "First," Smith wonders, "do the American people like canned music so well that they are willing it should replace the 'live' variety? And second, if so, does a democracy have any obligation to those workers who are displaced by technological improvements?"[67] Throughout the 1940s and into the 1950s, the term "live" was used more frequently (and increasingly without the quotation marks) to refer to musical performances and television broadcasts that were not recorded.[68] Even the AFM acknowledged the term's more modern meaning in *The National Crisis for Live Music and Musicians*, a report from 1955 on a crisis that promised to worsen as audiences grew more accustomed to experiencing music in a recorded form.[69]

For any number of reasons, most listeners of the era never experienced their favorite musical performers in a live setting. Instead, the musical tastes of audiences were increasingly shaped by the sounds that were etched on recordings and heard over and over again through speakers connected to turntables, jukeboxes, and radios. By the middle of the twentieth century, a variety of technological developments, cultural conditions, and economic factors had contributed to a growing preference among audiences for recorded music. Following the adoption of magnetic tape-recording technologies after the war, for example, the sound of recordings changed dramatically. Furthermore, the new vinyl records that had appeared by the end of the 1940s (notably the twelve-inch long-playing record introduced by Columbia in 1948 and the seven-inch single introduced by RCA in 1949) promised a more faithful representation of the original tape recording, especially when played on the latest "hi-fi" stereo systems. At the same time, the technical and artistic possibilities offered by "overdubbing" meant that the sounds that audiences were hearing on their favorite recordings did not necessarily represent, or "capture," a unique live performance from the past.

As documents of past live performances, recordings would continue to serve an authenticating function among select audiences (refer to the earlier discussion of *The Famous 1938 Carnegie Hall Jazz Concert*, for example). For many pop fans of the era, however, the notion of the "authentic" musical performance increasingly came to be associated with the formal properties of the recording itself and not a particular live performance. Recalling Benjamin, Albin Zak has described how, by the middle of the twentieth century, recorded music had acquired an "aura of the 'genuine.'" Recorded music, Zak explains, was no longer considered a "substitute for the real thing [i.e., live performance]; it *was* the real thing—not a replacement for live music, or a stand-in, but something different altogether." It had become, Zak notes, a "piece of shellac with a soul of its own."[70]

As described in the previous section, the AFM's public relations campaign sought to locate the authentic musical experience in live performance. In an effort to convince audiences of the value of "living music" in the theater, the AFM emphasized the *work* (i.e., the labor) that was required in establishing a form of "spiritual contact" between performers and an audience. By the 1950s, however, an "aura of the genuine" had come to be associated with the many musical performances that were readily accessible on mass-produced recordings. Reconceived as the "real thing" with a "soul of its own," the mechanical reproduction (i.e., "canned music") had been reimagined as a *work of art*.

As the listening habits of audiences continued to be conditioned by the sounds reproduced on recordings, one might be tempted to speak of the triumph of the recorded over the real, a shift in preference for the record over the live performance, or an "ideology of phonography" as eclipsing an "ideology of liveness."[71] The reality of the phonographic situation at midcentury reveals that, in addition to their status as objects worthy of disinterested interest, records were also used to (re)affirm the imagined authenticity of the live musical experience and many of the fundamental claims of the ideology of liveness. This can be seen most clearly in the increased marketing and promotion of live concert recordings beginning in the mid-1950s.

After introducing fans and critics to the modern live recording with *The Famous 1938 Carnegie Hall Jazz Concert* in 1950, Columbia was successful again in 1956 with the release of *Ellington at Newport*. Reading the liner notes on the back cover, potential record buyers may have been intrigued by George Avakian's recollections regarding the "girl who launched 7,000 cheers" during saxophonist Paul Gonsalves's solo on the song "Diminuendo and Crescendo in Blue."[72] Avakian provides a prosaic, almost cinematic, depiction of the events that unfolded over the twenty-seven choruses of Gonsalves's famed solo. In particular, Avakian notes that at "about his seventh chorus, the tension, which had been building both onstage and in the audience since Duke kicked off the piece, suddenly broke." At this point, Avakian continues, a "platinum-blonde girl in a black dress began dancing in one of the boxes (the last place you would expect that in Newport!) and a moment later somebody else started in another part of the audience. Large sections of the crowd had already been on their feet; now their cheering was doubled and re-doubled as the inter-reacting stimulus of a rocking performance and crowd response heightened the excitement."

With Avakian's notes serving as a guide, audiences are encouraged to attend to the musical performances captured on record while imagining the events of the day as they listen to "Diminuendo and Crescendo in Blue." Beginning around the seventh chorus, for example, some listeners might focus a bit more intently as they try to identify the moment when actress Elaine Anderson (the "platinum-blonde girl") begins to dance. As Gonsalves continues to improvise, listeners may almost sense the energy and excitement that was sweeping through the audience at Newport. Finally, Cat Anderson closes out the performance with a series of dramatic high notes. As *Ellington at Newport* fades out, the last thing that record listeners hear is the ecstatic reaction of the crowd.

In the standard historiography of jazz, the performance of "Diminuendo and Crescendo in Blue" transformed what had been a rather lackluster concert into what is now considered a legendary event and a concert that gave Duke Ellington's career a much-needed boost. But while it could be argued that *Ellington at Newport* "captured" a dynamic and historic musical occasion, it could also be argued that the presumed historicity of the concert has been shaped by the exhilarating stories that have been (and continue to be) told about the live record.[73] Attending to the sounds and marketing materials of *Ellington at Newport*, generations of listeners may continue to imagine how Ellington, his music, and his legacy were historicized on that summer day in Newport.

Along with *Ellington at Newport*, critically and commercially successful live albums such as *Ray Charles at Newport* (1958) and Muddy Waters's *At Newport 1960* (1960) point to the growing realization on the part of record companies that live recordings could be financially lucrative (including those, presumably, that were not recorded at Newport). These and many other live recordings of the era reflect a common titling convention that advertised a form of recorded liveness by aurally emplacing listeners "at" a particular venue or location. By the 1960s, the word "live" had started to appear on album titles, especially among independent labels specializing in jazz, soul, and rhythm and blues. John Coltrane's *Coltrane "Live" at the Village Vanguard* (1962) and B. B. King's *Live at the Regal* (1965) show how the term was gradually introduced into titles of the era (both with and without quotation marks).

In the early 1960s, James Brown's *"Live" at the Apollo* captured the attention of fans, critics, and people throughout the music industry. Shortly after its release in May 1963, the album (identified as *The James Brown Show*) was included as a "Pop Spotlight" in *Billboard* magazine, a collection of reviews reserved for "albums with sufficient sales potential."[74] At the time of the record's release, Brown had a song on the charts ("Prisoner of Love") and was widely recognized as a dynamic live performer with a committed and loyal fan base. The short review opens by noting, "Here's a wild album that should appeal to the many James Brown fans around the country." Words (and syntax) appear to elude the reviewer, who proceeds to describe the record in exceedingly vivid (and slightly suggestive) terms, noting that the "exciting set was recorded during an actual performance at the Apollo Theater, and the shouts of the crowd, the electric of the music bursting on the audience and their reaction for a dynamic 40 minutes or so." At the time, *Billboard* noted how distributors in some cities "report business at an unprecedented summer peak because of James Brown's 'Alive at the Apollo' which they say is selling like a single."[75] *The James Brown Show* rose as high as number 2 on the *Billboard* "Top LP's" chart (it could never overtake Andy Williams's *Days of Wine and Roses*). The success of Brown's album is even more remarkable when one considers that it does not feature new songs. Instead of new material, fans were being encouraged to buy live versions of songs that were already familiar to them from Brown's studio recordings.

Fans were not being encouraged to buy just the record; they were also being sold an experience. In his liner notes to the original LP release, producer Hal Neely acknowledges those fans "who have been fortunate to see [Brown] perform in person, I'm sure it was a thrill and I'm sure you agree that he is all talent . . . all showman . . . all entertainment."[76] After establishing the image of Brown and his live shows in the minds of potential record buyers, Neely turns his attention to everyone else, assuring "those of you who have never seen him work [that] this album will be a new, and exciting experience." For those fans who might know the songs but have never been to a concert, Neely promises that the album features the "actual recording of the midnight show and includes the actual 40 minutes of James Brown on stage."[77] In Neely's opinion, the album is "without a doubt one of the most exciting albums ever recorded at a live performance." Even more remarkable is the fact that "the producers and engineers have completely captured the James Brown personality, the James Brown sound, the James Brown feel." For audiophiles and fans who might have been justifiably skeptical of such bold claims, Neely admits that the "technical problems of recording a live performance in a packed house were almost insurmountable." However, Neely confidently asserts that by "using [an] AMPEX 350–2 tape machine with eight mikes" and mixed in "Stereophonic sound," the amount of "effort and time" devoted to producing the recording was "justified by the result."

Throughout Neely's liner notes, the recorded sounds, the concert experience, and the mythology surrounding James Brown's concerts become indistinguishable from one another. The recording acts as a sort of sonic portal that is capable of providing direct contact to the personality of the performer and the sound and feel of the original live experience. The tone and tenor of Neely's notes are not unique among live album releases of the era. Indeed, by the early 1960s, live recordings were commonly promoted for their purported ability to convey a sense of musical liveness. As Philip Auslander has pointed out, however, the experience of liveness provided by live recordings is "primarily affective." As a mediated experience of liveness, live recordings encourage in the "listener a sense of participating in a specific performance and a vicarious relationship to the audience for that performance not accessible through studio productions."[78]

It is important to keep in mind, however, that audiences and record buyers were being convinced of this affective experience of recorded liveness. From the "girl who launched 7,000 cheers" at Newport to the "electric of the music bursting" all over Brown's audience at the Apollo, record companies routinely promoted the affective capabilities of live recordings to consumers who demanded more and more recorded material. At the same time, the remarkable claims regarding the sonic and experiential qualities of contemporary live records served to reinforce the idea that a live performance offered a more authentic manner of experiencing music. This (re)affirmation of the ideology of liveness was being promoted, of course, through the production, promotion, and sale of recorded objects: the commercial live recording. As media scholar Keir Keightley has observed, for a generation of listeners whose experience of music had been shaped by records, the modern live recording offered a "perceived sense of spontaneous performance, emotional directness and audience interaction," qualities that were more commonly associated with the live concert experience.[79] By the middle of the 1960s, therefore, record companies were aggressively selling the ideology of liveness to audiences in the form of live records.[80]

The Grateful Dead, Live Recordings, and the Ideology of Liveness

In 1965, the Grateful Dead (then known as the Warlocks) played their earliest live shows in venues throughout San Francisco and the Bay Area. As a dance band that played multiple sets night after night, it might be tempting to assert that the Dead were somehow ineluctably interpellated within a prevailing ideology of liveness.[81] To do so, however, would serve to simply "read," or interpret, aspects of the Dead phenomenon against the expansive backdrop ("through the lens") of some hazy, inchoate conception of liveness.[82] Instead, *Live Dead* traces a critical history of the idea of liveness by considering how and why live recordings came to dominate the discourse of the Grateful Dead.

In chapter 1, I describe how, by the middle of the 1960s, the Grateful Dead were already being heralded as the premier live band of the San Francisco scene. Despite the musical and lyrical eclecticism, innovative formal designs, and unconventional recording and production techniques associated with the band's earliest studio albums, many fans and critics were skeptical that the Dead were capable of capturing the energy and intensity of their live concerts on record. The Dead were finally able to produce a distinctive form of recorded liveness with the release of *Live/Dead* in 1969, an artistic achievement and a critical success made possible by advances in multitrack recording and mixing technologies. Subsequent live recordings (including *Skull and Roses* and *Europe '72*) reveal how, by the early 1970s, the Grateful Dead were content to produce live albums as a way of satisfying the material demands of the record industry. As purported documents of "liveness," however, the band's official releases owe more to the production techniques commonly associated with studio recordings. Consequently, by the early 1970s, a growing number of fans and critics were beginning to question the perceived authenticity of the form of recorded liveness that the Dead were promoting on their major label releases.

Alongside the Grateful Dead's earliest commercially released live albums, fans also had access to a growing body of "unofficial" live concert recordings. Chapter 2 considers the community of tapers and the culture and economics of tape trading that had emerged by the early 1970s. More specifically, this chapter examines how, in the era of unauthorized "bootlegs," these amateur recordings—commonly known as "tapes"—offered fans an alternate version of recorded liveness, a version that was substantially different from what was packaged and sold on the Dead's official live albums. Drawing on the work of literary critic Susan Stewart, I examine how the tapes became meaningful through a variety of personal and historical narratives that served to connect fans to the original concert experience(s) via (what was imagined as) a more authentic version of recorded liveness. As the demand for live recordings continued to grow among fans, I also describe how, beginning in the mid-1970s, members of the Dead organization prepared to produce, market, and distribute recordings from the band's personal "vault" of unreleased material.

Chapters 3 and 4 examine how idea(l)s of recorded liveness continued to influence the Grateful Dead's creative and commercial endeavors throughout the 1980s. Chapter 3 considers the band's run of concerts at the Warfield Theatre in San Francisco and Radio City Music Hall in New York City in September and October 1980. Whereas the distinctive quality of liveness heard on the band's earliest commercial live releases owed much to the production techniques associated with the recording studio, *Reckoning* and *Dead Set*, two live double albums released in 1981, were recorded and mixed so as to suggest the sounds and textures of fan-produced recordings. Furthermore, advances in video technology, the introduction of home video systems, and the growing market for videocassettes and videodiscs suggested new approaches to experiencing and marketing liveness at the dawn of the new decade.

In chapter 4, I describe how, throughout the 1980s, members of the Dead's touring crew continued to document the band's live performances on a variety of recording mediums and formats while designated tape archivists worked to store, catalog, and maintain the Dead's growing library of concert recordings. At the same time, people throughout the Dead organization continued to explore the practical and logistical details of producing, marketing, and distributing live concert recordings from the vault.

In 1987, the song "Touch of Grey" introduced the Grateful Dead to a new (younger) generation of fans, many of whom were just learning about the era of the "hippies" and the associated (and increasingly romanticized) ideals of the San Francisco countercultural movement of the 1960s. Even as the band's recent studio records and concerts introduced newer fans to the history of the Dead (not to mention the Dead's legacy of liveness), an enormous trove of previously unavailable live concert recordings, known among traders and collectors as the "Betty Boards," began to circulate in the spring of 1987. As I describe in chapter 4, the remarkable history of this batch of tapes—their production, provenance, rediscovery, and resurrection—reaffirmed the significance of live recordings within an established discourse of liveness among Deadheads.

Following the critical and commercial success of "Touch of Grey" and the album *In the Dark*, the Grateful Dead renegotiated their contract with Arista Records in 1988. Among the many favorable terms of the new contract, the Dead were finally granted the right to sell and distribute materials from their personal vault of archival recordings. Chapter 5 examines the distinctive "languages of liveness" that were used to advertise and aestheticize the earliest official releases from the Grateful Dead's legendary vault. As I describe, the releases that appeared on the *From the Vault* series were evaluated, produced, and promoted according to a rationalized discourse that emphasized the superior sonic qualities and technical features of the multitrack recordings. In 1993, the band and tape archivist Dick Latvala introduced a series of compact disc releases called *Dick's Picks* that featured live performances that had been recorded using 2-track technologies. Whereas the recordings featured on the *From the Vault* series more closely resemble the sound and aesthetic of the band's professionally produced, major-label live releases, the compact discs included as part of the *Dick's Picks* series were shaped by the discourse of liveness that had come to be associated with fan-produced tapes.

Live recordings became the primary method by which the Grateful Dead would continue to promote the band's legacy of liveness following the death of Jerry Garcia in 1995. By the turn of the millennium, a vast (and growing) digital library of live concert recordings featuring the sounds of the Dead was readily accessible on the World Wide Web. But even as fans all over the world gained access to thousands of live recordings online, the Grateful Dead and their business partners continued to market and promote an "official" version of recorded liveness by producing a multitude of physical releases in a variety of (increasingly obsolete) formats. In chapter 6, I consider how, within the community and the culture of the Grateful Dead, live recordings have been valued not just for the sounds and stories that they transmit but also for their materiality.

For more than fifty years, live recordings have shaped and influenced the general history and popular mythology of the Grateful Dead. Many of the stories recounted in the following chapters may be familiar to some fans of the band. In narrating these stories, I have relied on numerous sources, including popular and scholarly writings, reviews and interviews, fanzines, blogs, and a host of audio and video recordings. At the same time, however, the versions of the stories told in *Live Dead* reflect details and information drawn from a variety of primary documents housed within the Grateful Dead Archive at the University of California at Santa Cruz, including business meeting minutes, internal memos, planning and promotional materials, contracts, recording logs, concert files, correspondence, and a host of other sources. Weaving together these various resources, *Live Dead* considers how live recordings of the Grateful Dead became meaningful, both for the band and their fans, as material expressions of various idea(l)s, including liveness, authenticity and historical meaning, the use and value of cultural objects, and the phantasmagoric power of recorded sound.

The Grateful Dead (1969) (*Left to right*: Bob Weir, Bill Kreutzmann, Tom Constanten, Phil Lesh, Jerry Garcia, Mickey Hart, Ron "Pigpen" McKernan)

"To Capture That Special Feeling"

RECORDED (AND RECORDING) LIVENESS
(THE WARNER BROS. YEARS, 1966–1973)

By early 1967, San Francisco was widely recognized as the geographic and spiritual center of the emerging counterculture in the United States. As news of the "hippies," "free love," and the mind-expanding potential of LSD ("acid") continued to attract (and alarm) people throughout the nation, music fans were also being introduced to the modern "psychedelic" rock sounds that were emanating out of the Bay Area. Published in the *Village Voice* in March 1967, Richard Goldstein's feature "The Flourishing Underground" introduced rock fans on the East Coast (especially those in and around New York City) to the many bands, venues, and countercultural ideals that formed the musical scene in San Francisco. In particular, Goldstein considers four groups from San Francisco: Jefferson Airplane, Quicksilver Messenger Service, Big Brother and the Holding Company, and the Grateful Dead.

Describing San Francisco as the "Liverpool of the West," Goldstein proclaims that, just as the Beatles and other bands associated with the British Invasion (including those not from Liverpool) had transformed popular music in 1964, the music currently being made in the Bay Area is the "most potentially vital in the pop world."[1] The value and vitality of the scene are even more remarkable, he suggests, given that most of the bands had yet to release any recordings. Indeed, when Goldstein's article appeared in March 1967, the only commercial albums by a group identified with the San Francisco scene were the first two releases by Jefferson Airplane: *Jefferson Airplane Takes Off* (released in December 1966) and *Surrealistic Pillow* (released in February 1967).

Ultimately, the paucity of recordings did not matter for, as Goldstein and other contemporary critics emphasized, the musical, cultural, and spiritual qualities ascribed to the San Francisco scene could only truly be experienced live. In a quote reproduced in Goldstein's article, Ralph J. Gleason, the noted jazz critic and early champion of the scene, suggested that the "important thing about San Francisco rock 'n' roll is that the bands here all sing and play live, and not for recordings. You get a different sound at a dance, it's harder and more direct."[2] The musicians also stressed the importance of performing live. Less than a year after moving to the city to join Big Brother and the Holding Company, singer Janis Joplin proclaimed that "San Francisco is live." "Recording in a studio," Joplin explained, "is a completely different trip. No one makes a record like they sound live."[3]

For Goldstein, no band better represented both the spirit of the San Francisco scene and the ideals associated with live performance than the Grateful Dead. In his opinion, there is "nothing convoluted in the lyrics, just rock 'n' roll lingua franca. Not a trace of preciousness in the music; just raunchy, funky chords."[4] Echoing Gleason, Goldstein notes that the Dead's "music hits hard and stays hard like early Rolling Stones, but distilled and concentrated."[5] Describing the band's live performances, he wrote that the Grateful Dead "sound like live thunder."

Goldstein admitted, however, that he had yet to experience the Grateful Dead in a concert setting. Instead, his description of the Dead sounding "like live thunder" was based on an experience he had while listening to recorded concert performances by the band. "I have never seen them live," Goldstein explained, "but I spent an evening at the Fillmore listening to tapes."[6]

For many readers, the image of Goldstein in the Fillmore Auditorium, one of the most iconic ballrooms of the San Francisco scene (operated by Bill Graham, the renowned concert promoter), listening to taped recordings of live performances by the Grateful Dead might have seemed odd. Was Goldstein alone, or was he a member of an audience? Did he dance to the taped performances, or did he sit and politely listen? What was the reaction to the abrupt cut in the "performance" when a tape ran out and had to be replaced?

Did he clap at the end of songs? (Obviously, it would make no sense to call out requests.)

At the same time, other readers may have been intrigued by Goldstein's account of the events at the Fillmore. Even before most audiences had heard music *by* (no less heard *of*) the Grateful Dead, Goldstein's evocative description of the recorded sounds that he heard that evening undoubtedly caught the attention of many people. On the one hand, Goldstein notes that, at the time, there were no commercial "recordings of [the Dead's] music, which is probably just as well because no album could produce the feeling they generate in a dance hall."[7] Of course, Goldstein's effusive description of the band's concerts was based on an experience he had while listening to recorded performances. On the other hand, therefore, Goldstein's reaction to the tapes would seem to suggest that recordings are capable of, in some way, "capturing" certain qualities or characteristics of the band's live sound, a "sound like live thunder."

In the fall of 1966, the members of the Grateful Dead—Jerry Garcia, Bill Kreutzmann, Phil Lesh, Ron "Pigpen" McKernan, and Bob Weir—signed a major label recording contract with Warner Bros. Records. A few months later, the band entered RCA Studios in Los Angeles to record their debut studio album. While the group had established themselves as a live dance band and had built a devoted local following in San Francisco, they were now committed to working within an industry that required a recorded commodity. In this chapter, I consider how the Grateful Dead sought to impart a sense of the live "feeling" on their earliest commercial releases. More specifically, I consider how, by adapting available recording technologies and traditional recording practices, the group learned how to produce a form of recorded liveness that was successful—both critically and commercially—in suggesting the sense and the sound of a Dead concert.

Searching for the Live Sound on Record
(*The Grateful Dead*, 1967)

Less than three weeks after Goldstein's article appeared in the *Village Voice*, Ralph J. Gleason's short piece "Dead Like Live Thunder" was published in the *San Francisco Chronicle*. Recalling Goldstein's vivid description of the group's live sound, the title of Gleason's article suggests that a sort of bicoastal critical consensus was forming around the band. At the same time, Gleason's article introduced readers to the band shortly before the release of their debut album, *The Grateful Dead*.

Gleason situated the Dead within the dance scene that had developed around the many clubs and ballrooms in the Bay Area. "At the dances at the Fillmore and the Avalon and the other, more occasional affairs," Gleason noted, "thousands upon thousands of people support several dozen rock 'n' roll bands that play all over the area for dancing each week. Nothing like it has occurred since the heyday of Glenn Miller, Benny Goodman, and Tommy Dorsey. It is a new dancing age."[8] Speaking with Gleason, guitarist and vocalist Jerry Garcia described the role of the Grateful Dead in relation to the dance scene, noting how "we still feel that our function is as a dance band and that's what we like to do; we like to play for dancers."[9]

The Grateful Dead regularly performed alongside many other local bands at venues such as Bill Graham's Fillmore Auditorium, the Avalon, the California Hall, and the Longshoreman's Hall (the latter being the site of numerous dances and events including, most notably, the three-day Trips Festival in January 1966). The Dead's performances at these and other venues often occurred as part of an expansive multimedia/multisensory experience that included not only music and dancing but also light shows, films, and other spontaneous "happenings." When the Grateful Dead became the house band for Ken Kesey's famed Acid Tests in December 1965, the immersive experience of the dance was augmented by an elaborate sound system. Developed by Kesey and other Pranksters, a makeshift tape delay system was often used to broadcast live and recorded sounds during the Acid Tests. These manipulated sounds would echo and reverberate throughout the venue as people danced to the improvisations provided by the Dead or simply stared off into space while tripping on LSD.[10]

Speaking to Gleason, Garcia described the band's approach to making music as "we'll take an idea and we'll develop it."[11] In an effort to enhance the mood of the dancers while also responding to the changing peaks of the collective "trip" of the dance, the Grateful Dead had become increasingly adept at developing, transforming, and connecting musical performances through improvisation. Of course, collective improvisation enabled the Dead to play for longer periods of time as they learned to shape their performances through a careful balance of contrasting dynamics, varying moods, and deliberate pacing.[12] Speaking of the band's approach to performing a traditional song like "Viola Lee Blues," Gleason asked Garcia if, "when you play it, do you play it the same way all the time?"

[JERRY GARCIA]: No, never.
[GLEASON]: Do you change that structure?

JERRY: Always. That's the part that's fun about it, because it's like we all have to be on our toes. All of a sudden there's something new entering and we all try and pick up on it. . . . Our ideas come from everywhere, and we have no bones about mixing our idioms or throwing stuff back and forth from one place to another. So you might hear some very straight traditional counterpoint, classical-style counterpoint popping up in the middle of some rowdy thing.[13]

Writing in the early rock publication *Crawdaddy* in November 1966, critic Gene Sculatti described the Grateful Dead's repertoire as a combination of "city blues, some old folk and early rock, with some strong originals."[14] He explained that, among "local dance-concert attendees," the band's cover of "In the Midnight Hour" is considered a highlight of their live shows. "The Dead's closing number is usually Wilson Pickett's blockbuster, and it is transformed into a type of half-hour (sometimes longer) 'Everybody Needs Somebody to Love' performed by the Dead's organist, Pig Pen."[15] In Sculatti's opinion, however, their cover of "In the Midnight Hour" is not even "the Dead at their best." As some of their "best accomplishments," Sculatti singles out other tunes that were sung by founding member Ron "Pigpen" McKernan, including the traditional blues song "Good Morning, Little Schoolgirl" and Howlin' Wolf's "Smokestack Lightning." Sculatti exclaims that the band's version of the country blues song "Sittin' on Top of the World" "jumps" while their cover of "Dancing in the Street" by Martha and the Vandellas is a "railroad trip."[16]

In many ways, the Dead's repertoire and instrumentation mirrored the musical influences and sound of most of the bands associated with the San Francisco scene, especially groups such as the Jefferson Airplane, Big Brother and the Holding Company, and Quicksilver Messenger Service. In describing the emergence of a musically distinct "San Francisco sound" alongside a culturally (and commercially) marketable "psychedelic" style of blues-based hard rock, musicologist Jan Butler has drawn attention to contemporary "tensions that emerged between the live-performance culture of 1960s San Francisco and the more studio-based scene in Los Angeles."[17] These tensions were stoked by early rock critics, many of whom (including Gleason and Goldstein) played an important role in promoting a discourse of liveness by which the scenes in San Francisco and Los Angeles were mapped on either side of the "live"/"recorded" divide. Among many contemporary rock critics and fans, for example, the music industry practices associated with Los Angeles were linked to notions of corporate control and a standardized approach to record production. By contrast, San Francisco came to be identified with many of the cultural, political, and artistic ideals associated with the emerging counterculture. In the minds of many people, therefore, the San Francisco music scene represented freedom and experimentation, idea(l)s that were enacted and affirmed not on records but as part of a live musical performance.

Even before the band entered the recording studio, the Grateful Dead were imbricated within a critical discourse of liveness, a discourse that was informed by a set of contrasting musical styles, modes of production, and cultural practices that were conveniently symbolized and connoted by the cities of San Francisco and Los Angeles. In Richard Goldstein's opinion, the style of rock music emerging from San Francisco "shoots a cleansing wave over the rigid studiousness of folk-rock" epitomized by The Byrds, The Monkees, The Mamas and the Papas, and other Los Angeles–based bands.[18] San Francisco rock, by contrast, "brings driving spontaneity to a music that is becoming increasingly classical, conscious of form and influence rather than effect. It is a resurgence which could smother the Monkees, drown the casual castrati who make easy listening, and devour all those one-shot wonders that float above stagnant water."[19] Goldstein weaves together the dualities of "live-versus-recorded" and "San Francisco–versus–Los Angeles" in describing how, "when [the Dead's] new album comes out, I will whip it onto my meagre record player and if they have left that [live] boulder sound at some palatial L.A. studio and come out with a polished pebble, I will know they don't live together in the Haight anymore."[20]

In late January 1967, Garcia, Pigpen, and the rest of the Grateful Dead—including Bill Kreutzmann (drums), Phil Lesh (bass guitar and vocals), and Bob Weir (vocals and guitar)—traveled from San Francisco to Los Angeles to record their debut studio album at RCA Studios. Following the standard protocol of the era, the sessions required an industry-affiliated producer, and the band selected David Hassinger, an engineer who had assisted on recordings by the Rolling Stones, the Electric Prunes, and others. A few months earlier, Garcia had been introduced to Hassinger during the recording sessions for Jefferson Airplane's *Surrealistic Pillow*, an album for which Garcia contributed guitar parts (he is also identified on the liner notes as a "spiritual advisor").

The instrumental backing tracks for the Grateful Dead's debut album were recorded live to four tracks; a short time later, vocal and instrumental overdubs were recorded during separate sessions. After hearing an early version of the record, Warner Bros. executive Joe Smith urged the band to return to the studio with the intention of producing a song that could be promoted as a single. Instead of returning to Los Angeles, the band gathered at Coast Recorders in San Francisco to record "The Golden Road (To Unlimited Devotion)," a joyful paean to the San Francisco scene that had been written a few weeks after the Dead's performance at the Human Be-In at Golden Gate Park on January 14.[21] The entire process of recording and mixing the album took less than a week to complete. Just a few months later, in March 1967, Warner Bros. released the Grateful Dead's debut record, *The Grateful Dead*.

Except for the newly composed "Golden Road," the songs included on *The Grateful Dead* are a good representation of the band's live repertoire at the time. Indeed, three of the songs on the album—"Morning Dew," "Good Morning, Little Schoolgirl," and "Viola Lee Blues"—had all been played during the band's performance at the Human Be-In. Speaking shortly after the album was released, Garcia explained that he thought the album "sounds just like us. It even has mistakes on it." "But it also has a certain amount of excitement on it," Garcia continued. "It sounds like we felt good when we were making it. We made it in a short period—four days—and it's the material we've been doing onstage for quite a long time. It sounds like one of our good sets."[22]

By the beginning of the next month, however, the band's expressed opinion of their debut album had changed dramatically. In April, Garcia and Lesh appeared on Tom Donahue's radio show on KMPX-FM in San Francisco where they acted as DJs, selecting some of their favorite recordings from an eclectic mix of performers and composers.[23] After playing Charles Mingus's "Wednesday Night Prayer Meeting," Donahue asked them if they planned to play any songs from their new record. "No . . . well . . . ," Garcia demurred in a singsong manner. Following a bit of nervous laughter, some jokes, and an awkward pause, Donahue asks, "How do you feel about the album yourselves personally?"

"I feel like it's a turd," Lesh responds. "It's where we were at the time," he explains, while also emphasizing that the "next [album] certainly won't be anything like that . . . in any way." Garcia describes the band's approach to recording their debut album as "sort of an attempt to try and sound like . . . the stuff that we do live with the same instrumentation and everything." "But that's impossible to do in a recording studio," Lesh interjects. "Right," Garcia agrees, "so we're not gonna bother doing that anymore."

Along with the band, many reviewers and fans also considered *The Grateful Dead* as a poor substitute for the group's more highly regarded live performances. Writing in *Crawdaddy*, critic Paul Williams remarked that the "more you've grown to love Grateful Dead live performances over the years the more difficult it must be to accept an album which is—though very beautiful—something completely different."[24] For Williams, the only track that even somewhat resembles how it might have been performed live is the ten-minute version of "Viola Lee Blues" that closes side 2. "Only 'Viola Lee Blues,'" he writes, "has any of the fantastic 'this is happening *now!*' quality of a good Dead performance; only 'Viola Lee Blues' takes you away as far as the long time Dead fan has grown accustomed to being taken."[25]

Following his exuberant exposé of the band in March in the *Village Voice*, Richard Goldstein was less enthusiastic in his review of *The Grateful Dead* in April, describing it as "straight, decent rhythm and blues—some of it so civil it passes for dull." In one of his most pointed critiques, he describes "The Golden Road"—the song that the band recorded in San Francisco—as "plain old rock with vocal harmonies that remind you of the Mamas and the Papas of all things." In spite of the folk-rock vocal stylings, Goldstein admires the sound of the recording, noting that all of the "prototechnics [*sic*] of the recording studio are forsaken for a straight, 'live' effect. It feels spontaneous; it sounds honest." [26]

Whereas Williams, Goldstein, and other critics lamented the diminished sense of liveness on *The Grateful Dead*, DJ Tom Donahue recognized the inherent technological limitations of the modern recording studio. Speaking with Garcia and Lesh on his radio program, Donahue observed how "it's the whole problem of trying to take what live sounds like and put it on some kind of tape, or disc or something." Nearly in unison, Garcia and Lesh responded that "you can't do it in the studio." "You might be able to do it," Garcia pointed out, "if you could record a rock and roll band live at the volumes we play at [in] places like the Fillmore, or something like that." Even if such recording technologies existed, Garcia imagined how the process of selecting and sequencing different performances would only be possible "maybe after [playing] about two or three months of every night at the Fillmore." Eventually, Garcia explains, "we'd start to get good cuts, good enough for an album, in terms of how clean they were and how much we like the performance on them and then we'd have something. But it would be such an expensive undertaking and long and everything."

Although the Grateful Dead would not return to the studio until later in the year, some members of the band imagined a very different approach when recording the next album. As Garcia explained to Donahue, "Since the first album is doing so nicely, we hope [Warner Bros. will] let us have a lot of time in the studio and next time we'll do a lot more studio stuff." And that is exactly what the Dead did.

Learning to Record Live (*Anthem of the Sun*, 1968)

In September 1967, the Grateful Dead—including Mickey Hart, a drummer and percussionist who had recently joined the band—along with producer David Hassinger returned to RCA Studios in Los Angeles to begin sessions for the group's second album. While working on their new album, the Dead spent a significant amount of time in the studio developing musical arrangements while also exploring the many possibilities (and limitations) offered by the 8-track recorder and the modern recording studio. Following some preliminary recording sessions at RCA, the band relocated to American Studios in North Hollywood, where they further immersed themselves in studio experimentation through October. Hassinger and the band also booked impromptu recording sessions in studios throughout New York City while on tour in December.

Having grown increasingly exasperated with the band and the sessions, Hassinger informed executive Joe Smith at Warner Bros. that he would no longer produce the album. In late December, Smith sent a letter to Danny Rifkin, the Grateful Dead's manager, in which he expressed his frustrations with the band and their "drawn out project," describing it as the "most unreasonable project with which we have ever involved ourselves."[27] Smith chastised the band, labeling them as an "undesireable [*sic*] group in almost every recording studio in Los Angeles" and claiming they had run "through engineers like a steamroller" during their time in New York City. Smith pressed the band to deliver the master tapes of the new record for a planned release in February 1968. "Your artistic control is subject to reasonable restrictions," he wrote, "and I believe that the time and expense involved along with your own freedom has been more than reasonable."

At the beginning of 1968, the Grateful Dead found themselves in a very enviable, yet precarious, situation. Following Hassinger's departure, they were free to produce and engineer their record on their own terms. However, even after many months in the studio, none of the band members had enough practical experience or technical knowledge necessary in recording, editing, and mixing a commercial album.

When they returned to the studio, the band enlisted Dan Healy to assist in producing and recording the sessions. Prior to becoming the band's live sound engineer in 1966, Healy had worked at Commercial Recorders, one of the few independent recording studios in San Francisco.[28] With Healy's assistance, the remaining studio sessions for what would become the band's second album, *Anthem of the Sun*, took place at Columbus Recorders in San Francisco, one of the few studios in the city that had an 8-track tape machine.

In addition to his mechanical expertise and experience, Healy was very familiar with the band's live sound. Under pressure to deliver an album to Warner Bros., Healy and the band chose to combine studio recordings made with Hassinger with live recordings that would be produced by the group. At the time, various crew members would often record the Dead's concerts using a 2-track stereo tape recorder. These self-produced live recordings served many purposes for the band. By recording their concerts, the group could review their performances as they sought to develop and grow as an improvising ensemble. At the same time, the band would sometimes review recordings of their long, free-form improvisations for musical ideas that could be developed further, perhaps into new songs. Given the circumstances following the departure of Hassinger, Healy and the group decided to record some of the band's upcoming concerts in the hopes of capturing performances that could be used on their forthcoming (and long overdue) album.

Around the same time that Healy and the band were beginning to record live performances for *Anthem of the Sun*, Jerry Garcia was quoted as saying, "I don't believe the live sound, the live excitement can be recorded."[29] Appearing in an article titled "Live Sound of the Grateful Dead," Garcia's assertion not only recalls his comments to DJ Tom Donahue in 1967 but also seems to reflect the opinion of many of the band's fans. As described by journalist Tony Leigh, "With raunchy chords and funky sounds, [the Dead] grip their live audiences with a burst of sound that patrons of San Francisco's famed Fillmore Auditorium maintain cannot be duplicated on records."[30] By early 1968, however, advances in multitrack recording provided musicians, producers, and engineers with a host of new approaches and strategies when recording music, both in a studio and live.

When the band returned to the road for a run of concerts in Northern California and the Pacific Northwest in January 1968, Healy brought along a modified 4-track tape machine to record the performances. The band and their road crew also transported the 8-track tape machine from Columbus Recorders to record a performance on February 14 at the Carousel Ballroom in San Francisco. As they worked toward completing the album, Healy and the group used portions of these and other live performances as a framework on which studio recordings were then superimposed or interspersed. As Phil Lesh would later explain, the collage-like approach by which the band produced *Anthem of the Sun* functioned as "both a means of extending the material through thematic improvisation, and a means of [transitioning] between live and studio recording."[31] At the time, it also seemed like the simplest (and cheapest) way to finish the record.

For the Dead's dedicated fans, most of the songs that appear on *Anthem of the Sun* would have been familiar from the band's concerts. The songs "Alligator" (cowritten by Garcia's longtime friend, the musician and writer Robert Hunter), "Caution (Do Not Stop on Tracks)," and "New Potato Caboose" (cowritten by Lesh and poet Robert "Bobby" Petersen), for example, had all been performed live since January 1967. The songs "Cryptical Envelopment" and "The Other One" (identified on the record as "The Faster We Go, the Rounder We Get") were introduced into the band's live sets in October following the addition of Mickey Hart. "Born Cross-Eyed," the remaining song on the album, was probably written and composed in the studio, most likely during sessions that had been produced by Hassinger.

There are no breaks between the songs on each side of *Anthem of the Sun*. On the one hand, of course, this feature can be interpreted as an acknowledgment of (and expansion on) the innovative approach to song sequencing employed by the Beatles on *Sgt. Pepper's Lonely Hearts Club Band* (1967). On the other hand, the practice of connecting songs, typically through collective improvisation, was something the band routinely did as part of their live performances and was a practice that audiences and critics had come to expect, admire, and value.[32] During the band's concerts at the time, for example, the song "Alligator," a bouncy, lighthearted tune sung by Pigpen, would often segue into "Caution," a propulsive, blues-based song that typically served as a vehicle for extended improvisations. Lasting over twenty minutes, this song pairing appears as the second side of *Anthem of the Sun* and includes numerous sections of improvisation. The form of this expanded musical performance, however, is the result of numerous edits and carefully coordinated mixing decisions that blend together numerous live and studio recordings.

Figure 1.1 reproduces a sheet created by the band when mixing side 2 of *Anthem of the Sun*. To be sure, there is a tremendous amount of information on this page, information relating to dynamics, equalization, mixing, and panning. The circled numerals arranged vertically on the left side of the image reveal how the band sequenced the various live and studio recordings to arrive at the syncretic "performance" that appears on side 2 of the album. As indicated on the top left-hand corner of the page, the song "Alligator" begins with material identified as having been recorded in the "Studio," material that lasts for the first three minutes and fifteen seconds. During live performances, a rhythmic breakdown featuring the two drummers would often serve as a transition between the opening "song" portion of "Alligator" and the open-ended improvisatory sections that followed. This is also what happens on *Anthem of the Sun*, yet, as seen on figure 1.1, the percussion

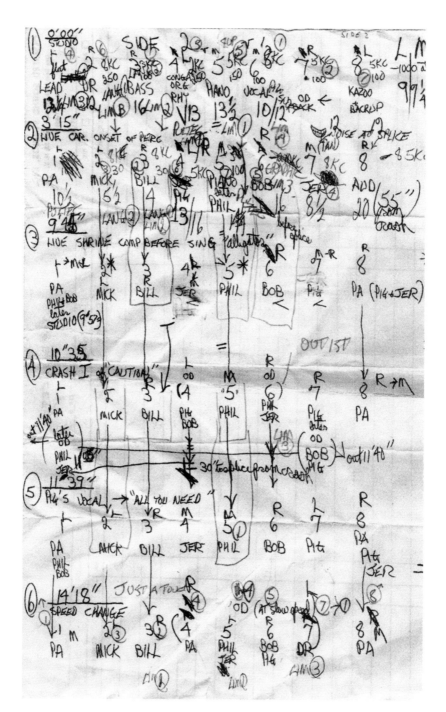

FIGURE 1.1. Production notes for side 2 of *Anthem of the Sun*

transition that appears at 3:15 (the "onset of perc." identified by the numeral 2) is drawn from live performances recorded on 8-track at the Carousel Ballroom on February 14 ("Live Car."). Number 3 identifies another edit at 9:45, a section of an instrumental "comp before [singing] 'Alligator'" that was recorded live at the Shrine Auditorium in Los Angeles in November 1967 ("Live Shrine"). The circled numeral 4 at 10:35 marks the moment when the song "Caution (Do Not Stop on Tracks)" finally emerges from "Alligator" (as it usually would in live performances). As with "Alligator," the version of "Caution" that appears on *Anthem of the Sun* is compiled from various live recordings that were spliced together and overlaid with numerous vocal and instrumental overdubs.

Despite the extensive use of live recordings, fans and critics undoubtedly recognized that *Anthem of the Sun* was a product of the recording studio. Beginning with "Cryptical Envelopment," the first track on side 1, listeners are immediately placed within an exaggerated and wholly fabricated sound space. As heard on the recording, Garcia's vocal track is panned hard to the left with the organ and electric guitar tracks panned hard right.[33] A trace of reverb on Garcia's lead vocals can be heard in the right channel, creating a fading trail across the stereo field. Organized as a traditional AABA popular song form, the bridge of "Cryptical Envelopment" (at 0:43) marks a dramatic shift in texture and tone as Garcia's vocals are now heard through a rotating speaker, giving his voice an otherworldly, warbling effect. The sense of space changes, too, as Garcia's vocals and the electric organ both shift to the center of the stereo field; the bass guitar occupies most of the space on the left side while an acoustic guitar can be heard in the right channel. Garcia's vocals remain in the center of the stereo field when the A section returns at 1:05.

As the introductory section of the suite that opens side 1 of *Anthem of the Sun* (identified as "That's It for the Other One"), "Cryptical Envelopment" segues into "Quadlibet for Tender Feet"/"The Faster We Go, the Rounder We Get," a performance that, among fans, is better known as "The Other One." As with the pairing of "Alligator" and "Caution," in live performances the band would often improvise a musical segue from the carefree, relaxed mood of "Cryptical Envelopment" into the faster, more aggressive tone of "The Other One," sung by Bob Weir. When re-creating this transition for the album, the band drew on recordings from multiple live performances to create a constantly shifting sonic tapestry as recorded sounds from various concerts emerge, blend, recede, and disappear.[34] Next, a section of musique concrète ("We Leave the Castle") featuring a prepared piano adds to the dizzying kaleidoscope of sounds heard on the album. Serving as a transition to

"New Potato Caboose," "We Leave the Castle" was performed by Tom Constanten, a friend of Lesh.[35] Following his work on the album, Constanten briefly joined the band.

Anthem of the Sun was finally released in July 1968. As part of the album's promotional campaign, Warner Bros. turned what had been a point of contention between the label and the band—the extended delays in delivering the record—into a selling point. In ads that appeared in numerous trade publications and popular music magazines, Warner Bros. emphasized the amount of time and the attention to detail that went into completing *Anthem of the Sun*, noting that here was an "album one year in the making" and one that was so "sonically advanced to the point of making you rediscover your body."[36] In August, *Rolling Stone*, the recently formed music and culture magazine based in San Francisco, offered a free copy of *Anthem of the Sun* to every new subscriber.

In a gushing review in *Rolling Stone*, critic Jim Miller praised the first side of *Anthem of the Sun* as a "masterpiece of rock."[37] Miller notes how, over the course of the album, the "studio with its production work dissolves into live performance, the carefully crafted is thrown together with the casually tossed off, and the results are spliced together." In a comparison that almost certainly made Lesh and Constanten giddy, Miller writes that, much like the "mixture of electronic and serious music" in *Déserts*, a composition by Edgard Varèse (a pioneer of electronic and tape music), the Dead "have achieved a comparable blend of electronic and electric music." Miller admits, however, that the vocals are the weakest part of the album. Aside from that "minor quibble," he considers *Anthem of the Sun* as the Dead's "personal statement of the rock aesthetic."

Stepping outside of the historical exposition for a moment, Miller's evocation of a "rock aesthetic" recalls aspects of Theodore Gracyk's "aesthetic of rock" as described in the introduction. It will be recalled how, as a consequence of his general philosophy of art, Gracyk had serious doubts that, when "given a choice between any band's best studio work and their live recordings," fans would prefer live albums.[38] The Grateful Dead, Gracyk notes, "are the exception that proves the rule," and "for all their reputation as a free-flowing live ensemble, the group often adopts a calculated construction of music in the studio."[39] In support of his argument, he considers the structure, construction, and sound of *Anthem of the Sun*. Quoting Garcia, Gracyk suggests that, prior to their work on *Anthem of the Sun*, the band had no sense of "record consciousness." Unlike the live approach that the band adopted for the first record (what Gracyk refers to as a "realist attitude" to recording), *Anthem of the Sun* marks the moment when the band first achieved "record consciousness" and were, in Gracyk's words, "keenly aware of themselves as recording artists."[40]

It is important to recognize, however, that so much of what Gracyk identifies with an emerging sense of "record consciousness" on *Anthem of the Sun* was actually motivated by (and is reflective of) the band's live performance practices. The novel musical forms, extended improvisations, segues, experiments with noise, and overall sense of "trippiness" associated with the album (Garcia remarked that the record was "mixed for the hallucinations") come directly from—often times literally—the band's live performances.[41] Referring to the meticulously constructed amalgamation and arrangement of live and studio recordings that form *Anthem of the Sun*, Phil Lesh has described the album as a "metaphor for the manifestations in our live performances."[42]

At the same time, however, it is important to remember that *Anthem of the Sun* is an album born out of necessity and constructed out of convenience. The Dead had to provide a record to their label. By delivering an album, the band not only would satisfy a contractual obligation to Warner Bros. but also could begin to pay off the debt they had accrued while recording and experimenting in studios across the country. Following Hassinger's departure as producer, Dan Healy provided the technological know-how in the studio that the band lacked. Furthermore, and most important, by recording the band's concerts, Healy simply adopted and adapted what was already an established practice of the band's live performances. With the improvements in sound quality and mixing capabilities offered by multitrack recorders and mixing consoles, the Dead were now able to record and mix higher-quality live recordings such as those that were included on *Anthem of the Sun*.

The band utilized an 8-track machine to record a concert on February 14, 1968, at the Carousel Ballroom in San Francisco. Referring back to figure 1.1, the number 2 on the left side of the image corresponds to the location where recordings produced at the Carousel had been edited into the performance of "Alligator" on side 2 of *Anthem of the Sun*. Reading from left to right, a series of vertical slashes and a sequence of Arabic numerals identify the recorded performances featured on each of the eight tracks. Immediately below the note "Live Car." ("Live Carousel"), for instance, the number 1 refers to track 1, a track that features the mix that was sent to the public address ("PA") system and that would have been broadcast throughout the venue. At this time in the band's performance history, most (if not all) of their live instrumental sound came from the amplifiers onstage; the mix included on track 1 is probably composed of multiple vocal parts. Continuing across the page, track 2 was assigned to Mickey Hart and track 3 was for Bill Kreutzmann (most likely, each drummer was recorded using a single overhead microphone). Track 4 was reserved for Pigpen's lead vocals, track 5 for Phil Lesh's bass, track 6 for Bob Weir's guitar, and track 7 for Garcia's guitar. Finally, track 8 was used to capture the sound of the audience ("AUD"). Featuring a blend of crowd noise, stage amplification, and the performances that were projected over the PA system, track 8 offers a recorded representation of the Carousel Ballroom from the perspective of someone in the audience. During the production of *Anthem of the Sun*, the performances on tracks 1 through 7 would have been evaluated according to a variety of musical and technical standards. Mixed alongside the musical performances on tracks 1 through 7, the sounds and textures captured on track 8 provided record listeners with a sense of the "live feel" that the Dead were seeking to evoke/invoke on *Anthem of the Sun*.

Anxious to explore the possibilities afforded by the multitrack recorder, the band used the 8-track machine to tape a run of shows in August 1968 at Bill Graham's Fillmore West (formerly the Carousel Ballroom) and concerts at the Shrine Auditorium in Los Angeles.[43] Following their brief sojourn in Southern California, the band returned to the Bay Area to begin recording material for their third studio album.

Recording sessions for what would become *Aoxomoxoa* took place at Pacific Recording Studio in San Mateo, approximately twenty miles south of San Francisco. The record was produced by the Dead with the assistance of Betty Cantor and Bob Matthews, both of whom were closely acquainted with the band. In addition to working at Pacific Recording, both Cantor and Matthews were sound engineers at local venues and had assisted Dan Healy with the multitrack recordings of the Dead's performances in February at the Carousel. Cantor and Matthews were joined by Ron Wickersham, an employee of Ampex (the main industrial designer of tape-recording technology in the United States), who was at work in the studio building a mixing console that would accommodate the new 16-track recorder that was scheduled to arrive sometime before the end of the year.[44]

Unlike the chaotic recording sessions for *Anthem of the Sun*, sessions for the new album began smoothly. Robert Hunter was beginning to emerge as the Dead's primary songwriter; indeed, all the songs that would eventually appear on their forthcoming album were cowritten by Hunter. Whereas songs such as "China Cat Sunflower" and "St. Stephen" had been introduced to concert audiences earlier in the year, most of the songs on the album were composed and arranged in the studio. The sessions were not without their share of drama, of course, as Weir and Pigpen were (briefly) kicked out of the band. Despite this momentary personnel upheaval, band biographer Dennis McNally has remarked that the process of recording the new album "had gone so remarkably well that it could almost be described as efficient."[45]

"As Good as We All Hoped It Would Be" (Live/Dead, 1969)

The efficiency in the studio was overturned when the 16-track recorder arrived from Ampex in late December. By the beginning of 1969, it had become clear that, in McNally's words, the "possibilities opened by sixteen tracks had become something of a quagmire for a bunch of very stoned musicians."[46] Instead of simply transferring the tracks they had already produced on the 8-track recorder, the band chose to record new tracks for every song using the 16-track machine, the Ampex MM-1000. As the band began to rerecord tracks in the studio, they also used the 16-track machine to record select live performances, beginning with a New Year's Eve show at the Winterland in San Francisco.

Following the closure of Pacific Recording, the band acquired the 16-track recorder and continued to work on their new record at the similarly named Pacific High Recording, a studio in San Francisco. After a lengthy period devoted to mixing, the Dead released *Aoxomoxoa*, their third studio album, in June 1969. While Warner Bros. made a modest attempt at promoting the song "Dupree's Diamond Blues" as a single, the album was received by most fans and critics with a collective shrug. Writing in the *New York Times*, for example, critic Robert Christgau suggested to new fans that the "easiest introduction [to the band] is probably the first side of either of their two most recent albums," although, he admitted, "it's better to see them live."[47] In a cover story in the August issue of *Rolling Stone*, journalist Michael Lydon observed that, while all of the band's "records have fine moments," "none of them are as open and vital as the Dead live, even accounting for the change in medium."[48] Lydon mentions, however, that a "double record album of live performances . . . is planned" for release.[49]

The live record hinted at by Lydon was subsequently released in November 1969 as *Live/Dead*, a double album featuring performances recorded earlier that year. In late January, the band (along with recording engineers Betty Cantor and Bob Matthews) used the Ampex 16-track machine to record two shows at the Avalon Ballroom and a run of concerts from February to March at the Fillmore West. Released just a few months after *Aoxomoxoa*, *Live/Dead* quickly became the band's highest-charting album to date, rising as high as number 62 on the *Billboard* album chart.

For many critics and fans, *Live/Dead* was the album they had been hoping for and imagining since 1966. Writing in the *San Francisco Examiner*, Ralph Gleason described *Live/Dead* as "far and away the best thing the Dead have offered on record in terms of getting across what the band really sounds like" in concert.[50] In a review in *Rolling Stone*, critic and musician Lenny Kaye noted that *Live/Dead* "explains why the Dead are one of the best performing bands in America, why their music touches on ground that most other groups don't even know exists."[51] Following a vivid and detailed examination of the album's design and sound, Kaye boldly suggests, "If you'd like to visit a place where rock is likely to be in about five years, you might think of giving *Live/Dead* a listen or two."

By 1969, the Grateful Dead had yet to tour outside of North America; *Live/Dead* therefore offered audiences throughout the world a form of access to the band's renowned live performances. Writing in the British publication *Melody Maker*, for instance, reviewer Richard Williams admitted that he "wasn't expecting too much from [*Live/Dead*], having been bored silly by the Dead on their previous three albums."[52] "But all the fuss is clarified on this double-album," he continues. Listening to *Live/Dead*, Williams remarks in closing, "you can glimpse what all the fuss has been about."

Critics and fans recognized that the song sequencing on *Live/Dead* resembled the dynamic pacing of the band's more memorable live performances. Kaye observed how "one of the finer things about the record is that the cuts seem to have been chosen with a great deal of care." As with the band's best live performances, the song selection and sequencing on *Live/Dead* highlight the "group's quite considerable ability in tying together differing song-threads, letting them pass naturally into one another, almost as if they had been especially designed for such a move." Indeed, the two records of *Live/Dead* were originally pressed utilizing automatic sequencing whereby side 1 was paired (on the same record) with side 4 while side 2 was paired with side 3. Although there would still be a short break in the music as sides 2 and 4 fell into place on the record player, listeners could experience longer, more expansive musical journeys without having to flip records as often.[53] Referring to the sequence of songs beginning with "St. Stephen" to "The Eleven" and "Turn on Your Love Light," Kaye describes the production as "beautifully conceived," with "each piece clicking together perfectly."[54]

In a remarkable review published in the underground newspaper *San Francisco Good Times*, the author, black shadow, exclaims that the "programming of the record is perfect, too—which it should be, since it just duplicates a typical Dead set." Narrating the tracklist, black shadow describes how *Live/ Dead* opens with the songs

> "Dark Star" and "Saint Stephen" to get you centered and calm, "The Eleven" to get you standing up and . . . dancing, sliding into "Lovelight" which blows your mind and gets you so whacked out jumping and bopping that you're glad to fall on the floor and just listen to "Death Don't Have No Mercy." Now the acid (or whatever) is probably coming on heavy, so the Dead (ever heedful of your state of consciousness) get into "Feedback." Then, finally, "We Bid You Goodnight" gives you back your head again and sends you out into the night. Whew![55]

Along with the album's standout musical performances and dynamic pacing familiar from the band's live concerts, most fans and critics, whether they recognized it or not, were also responding to the *sound* of *Live/Dead*. *Live/ Dead* is not only the first live album to be recorded and mixed on 16-tracks but also is one of the earliest 16-track recordings to be commercially released. When *Live/Dead* came out in November 1969, record buyers and radio listeners may have been familiar with only a handful of albums and singles that had been recorded and mixed on sixteen tracks, including *Aoxomoxoa*; the eponymous album by Blood, Sweat & Tears (released in December 1968); and Frank Zappa's *Hot Rats* (from October 1969).

By the end of the 1960s, advances in recording technologies and methods of recording enabled engineers and producers to craft vibrant recordings that captured the complex sounds, dense textures, and extreme volumes of contemporary rock music. The Grateful Dead and their recording crew quickly recognized the opportunities and advantages that were offered by the Ampex MM-1000. From a practical perspective, the 16-track machine could accommodate all the instrumental and vocal resources of a band that, by 1969, had grown to seven members. From an aesthetic (not to mention commercial) perspective, the multitrack recorder allowed the band to mix and sculpt live performances utilizing techniques they had learned and developed in the studio. When tracking the original live performances that would appear on *Live/Dead*, the band and their recording engineers reserved four tracks for vocals; five tracks for drums and percussion played by Kreutzmann and Hart; two tracks for Lesh's bass guitar; and single tracks for Tom Constanten's electric organ, Garcia's guitar, and Weir's guitar. As they prepared to produce live recordings on the 16-track machine, Cantor, Matthews, and the band were clearly focused on the quality of the musical performances and the technical aspects of the recording process, for even with two tracks still available, they did not assign any microphones to record the audience. Whereas the multitrack recordings the band had produced at the Carousel Ballroom in 1968 acknowledged the sounds of the audience as an element of recorded liveness, the sound of the modern multitrack live recording as represented by *Live/ Dead* was accompanied by the (relative) silencing of the audience.[56]

Side 1 of *Live/Dead* introduced listeners to the expanded sound world offered by multitrack recording.[57] The opening is incredibly quiet (it is possible to hear the "humming" of an amplifier), and every sound seems to shimmer with a delicate intensity. As the record fades in, the band is in the midst of concluding one musical journey and looking to embark on another. Suggesting a possible direction, the bass takes the lead while a guitar, played by Weir, lightly plays a series of open-voiced chords. Playing in the instrument's middle and upper registers, the tone of the bass, in addition to being a bit louder, is full, expansive, and remarkably clear. Another electric guitar enters, played by Garcia. With its "gritty" timbre, Garcia's part complements the clean tone of Weir's guitar. The music continues to build as Lesh and Garcia improvise countermelodies over Weir's ringing guitar chords.

Until this moment, the sound of the recording has been dominated by the lower and middle registers of the bass, guitars, and drums. However, with a few clicks on the hi-hats (in the right channel) and a series of strokes on the ride cymbal (in the left channel), the frequency range of the performance expands dramatically. Accompanied now by the added brightness and brilliance provided by the cymbals, the guitars and bass continue their freely evolving collective improvisation on the song "Mountains of the Moon."

The music seems to float as the instruments blend and weave around one another. At 0:56, Lesh finally establishes a pulse by playing a well-defined rhythmic figure. The band begins to coalesce around the beat until, at 1:18, Lesh and Garcia, after getting the attention of Weir, play the distinctive riff that opens the song "Dark Star." Even as the performance continues to grow and evolve over the next twenty-two minutes (taking up all of side 1), the mix of "Dark Star" preserves the sense of sonic intimacy that was gradually revealed at the song's opening. As with all the performances on *Live/Dead*, "Dark Star" captures the extreme dynamic range and dramatic intensity that critics had been raving about and fans had come to expect of the band's live performances. "It's all here," black shadow assured readers at the end of his review of *Live/Dead*, "and it's as good as we all hoped it would be."[58]

Upon its release, *Live/Dead* offered listeners a recorded musical experience that was imagined (and promoted) as the "next-best-thing" to a Dead concert. Of course, what fans and critics heard (and may continue to hear) on *Live/Dead* are not the original sounds of specific live performances. Instead, we hear how the original sounds created during particular live performances have been carefully mixed and painstakingly edited according to production standards that performers, industry executives, and listeners had come to expect of contemporary commercial studio recordings. The various recording, engineering, and mixing decisions that were made during the production of *Live/Dead* constructed an idealized representation of the band's live sound and provided a sonic template for the Dead as they sought to (re)produce their unique form of liveness on subsequent live recordings.

The Dead Come Alive (1970–1972)

By the middle of 1970, fans and critics across the country and around the world acknowledged that, of all the albums the Grateful Dead had released, *Live/Dead* had come the closest to representing the band's live sound on record. After the band's attempts to capture, incorporate, and perform liveness on their earliest studio recordings, the newly expanded sound world offered by the 16-track machine allowed for greater clarity in recording and provided greater flexibility in molding and mixing the performances in postproduction. For fans and critics who had experienced the Dead in concert, *Live/Dead* was considered a very good approximation of the band's live sound. At the same time, for those people who had never experienced the Grateful Dead in concert, *Live/Dead* provided an idealized representation of the group's shows. Among fans and critics, the album offered proof that the Grateful Dead were capable of capturing an element of "liveness" on record. Furthermore, the commercial and critical success of *Live/Dead* proved to Warner Bros. that the Dead had a devoted fan base that would purchase records, especially when provided with a product that was deemed to be a more accurate representation of the band's live concerts.

When *Live/Dead* was released in November 1969, however, the version of the Grateful Dead that audiences were hearing on record did not resemble the version of the band they were hearing in concert. To be sure, songs that had traditionally served as vehicles for extended group improvisations continued to be performed in concert, songs such as "Dark Star," "The Other One," and "Caution." By late 1969, however, the band had introduced a number of new songs to their concert setlists, most of which were cowritten with Robert Hunter. Hunter's most recent songs—such as "Uncle John's Band," "Casey Jones," "Dire Wolf," and "High Time"—were often set against the backdrop of a mythic, imagined American past. Following the evocative, abstract imagery of his earlier lyrics, Hunter's latest songs were populated by a host of complex and colorful characters, all of whom are described in stories of love and loss, life and death, and good and bad.

In February 1970, the band (minus Tom Constanten, who had recently left the group) returned to Pacific High Recording Studios to begin sessions for their next studio album, *Workingman's Dead*. With a greater emphasis on vocal harmonies, the prominent use of acoustic instruments, and the evocative wail of the pedal steel guitar (played by Garcia), the tone of *Workingman's Dead* recalls the "Bakersfield" sound of country artists such as Buck Owens and Merle Haggard. Indeed, Haggard's song "Mama Tried" had recently been introduced into the band's live repertoire. Stylistically, *Workingman's Dead* also sits comfortably alongside recordings of a number of contemporary bands and songwriters, including the Band; Bob Dylan; Kris Kristofferson; Crosby, Stills, and Nash; and others.[59]

As the Dead continued to grow and develop as a band and as a business organization, sound engineers Bob Matthews, Betty Cantor, Ron Wickersham, Owsley "Bear" Stanley (the band's earliest live sound mixer), and instrument builder Rick Turner were active in a company called Alembic. For all practical purposes, Alembic served as the Grateful Dead's instrument technicians, builders, sound reinforcement designers, and recording crew engineers.[60] *Workingman's Dead* was recorded on Alembic's 16-track machine and was produced by the band, Cantor, and Matthews. Given the Dead's history and reputation in the recording studio, Bob Matthews noted how "*Workingman's Dead* was done very quickly," explaining that the band and crew "went into the studio first and spent a couple of days basically rehearsing—performing— all the tunes, recording them on 2-track." As Matthews recalled:

> When that was done, I sat down and spliced together the tunes— beginning of Side One to end of Side One; beginning of Side Two to end of Side Two. I got that idea from listening to *Sgt. Pepper*. Before we even start, let's have a concept of what the end product is going to feel like, sequencing-wise. We made a bunch of cassette copies and gave them to the band. They rehearsed some more in their rehearsal studio, and then they came in and recorded. But at all times there was the perspective of where we were in the album.[61]

Much like on the band's debut record, the instrumental backing tracks for *Workingman's Dead* were recorded live in the studio; vocal parts and select instrumental overdubs were recorded later. After a short time spent mixing the record, the album was released in June 1970. Given the group's efficiency, focus, and clear sense of direction, *Workingman's Dead* marks the moment when the band finally attained the sense of "record consciousness" to which they had been aspiring since 1967. "*Workingman's Dead*," Garcia recalled many years later, "was our first true studio album."[62]

In his review in *Rolling Stone*, Andy Zwerling wrote that "*Workingman's Dead* is an excellent album. It's a warming album. And most importantly, the Dead have finally produced a complete studio album."[63] Zwerling's opinion was shared by numerous critics and fans, both old and new. With the song "Casey Jones" in heavy rotation on FM radio, *Workingman's Dead* peaked at number 27 on *Billboard*'s album chart; the song "Uncle John's Band" rose as high as number 69 on the singles chart. Aided by an extensive promotional campaign, *Workingman's Dead* had already sold close to a quarter of a million copies a month after it was released.

Less than four months later, the band released another studio album: *American Beauty*. In many ways, the lyrical themes and musical arrangements explored on *Workingman's Dead* carry over into the songs, on *American Beauty*. (Drummer Bill Kreutzmann has even admitted, "I often get *Workingman's Dead* and *American Beauty* mixed up with each other.")[64] Building on the momentum of *Workingman's Dead*, *American Beauty* rose as high as number 30 on *Billboard*'s album chart as the song "Truckin'" peaked at number 64 on the singles chart. On the strength of songs such as "Uncle John's Band" and "Casey Jones" (on *Workingman's Dead*), along with "Ripple," "Sugar Magnolia," and "Truckin'" (all on *American Beauty*), the band finally had radio hits. By the spring of 1971, the Grateful Dead appeared to have recreated themselves as a commercially and critically successful "album band" capable, it seemed, of producing hit records with apparent ease.

The commercial and critical acclaim that accompanied *Workingman's Dead* and *American Beauty* contributed to larger audiences for the band's live performances. To accommodate their growing fan base, the Dead maintained a tireless touring schedule. While the band and their crew continued to produce lower-fidelity concert recordings on 2-track, the Dead used the 16-track machine to record live performances on only two occasions in 1970: once to record a television special in February and again for the band's New Year's Eve concert at Winterland in San Francisco. In 1971, however, Bob Matthews and Betty Cantor joined the band on the road to record shows on the East Coast, beginning in February in Port Chester, New York, and in April for a run of concerts at the Manhattan Center and Bill Graham's Fillmore East in New York City. Between these performances, Alembic and the band also used the 16-track machine to record a concert on March 24 at the Winterland in San Francisco.

Select performances from these shows were included on the band's next commercial live recording, *Grateful Dead*, an album that has since come to be known among fans as *Skull and Roses*.[65] By 1969, the band's live shows had started to assume a relatively standard form, and when it was released in 1971, *Skull and Roses* was sequenced to suggest the form of a "typical" Grateful Dead concert. As drummer Bill Kreutzmann has noted, now that the band had "more accessible tunes alongside our wilder jam vehicles, we broke apart the live show into different sections."[66] More specifically, the band's concerts at this time were presented as two sets where the first set was devoted to performances of "accessible tunes" (both originals and covers) and featured very few, if any, extended group improvisations. Following an intermission, the second set, as described by Kreutzmann, "was more open and free, with a lot more jamming and improvisation."[67] It was during the second set that the band would typically "stretch out" on songs such as "Dark Star," "The Other One," and other improvisational vehicles that would have been familiar to longtime fans. As Kreutzmann has acknowledged, this was the concert "format we kept for the rest of our career."[68]

Released as a double album, each record of *Skull and Roses* offers a condensed representation of what could be imagined as a typical Grateful Dead concert.[69] Sides 1 and 3 both represent prototypical "first sets" and feature newly recorded original songs ("Bertha" and "Playing in the Band") as well as many covers, including Merle Haggard's "Mama Tried," Kris Kristofferson's "Me and Bobby McGee," and Chuck Berry's "Johnny B. Goode." Sides 2 and 4, by contrast, are conceived as "second sets." Side 2, for example, fades in as the final strains of "Cryptical Envelopment" give way to a drum solo before transforming into an extended improvisation on "The Other One." Side 4 also features songs that were commonly heard during the band's second sets, including "Wharf Rat" (cowritten by Garcia and Hunter) and an extended jam on Buddy Holly's "Not Fade Away" that segues into the traditional song, "Goin' Down the Road Feelin' Bad."

In addition to the song sequencing, *Skull and Roses* is mixed in a manner that is designed to evoke the spatial experience of a contemporary Grateful Dead concert. As with most pop and rock recordings, the bass, drums, and lead vocals are mixed down the center of the stereo image.[70] Bob Weir's rhythm guitar is heard on the right channel while Garcia's guitar parts are often panned to the left. The resulting stereo image corresponds to what audiences would have seen at that time when attending a Grateful Dead concert, with Garcia on stage right and Weir to his left. As on *Live/Dead*, there is very little audience noise on *Skull and Roses*. At times, sounds from the crowd are mixed in at the end of songs ("Bertha") or are used as a fade-in before being quickly faded out as the song begins ("Me and My Uncle").

Despite being sequenced to resemble the form of a standard concert and mixed to suggest the perspective of someone in the audience, the addition of numerous vocal and instrumental overdubs strongly suggest that the band did not consider *Skull and Roses* to be a realistic depiction of the live concert experience(s). To be sure, audiences were certainly aware that what they were hearing on *Skull and Roses* was not (just) what was recorded at the original concerts. Despite not having played during these shows, for instance, organist Merl Saunders is identified in the liner notes as playing on the songs "Bertha," "Playing in the Band," and "Wharf Rat." Saunders's performance on "Wharf Rat" is especially poignant as his electric organ overdubs underscore the range of emotions expressed in the lyrics. The dramatic arc of "Wharf Rat" reaches a climax when Garcia sings "I'll get up and fly away . . . ," a performance made even more harrowing by Garcia's double-tracked vocal part recorded in postproduction. Featuring heavily edited performances of many of the band's most recent songs, *Skull and Roses* could arguably be considered a studio album masquerading as a live record.

Skull and Roses sold over half a million copies within a month of its release and became the band's first record to be certified Gold. By the end of 1971, the Grateful Dead had emerged as one of the most popular and lucrative acts signed to Warner Bros. Building on their recent successes and newfound respect among executives at Warner Bros., the band, led by their tour manager, Sam Cutler, convinced the label to finance an overseas tour; in April 1972 the Dead, their crew, along with many family members and friends set off for a tour of Europe. The Dead and Warner Bros. also agreed that all the concerts of their European tour would be recorded by Alembic for yet another commercial live record. Along with their instruments and sound system, the band shipped a massive amount of recording equipment to Europe in the spring of 1972. Upon arriving in England, the recording gear was installed into a specially designed truck that would serve as a mobile recording unit. Produced by the band and Betty Cantor and engineered by a new Alembic employee, Dennis Leonard, all of the shows from the Grateful Dead's European tour were recorded using a 16-track machine.

In November 1972, the band released *Europe '72*, a triple album featuring performances compiled from their recent tour. *Europe '72* includes versions of songs by Hunter and Garcia that would become staples of the band's live repertoire for many decades, including "He's Gone," "Brown-Eyed Woman," and "Tennessee Jed." The album also features songs cowritten by Weir and Hunter, including "Jack Straw" and "Sugar Magnolia." With the exception of a spacey, ethereal instrumental passage from a performance of "The Other One" (identified as "Epilog/"Prelude," spanning sides 5 and 6), *Europe '72* does not include any group improvisations or extended "jams" that audiences had come to expect of the band's concerts, especially as part of the second set.

As with *Skull and Roses*, the recorded live performances that were included on *Europe '72* were heavily augmented by overdubs, including most of the lead and backing vocals. Bob Matthews (who was responsible for mixing the band's live sound during the tour) recalls how, after returning to the United States, the band re-created their stage setup in Alembic's studio in San Francisco and rerecorded many of the original vocal performances. With seemingly very little concern for verisimilitude, Matthews explained that the "band wanted the albums to sound as good as they could make them. They weren't purists at all."[71] Indeed, one could be forgiven for forgetting that *Europe '72* is even a live album, for Matthews and the band included very little crowd noise in the final mix. Even with the addition of two new band members—keyboardist Keith Godchaux and vocalist Donna Jean Godchaux—the mix of *Europe '72* is nearly identical to that heard on *Skull and Roses*. The recording of "Jack Straw," for instance, provides a vivid representation of the audience perspective first established on *Skull and Roses*, with Garcia's vocals and guitars heard on the left channel and Weir's vocals and guitars on the right.[72]

The Grateful Dead's growing reputation for liveness was reflected in the design, promotion, and marketing of *Europe '72*.[73] Numerous photographs included in an accompanying booklet establish the scene and the setting of the band's concerts in the mind of the record listener. Alongside Mary Ann Mayer's images of the band and the crew exploring famous landmarks, the booklet also includes dramatic and lighthearted photographs of the band in midperformance, location shots from select venues, and pictures of fans camping out or standing in line waiting to enter a venue. In the mystical liner notes attributed to the "Choirmaster," Willy Legate, a longtime friend of Garcia, proclaimed that "THERE IS NOTHING LIKE A GRATEFUL DEAD CONCERT." Legate's phrase—part observation and part prophecy—would come to be associated with the band for the rest of their existence (and beyond).

Legate's hyperbole was echoed in the promotional campaign for *Europe '72*. In a letter to radio stations that accompanied prereleases of the songs "Ramble on Rose," "Jack Straw," and "Mr. Charlie," Joe Smith (now the president of Warner Bros.) wrote that the "Grateful Dead have been considered by many to be the greatest live band in the world. Warner Bros. has long believed this of the Dead and have tried with some success on two previous live albums to capture that special feeling contained in the phrase 'Grateful Dead Dance Concert.' What you have in your hand is a portion of our latest, and to our way of thinking, best effort at a vinyl version of the Dead live."[74]

Many record buyers appeared to agree with Smith's opinion. Within a few weeks of its release, *Europe '72* had sold over half a million copies and was the band's second consecutive record to be certified Gold. With *Europe '72*, the various ideals relating to the authenticity of live performances ("THERE IS NOTHING LIKE A GRATEFUL DEAD CONCERT") and the representational capabilities of live recordings ("best effort at a vinyl version of the Dead live") were combined, interwoven, and marketed to fans who were eager to experience (perhaps even reexperience) that "special feeling," that elusive sense of liveness, that critics and the band had been alluding to for years.

Other people, however, were beginning to grow weary of the Dead's steady stream of live records. Having previously described *Live/Dead* as "a place where rock is likely to be in about five years," Lenny Kaye, in his review of *Skull and Roses*, lamented that "there's nothing here that doesn't really amount to filler at an average Dead performance."[75] Given the commercial success that accompanied the group's recent studio records, Kaye, along with many other fans, expressed nostalgia "for them golden days of yore, when not much of anything could be predicted from the group except that they would inevitably try through the course of each performance to take you some place you'd never been before."[76] "But ever since the pyrotechnics of *Live/Dead*," Kaye recalls, "our boys seem to have backed away from such experimentation and confrontation, and the result is a mixture of pleasant good-time music and solid solos."[77] *Skull and Roses* "can't quite be called bad," Kaye suggests, "but it still can provide a bit of a letdown for those who have come to expect only great things" from the Grateful Dead.[78]

In his review of *Europe '72* in *Crawdaddy*, Patrick Snyder-Scumpy bluntly remarks that the band's "seemingly interminable procession of live recordings has become rather boring."[79] For some time, he notes, "the goal of a live rock act was to reproduce in concert the sound of their recordings. The Grateful Dead, who built their reputation and gathered a following with their live act, have reversed the old equation and have made their records sound like their concerts by the obvious stratagem of taping their live performances and then releasing them."[80] Snyder-Scumpy recognizes how the Dead had adapted modern studio recording techniques and mixing strategies to create a distinctive sound, a sense of "liveness," on record. But whereas this recording approach sounded novel and fresh when it first appeared on *Live/Dead*, the band's recent live recordings seemed formulaic, predictable, and overly "slick," all qualities that had never been attributed to the band or their live performances. In Snyder-Scumpy's opinion, the Dead have traded "exuberance and unpredictability for expertise and precision." Concluding his review, he recalls how *Live/Dead* "was a moment of brilliant sprinting and I, for one, am waiting for a new sprint, another burst of energetic creativity that will again expand the frontiers of rock music."[81]

(A Live) *History of the Grateful Dead, Volume One* (1973)

Despite the misgivings of many critics and fans, the Grateful Dead released another live album in 1973. Featuring recordings made at the Fillmore East in February 1970, *History of the Grateful Dead, Volume One (Bear's Choice)* was compiled by Owsley "Bear" Stanley and was the last record that the Dead owed to Warner Bros. It is fitting that the band selected Bear (as he was generally known) to oversee their final album on the label. In addition to being independently wealthy, Bear was also (in)famous as a chemist and was well known among hippies and law enforcement for making some of the highest-quality LSD in the United States (perhaps the entire world).

Bear was also incredibly interested in sound, and beginning in the late 1960s, he often recorded the Dead's concert performances while serving as their live sound technician. For many years, Bear and the band sought to create a public address system that could handle the extreme volumes and dynamic contrasts that were an integral part of the Grateful Dead's performance practice. When fans and critics referred to the power and intensity of the band's concerts (such as Richard Goldstein's memorable remark that the band sounded "like live thunder"), they were most certainly referring to the live sound made possible by Bear. As a founder and co-owner of Alembic, Bear continued to work with the band into the 1970s.[82]

As the producer of the Grateful Dead's latest live album, Bear compiled a unique portrait of the band, one that hearkened back to their roots in early rock and roll (including a version of the Everly Brothers' "Wake Up Little Susie"), country blues ("Katie Mae"), electric blues ("Smokestack Lightning"), rhythm and blues ("Hard to Handle"), and country folk ("Dark Hollow"). "Black Peter," a song featured on *Workingman's Dead*, is the only original song to appear on the album. The recordings included on *History of the Grateful Dead* capture the band performing shortly after the release of *Live/Dead* and just before they would enter the studio to record *Workingman's Dead*. Featuring more performances by Pigpen than any of the band's previous live albums, *History of the Grateful Dead* is also a tribute to one of the band's founding members who had passed away following a long illness in March 1973.

There is an unpolished quality to *History of the Grateful Dead* that distinguishes it from the band's previous live albums. The packaging of *History of the Grateful Dead*, for example, seems rather bland, especially when compared with the vibrant cover art and novel designs of the band's earlier live records. While artist R. D. (Bob) Thomas's "marching bears" would become an enduring image in the iconography of the Dead, the graphic design of *History of the Grateful Dead* pales in comparison to Thomas's vivid painting that adorns the cover of *Live/Dead* or Alton Kelly's instantly recognizable covers for *Skull and Roses* and (with Stanley Mouse) *Europe '72*.

At the same time, *History of the Grateful Dead* does not sound like the band's previous live albums. There is an informal sense of "looseness" to many of the performances, a quality that, for some listeners, may suggest a more authentic representation of the original concert experience. The record opens with a few notes on an acoustic guitar as an audience member yells out to Pigpen, "Take a solo!" Pigpen, who almost never played guitar during the Dead's live performances, replies, "Whaddya think I'm tryin' to do, man?," a response that elicits laughter from the audience at the Fillmore East. "Let me make my mistakes on my own," Pigpen continues. "I don't need your help." Sure enough, during the second verse of the song "Katie Mae," Pigpen announces from the stage that he just "made a mistake." Many of the recorded performances featured on *History of the Grateful Dead* include stage banter between band members or moments during which the performers are heard tuning or "noodling" on their instruments. In one instance, Bob Weir suggests that the band play the song "Dark Hollow," to which Garcia asks, "Do you know the words?"

In terms of its design and sound, *History of the Grateful Dead* resembles the "gritty," vérité aesthetic often associated with unauthorized "bootleg" live records. Featuring mistakes, stage dialogue, and crowd noise, *History of the Grateful Dead* could, in many ways, be considered an "official" bootleg album. In contrast to the meticulously produced, studio-enhanced live albums that the band had previously released, *History of the Grateful Dead* exhibits an alternative aesthetic of recorded liveness, one that, as I examine in the next chapter, emerged within a community of fans that sought to capture and preserve a document of liveness that had not been edited, overdubbed, or "fixed in the mix."

The Grateful Dead (1977) (*Left to right*: Donna Jean Godchaux, Keith Godchaux, Phil Lesh, Bill Kreutzmann, Bob Weir, Jerry Garcia, Mickey Hart)

"The Next Best Thing to Being There"

TAPES, TAPING, AND AN ALTERNATIVE
AESTHETIC OF RECORDED LIVENESS

With the release of *History of the Grateful Dead, Volume One* in July 1973, the band satisfied the terms of their recording contract with Warner Bros. A few months later, the Grateful Dead released *Wake of the Flood*, their first studio album since 1970 and the first recording produced by the band's new company, Grateful Dead Records.[1] In an interview with journalist Cameron Crowe, Jerry Garcia explained how the band had "planned for over a year to form our own record manufacturing and distributing company so as to package and promote our stuff in a more human manner."[2] Along with the members of the band and their touring crew, the expanding Grateful Dead organization included various administrative, marketing, and promotional personnel, all of whom helped in managing the day-to-day business operations. "There are a lot of people on our payroll," Garcia explained, "and we can't really count that much on record royalties to take care of business. The live shows we do are the main source of income for the band, and we've been playing an awful lot to pay off our overhead."[3] By forming their own company, Garcia imagined how the band might achieve a greater balance between recording and playing live, explaining that "if the records cover a larger share of our overhead, then we can pick and choose on our live shows. We can experiment a little bit and play the really groovy shows."[4]

Without a doubt, the band had recently played some "really groovy shows." In June, the Grateful Dead played two sold-out concerts co-headlining with the Allman Brothers Band at RFK Stadium in Washington, DC. In July, the Dead and the Allman Brothers Band played alongside The Band at the Summer Jam at Watkins Glen in New York, a single-day festival that attracted over 600,000 people. If the band's tenure on Warner Bros. is remembered as a period during which they learned to navigate the obligations and expectations of the record industry, the present version of the Dead, it would seem, commenced with a renewed focus on playing live.

The Dead's commitment to providing the best possible concert experience for their fans was reflected in the amount of research and development they devoted to their live sound, work that was undertaken by members of the crew, including Owsley "Bear" Stanley and Dan Healy. A group of sound engineers and designers at Alembic, notably Ron Wickersham and Rick Turner (an instrument designer and sound engineer), also assisted in creating some of the most sophisticated and powerful sound systems of the era. As described in the newsletter that was mailed to fans in June 1973, the sound system used by the Dead that summer weighed approximately thirty thousand pounds and required a semi-trailer to transport.[5] A few months later, *Rolling Stone* published a short piece on Alembic in which Turner provided a detailed account of the Dead's current sound system, describing the unique design, the number and sizes of the many speakers, the various wattages, and the use of phase-canceling microphones.[6]

The band's live PA system continued to evolve, and by the middle of 1974, it came to be known among the Dead and their fans as the Wall of Sound (figure 2.1). As described in a newsletter from December 1974, the Wall of Sound was a "combination of six individual systems, each being electronically separate and having a specific purpose and function. No two musical 'voices' go through the same system. Thus the vocals, piano, drums, lead guitar, rhythm guitar and bass each have their own channel(s) of amplification. This separation is designed to produce an undistorted sound, a clean sound in which qualities like 'transparency,' 'brilliance,' 'presence,' and 'clarity' are substantial musical dimensions."[7] Weighing close to seventy-five tons, the band's mammoth system was capable of producing an "acceptable sound at a quarter of a mile and a fine sound up to five or six hundred feet, where it

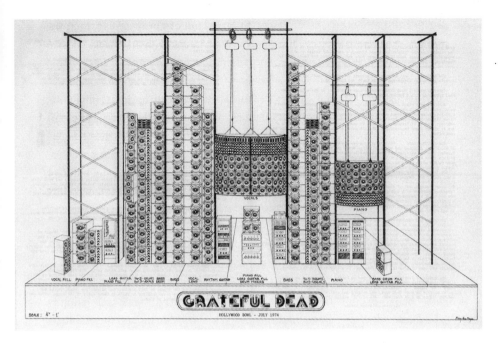

FIGURE 2.1. The "Wall of Sound" (Dead Heads Newsletter, July 1974)

begins to be distorted by wind." "A sound system could get the same volume from half as much power," the text boasts, "but it wouldn't have the quality."

By 1973, the Dead had transitioned from playing in ballrooms, college auditoriums, and other medium-sized halls and were now regularly performing in arenas and stadiums. The constantly evolving designs and various configurations of their sound system were carried out by the band and their crew to ensure that the entire audience, even those people farthest from the stage, could enjoy a high-quality audio experience of the concert. As the venues got bigger, concertgoers certainly appreciated the clarity and power of the Dead's live sound system.

For many fans who were unable to see the Dead perform, the enhancements made to the band's live sound were noticeable on many of the live recordings that were becoming increasingly available around this time. To be sure, these were not official live albums produced by the band but instead were amateur recordings made by members of the audience who, in most instances, had smuggled equipment into the venue, including tape machines, microphones, cables, batteries, and multiple reels of tape. Despite the policies of many bands (and venues) that prohibited the recording of live performances, the practice of taping the Dead's concerts had become so pervasive that, by the middle of the 1970s, most tapers made little effort to conceal their equipment. In a radio interview from September 1973, Bob Weir describes looking out from the stage and seeing a "forest of microphones" aimed toward the band's massive PA system.[8] As more fans taped the Dead's concerts (including shows that were broadcast on radio), many of these recordings began to circulate within an active community of collectors and traders. Through the generosity of people who were willing to copy, share, and trade audience-produced tapes, fans throughout the country and around the world suddenly had free access to a growing library of live recordings of the Grateful Dead, including concerts from early in their career as well as shows from the latest tour.

Taping and tape trading represent some of the most significant and influential practices that originated with, and were nurtured by, fans of the Grateful Dead. Fan-produced live recordings—often referred to simply as "tapes"—have been called the "sacred talismans that unite the tribe" of Deadheads.[9] In contrast to the band's officially released live albums (such as *Live/Dead*, *Skull and Roses*, and *Europe '72*), David Shenk and Steve Silberman have observed, "one of the most attractive things about tapes is that they offer whole shows, with mistakes, warm-up tunes, and the spontaneous development of musical architectures intact."[10] Echoing the opinion of many fans, John Dwork has asserted that "the tapes have power," for "as every Deadhead knows, the Dead's studio records barely scratch the surface of the *real* Grateful Dead Experience." "The true magic," Dwork claims, "is found in and around the band's live concert performances. And as we all learned quickly, concert tapes were and are the next best thing to being there."[11]

Dwork's recollection that he and other people "learned" how to appreciate the value and meaning of the Dead's live recordings is revealing for, as I describe in this chapter, the interrelated practices of taping, collecting, and trading were shaped by the ideals and associated discourse of liveness that had developed around the band beginning in the mid-1960s. Drawing on the work of literary critic Susan Stewart, I consider the tapes as forms of "souvenirs" made meaningful according to a variety of personal and historical narratives of liveness, narratives that served to connect listeners to the original concert experience and, in many ways, to connect fans to the band. The practice of taping established a novel relationship between the Dead and their fans, a relationship that would develop and evolve over the course of the band's existence and beyond.

Taping emerged at the same time that the practice of "bootlegging" and the manufacturing of "bootleg" records first came to the attention of people throughout the music industry. Therefore, before examining the complex meaning(s) and aesthetic discourse that formed around fan-produced tapes and tape trading, it is worth considering how the band and members of the Grateful Dead organization reacted to having their live concerts recorded at the dawn of the bootleg era.

Busting (and Besting) the Bootleggers

On December 31, 1970, portions of the Grateful Dead's concert at the Winterland Arena in San Francisco were broadcast live on local television and radio stations. At one point during the performance, Phil Lesh spoke directly to the audience, observing that there were "some bootleggers among you back here!" Jerry Garcia requested that the light crew "put a spotlight on the microphones out there" in the audience while Lesh urged the band's road crew and the staff at the Winterland to "find out who these people are, [and] follow the cords from those microphones." Garcia jokingly refers to the presence of "Underground Records, Incorporated," at which point Lesh, adopting the cadence and delivery of an advertising pitch-man, exhorts the audience to "find this [bootleg] for ten dollars at your local record store!"[12]

Of course, the fact that we can listen to this exchange between Garcia and Lesh (along with the musical performances) means that people *were* recording the band's concert that night. And although the Dead may have busted a few fans who were recording inside the venue, just as many people (if not more) were taping the concert as it was being broadcast on the radio. Not surprisingly, the practice of concert taping was interpreted by most members of the Dead organization at that time as the actions of "bootleggers." For a band that had come to symbolize most, if not all, of the antiestablishment and anticommercial ideals of the 1960s counterculture, it seems that there was a limit to what the Dead would tolerate from their fans. As the incident from the Winterland suggests, the band would not tolerate having their music—their liveness—"ripped off" by bootleggers.

More than a year before the Dead's New Year's Eve concert in 1970, bootleg recordings featuring some of rock's top performers began to appear in independent record stores across the country. Generally considered as the first major bootleg of the rock era, *Great White Wonder*, a compilation of unreleased studio and demonstration ("demo") recordings of Bob Dylan, came out in July 1969.[13] Later that year, another bootleg caught the attention of fans, critics, and people throughout the music industry. Released on Lurch Records in December, the bootleg album *Live R Than You'll Ever Be* included performances by the Rolling Stones that were recorded during a concert at the Oakland Coliseum in November. Following the concert, the recordings were transferred to vinyl, pressed, and distributed in a plain white jacket that featured the album title stamped in ink. The name of the band does not appear on the cover. Instead, on some pressings, the album is attributed to "The Greatest Group on Earth," a riff on "The Greatest Rock and Roll Band in the World," a phrase that Sam Cutler, the Stones' tour manager, used when introducing the group during their 1969 tour. It was reported that Cutler was so impressed with *Live R Than You'll Ever Be* that he bought copies for himself and the members of the Stones.[14] Released in time for the Christmas holiday, the album sought to capitalize on the excitement and anticipation that accompanied the Stones' 1969 tour and the recent publicity following the tragic events at the Altamont Speedway Free Festival.

Like Cutler, many reviewers were impressed by the exceptional sound quality of *Live R Than You'll Ever Be*, a quality that was even more remarkable given that the performance was recorded by a member of the audience using a handheld microphone and a portable tape machine. In a review of the album in *Rolling Stone*, critic Greil Marcus noted how, as a "bootleg disc and as pure music, [*Live R Than You'll Ever Be*] is almost unbelievable."[15] Marcus describes the sound quality as "superb, full of presence, picking up drums, bass, both guitars and the vocals beautifully." "The LP is in stereo," Marcus continues, but "while it doesn't seem to be mixed, the balance is excellent." For Marcus, the album "captures every thrill of the Stones live on stage . . . and in fact it offers more . . . than the concerts did—because it sounds even better." "It is," Marcus asserts, "the ultimate Rolling Stones album."[16]

Given the proliferation of bootlegs by 1970, it is ironic that some of the earliest unauthorized live recordings of the Grateful Dead did not appear on labels like Garcia's fictional (yet entirely plausible) "Underground Records, Incorporated" but were produced, instead, by a major label. In October 1970, MGM Records released *Vintage Dead*, an album featuring traditional songs and cover versions that had been recorded at the Avalon Ballroom in San Francisco in 1966. The recordings that were used for *Vintage Dead* were originally produced by Robert Cohen who had worked as a sound engineer at the Avalon. As part of an agreement with Together Records, an independent label from Los Angeles, the members of the Grateful Dead authorized the use of Cohen's recordings for a retrospective album of the San Francisco scene, an album that would include live performances of the Dead, the Jefferson Airplane, and other bands. Together Records went out of business, however, and MGM acquired Cohen's original tapes. In November 1970, Sunflower Records, an imprint of MGM, released material from Cohen's tapes on an album titled *Vintage Dead*. Other performances from these tapes appeared in 1971 on *Historic Dead*, also released on Sunflower.[17]

Unlike the multitrack recordings that were used in the production of *Live/Dead*, the live performances that appear on *Vintage Dead* were most likely recorded on a 2-track stereo machine. While the sound quality of *Vintage Dead* is very good, it does not come close to matching the quality of the band's official live releases. Therefore, in an effort to attract potential record buyers who might be skeptical of the sound quality, MGM promoted *Vintage Dead* as a historical document of the San Francisco scene before the Summer of Love.

In the accompanying liner notes to *Vintage Dead*, Robert Cohen (quoting Chet Helms, the well-known San Francisco promoter and manager) proclaims that "in the beginning there was the Grateful Dead. And the Avalon Ballroom was part of that beginning."[18] It was while playing for dancers at the Avalon in 1966 that the Dead first gained a reputation as a live band and, as Cohen explains, "this is why I recorded them." Cohen remarks that "Jerry Garcia once said, 'I don't believe the live sound, the live excitement can be recorded.'"[19] "Well, here it is," Cohen assures record buyers, "in its liveness, pressed on acetate for those who were not there." Despite the album's "rawer" sound quality, *Vintage Dead* was a modest commercial success for MGM. Although the band would not receive any royalties from record sales, *Vintage Dead* peaked at number 127 on the *Billboard* album chart in December 1970, just a few weeks before Garcia and Lesh called out suspected bootleggers during their New Year's Eve concert at the Winterland.

In an interview with Charles Reich and Jann Wenner published in *Rolling Stone* in 1972, Garcia dismissed the recordings that appear on *Vintage Dead*, explaining that there is "no point in going back to the past, for one thing, and for another thing, those performances weren't meant to stand around forever. They were for *that night*. And if you were stoned and there that night, that was probably *exactly* what was happening, but it's not happening *now*. It's just a source of embarrassment."[20] Despite Garcia's misgivings, an underground market for live recordings of the Grateful Dead had started to form by the early 1970s. Given this new market, it was the opinion of everyone associated with the Dead's expanding business organization that the band, and not the bootleggers, should be the ones to reap the financial rewards of what Robert Cohen so intriguingly described as the band's sense of "liveness."

This was probably the attitude of the Dead toward bootleggers and bootlegging when Sam Cutler became the band's tour manager in early 1970. As the former road manager for the Rolling Stones, Cutler, as mentioned previously, had been introduced to the burgeoning market and the improved sound quality of bootlegs with *Live R Than You'll Ever Be*. Cutler, therefore, certainly understood the promotional value and economic opportunities associated with such recordings. If there was a market for amateur-produced live recordings of the Dead (and there certainly was), then the Grateful Dead organization should, at the very least, have some control over how such recordings were distributed.

For the time being, this meant cracking down on tapers in the audience, a job that was tasked to Cutler and the band's road crew. There are numerous accounts beginning in 1970 of tapers being harassed by Cutler and other members of the crew.[21] Often, tapers were urged to stop recording; frequently, however, the crew would confiscate equipment and even cut the many microphone cables that were strewn throughout the venue. In a recording of a concert from Temple University in Philadelphia, Pennsylvania, on May 16, 1970, Cutler can be heard demanding a tape from an audience member ("I want the tape! I want the tape!") while the band is performing the song "New Speedway Boogie."[22] Cutler identifies himself as the band's manager and offers to pay for the tape. The recording stops for a moment, suggesting that the taper took up Cutler's offer of money or promised to stop recording (perhaps both). However, the recording starts again (the band is still playing "New Speedway Boogie"), at which point Cutler returns and demands that the taper "turn it off, turn it off!" (It is unclear what happened next as the recording comes to an abrupt stop.) At times, members of the band were more tolerant of taping. In a remarkably clear audience recording made by taper Rob Bertrando of a concert at the Hollywood Palladium in Los Angeles on August 6, 1971, Bob Weir can be heard calling out to someone in the audience, saying, "Hey, you down there with the microphone, if you want to get a decent recording you gotta move back about 40 feet. It sounds a lot better back there."[23]

By most accounts, however, Cutler, the crew, and the band had very little patience for tapers and were even less tolerant of people caught selling bootleg records. In an account published in the influential underground newspaper the *East Village Other* in 1971, Basho Katzenjammer describes how Cutler and members of the Dead's "goon squad" confiscated bootleg records that were being peddled at a concert in New York City. While crew members sometimes did return the contraband materials to the duly chastened offender, Katzenjammer also describes how Cutler, after seizing the records of one bootlegger, proceeded to give them away to audience members as part of an effort to "liberate those bootlegs."

Katzenjammer's piece, titled "Grateful Dead Pig Backlash," is a trenchant critique of the band and their relationship to tapers and bootlegging. Reflecting the confrontational tone and radical politics of contemporary publications associated with the underground press, Katzenjammer asserts that the "biggest piece of shit spewing from [Sam] Cutler's mouth is about the *reasons* the Dead have for being so pissed [about bootleg records]: they don't like the *quality*." "The 'quality'?" Katzenjammer exclaims. "Anyone who has bought a bootleg recently will know and agree that the bootleg stereo album called 'Grateful Dead' is one of the best underground products yet."[24]

For Katzenjammer, the actions and behavior exhibited by the band's crew toward bootleggers and tapers suggest another motive: "Money. That's the whole story, isn't it?" In their attempt to control taping and thereby limit the manufacturing and availability of bootleg records, Katzenjammer accuses the band of using "strong-arm shit to ensure that you get every last penny that you deserve" even as "you turn your back on your poor [fans]."

Responding to the band's claim that they are being ripped off by bootleggers, Katzenjammer reminds readers that the Dead are already part of the "biggest rip-off industry," the popular music industry. For bootleggers, "it's the same rip-off [but] on a smaller scale." Ultimately, bootleggers "give the eager little music freak what he [*sic*] wants and charge him what the stores charge." Furthermore, bootlegs are great publicity for, as he notes, "more people become Dead freaks as they hear more and more of the group, be it on bootleg or straight [i.e., an officially released] production."[25] Perhaps this is why, according to rumors, "the Dead have been looking for bootleg manufacturers for some time now with the object in mind of collaborating to produce one or more bootlegs."

Even as the band's crew continued to confiscate recording equipment and cut microphone cables, more people started to tape the Dead's concerts. As part of the radio interview from September 1973 during which Bob Weir remarked on the "forest of microphones" at their concerts, one of the interviewers asked if he was familiar with the "Free Underground Tape Exchange," an organization based in New York City that facilitated the trading of live recordings by the Grateful Dead. "Are you agreeable to that kind of thing?" the interviewer asked. "I mean taping, provided that it isn't done with the intention of making [bootleg] albums?" Keyboardist Keith Godchaux thought it was "far out," and band manager Jon McIntire observed that, "as far as I can tell, the people who are really into [trading tapes] just really like the music and that's the reason they do it." Weir responded that he was fine with the practice of trading "as long as they don't try to make a lot of bread off of it . . .

because most of those performances and the recordings are just not up to any sort of quality standards." Ultimately, however, Weir concluded that "if they want to tape [the show] and take it home and listen to it and roll one, it's perfectly fine by me."

Dead Relics

A few weeks after Weir spoke on the radio, the community of tapers, traders, and collectors grew even larger. In October 1973, *Rolling Stone* published a short article on Les Kippel, a taper based in New York City and the man behind the First Free Underground Grateful Dead Tape Exchange (the complete name of the organization mentioned by Weir's radio interviewer). In the article, titled "Mr. 'Tapes' of Brooklyn," Kippel boasts to journalist Charley Rosen of his collection of "over 500 hours of Grateful Dead tapes," including "more than 100 concerts from early 1968 right up to Watkins Glen [from July 1973]."[26] While some people may have been impressed by the size of Kippel's tape collection, what probably caught the attention of most readers was the fact that these and other live recordings were available for free through a handful of tape exchanges that had recently been established. "A lot of people want to set up exchanges," Kippel explained. "I tell them to get [business] cards made up with their telephone numbers on it, but I also insist it says 'free' on them."

By 1973, the First Free Underground Grateful Dead Tape Exchange and the Hell's Honkies Grateful Dead Tape Club were just a few of the growing number of "clubs" and "exchanges" that had formed to facilitate the sharing and trading of live concert recordings of the Grateful Dead.[27] Following the publication of Rosen's article in *Rolling Stone*, Kippel received letters from people who were interested in trading tapes and establishing their own exchanges. In response to the growing interest in tapes, in late 1974 Kippel began to publish *Dead Relix*, a newsletter devoted to the practice and culture of tape trading. With Kippel as the publisher and Gerald "Jerry" Moore, another New York City taper, as editor in chief of the early fanzine, *Dead Relix* quickly became an important resource for the rapidly expanding community of traders. In addition to publishing contact information for various traders and exchanges throughout the country, the earliest issues contained a great deal of practical information on how to record concerts, including articles on equipment, advice on where to set up to achieve the best sound quality, and how to avoid being caught by security or the band's crew members.

When it came time to decide on a name for their organization, Kippel recalls how he and other tapers agreed that "they are DEAD tapes, sort of like relics, so why not [call it] DEAD RELICS?"[28] Kippel's analogy suggests that tapes are connected to the past and, like many traditional relics, possess some sort of sacred quality or spiritual significance. But whereas the term relic is often used when referring to a unique historical object, there is nothing especially unique about the many tapes that were being copied and traded among collectors and fans.[29] Instead, as mass-produced objects associated with a specific event or experience, tapes of live recordings function more like "souvenirs" than as relics/*Relix*.

In her critical study of various "objects of desire," Susan Stewart considers souvenirs as repositories of meaning that perform and display "traces of authentic experience."[30] Much like a souvenir that one might purchase at a gift shop while traveling, tapes authenticate an experience. "We do not need or desire souvenirs of events that are repeatable," Stewart writes. "Rather," she continues, "we need and desire souvenirs of events that are reportable, events whose materiality has escaped us, events that thereby exist only through the invention of narrative."[31] Stewart's eloquent and poetic meditation on the desire and need for souvenirs is especially relevant when considering the place and function of tapes according to the various stories and narratives of liveness within which they became meaningful.

Following Stewart, the tape, like the souvenir, "speaks to a context of origin," a specific concert performance by the Grateful Dead.[32] As an improvising band whose set lists changed from night to night, the Grateful Dead's unique live performances were, of course, already imbued with a tremendous amount of meaning and significance among fans. For collectors, live tapes prove (and subsequently reaffirm) the idea that, as Willy Legate wrote in the liner notes to *Europe '72*, "THERE IS NOTHING LIKE A GRATEFUL DEAD CONCERT."

But while tapes may speak to a "context of origin," they can only do so through a "language of longing."[33] As Stewart notes in regard to souvenirs, the tape "is not an object arising out of need or use value; it is an object arising out of the necessarily insatiable demands of nostalgia."[34] As the subject of desire and longing, the original live event is and forever will be elusive. But in what Stewart calls a "transformation of materiality into meaning," the tapes become linked to the originating concert through a variety of idealized (and historicized) personal narratives. Stewart has described how souvenirs, much like tapes, represent a "conservative idealization of the past . . . for the purposes of a present ideology."[35] Of course, the related practices of taping and trading live recordings developed within the ideology of liveness that had shaped so much of the popular and critical discourse relating to the Grateful Dead.

By the early 1970s, tape trading had become another way that fans of the Grateful Dead (and other bands) could exhibit the extent of their "fandom." Even among the community of traders, fans acquired recordings for a variety of reasons. Some fans, for instance, collected tapes of concerts they attended while others sought out historically significant recordings or those deemed to be the "best-sounding." Some people, of course, simply wanted to collect as many recordings as possible. Whatever the degree of commitment and participation, the practice and appeal of tape trading are informed by an ideology that privileges the live concert experience. As Lee Marshall has noted, the "aesthetic justification" for collectors of live noncommercial recordings "stems from the understanding that music is a 'live' artform."[36] Such an understanding (or belief) is rooted within a general ideology of musical liveness that, in the United States, stretches back to the early twentieth century. The act of taping and the practice of trading, therefore, both serve to reinforce the already well-entrenched belief that a live performance represents a more "authentic" way of experiencing music.

While there may be nothing like a Grateful Dead concert, the activity of tapers and the burgeoning community of traders that developed in the early 1970s suggests that, for many fans, live recordings of the Grateful Dead not only functioned as recorded documents of a past event but also exhibited their own sense of liveness. As described in chapter 1, *Live/Dead* proved to fans and critics that the "special feeling" of a Grateful Dead concert could be captured on recordings. The increased activity of taping that followed the release of *Live/Dead* in 1969 (not to mention the release of *Live R Than You'll Ever Be*) can be understood as being motivated, in part, by the belief that—even without a multitrack recorder—tapes could still impart a sense of the liveness associated with the original concert. At the same time, the implicit acknowledgment on the part of tapers and traders that a sense (a "feeling") of liveness could be circulated via recordings underscores the continued commodification of live recordings, a practice that had been promoted by the music industry on albums such as *Ellington at Newport*, James Brown's *"Live" at the Apollo*, and, most recently, *Live/Dead*. Instead of challenging the hegemony of the music industry, Lee Marshall has described how tapes and other "unauthorized recordings exist within rock music as a discursive necessity."[37] Along with bootleg recordings produced for a profit, even fan-produced live recordings that are freely traded "reinforce the ideology that creates the value of the music industry's commodities, thus maintaining the industry's dominant position."[38]

One can acknowledge, of course, the dialectical and self-affirming interrelationships that exist between the music industry and the culture and practices relating to unauthorized recordings. However, it is important to recognize how and why unauthorized recordings of the Grateful Dead came to be valued among fans. In the opinion of many fans, tapes provide a more authentic recorded document of the Grateful Dead concert experience, especially in comparison to the band's commercially released live albums (most of which featured a variety of overdubs made in postproduction). In describing the appeal and allure of unauthorized bootleg recordings, Mark Neumann and Timothy A. Simpson have observed how such recordings (including Dead tapes) promise fans a chance of "getting closer to the 'authentic,' the 'real,' and overcoming the distances set by the commercial recording industry."[39] At the same time (and unlike the Dead's commercial live albums), many unauthorized recordings document complete concerts, a practice that was motivated by the belief that every live concert offered a unique experience. Although most tapes may document only a portion of a concert (due, for example, to equipment malfunctions, running out of tape, or being busted by the band's crew), it is reasonable to assume that the act of taping was originally undertaken with the intention of recording and preserving as much of the concert as possible.

The documentary impulse that motivated the act of taping, therefore, stands in stark contrast to how the band conceived of their commercially released live albums. Recall from the previous chapter how Jerry Garcia, when speaking with DJ Tom Donahue in 1967 about the possibility of capturing the band's live sound on record, remarked that, even if contemporary technologies were capable of adequately recording a rock band in a live setting, it would still require playing "about two or three months of every night . . . [before] we'd start to get good cuts, good enough for an album." Even before the band had recorded their first live album (and even before the multitrack recording technology existed that could make such a project possible), Garcia appeared to envision the group's live recordings as compilations and not, necessarily, as documents of a unique concert experience.

In the opinion of many tapers and traders, unauthorized live recordings were valued for their imagined ability to impart a more authentic sense of the live concert experience. Compared to the band's carefully produced, meticulously engineered, and heavily edited official live albums, live audience recordings often feature a considerable amount of crowd noise and between-song banter by the performers, the audience, or both, qualities that add to the perceived sense of realism that came to be associated with tapes.[40] The growing appeal and the increased demand for audience-produced tapes suggested that fans were willing to accept recordings whose sound quality may not have risen to the exacting standards of the Dead. On the one hand, the sound quality of audience recordings could vary dramatically and depended on a number of factors, including the knowledge and experience of the taper, the quality of the equipment used to record the concert, and the location of the taper within the venue. On the other hand, the "rougher" aesthetic associated with audience recordings contributed to a quality of realism that was valued by many tape collectors and traders.

In addition to the many audience recordings that were being produced at the time, traders and collectors also had access to a body of recordings known as "soundboards." Soundboard recordings capture the performances that were broadcast over the public address system and were typically produced by patching cables directly into the venue's (or the band's) mixing board. Featuring the mix of instruments and vocals that was projected throughout a venue, soundboards do not exhibit the same type, or form, of "liveness" as audience recordings. However, soundboards—especially those that had been produced by the band—would come to be valued among collectors and traders for their sonic clarity and fidelity.

The practice of taping and the increased activity of tape trading also meant that fans could potentially hear recordings of the band's live performances— as audience recordings or soundboards—within days of the original concert. Unlike the methodical and drawn-out process of releasing records within the established music industry, the underground industry of tapers and traders could satisfy the needs of fans who desired recordings of the band's most recent performances.

Whereas record companies and bootleggers have a clear financial incentive in marketing liveness to fans via commercially produced live recordings, tapers and traders affirm the symbolic significance of live recordings by re-placing them within an alternative system of exchange. Many critics and scholars have described how the tapes function as a form of currency within an "exchange economy" as opposed to the market economy in which musical recordings are traditionally bought and sold.[41] On the one hand, of course, the contrasting economies distinguish between those products that are affiliated with the record industry (commercially produced recordings) and those objects that are produced and exchanged outside of the traditional industry ("tapes"). On the other hand, the practice of trading also serves to distinguish "tapers" and "tapes" from the "secret recording industry" represented by "bootleggers" and "bootleg records." Indeed, early traders were sure to identify their recordings as "tapes" and not "bootlegs."[42] Beginning with their first issue, the editors and publishers of *Dead Relix* emphasized that they do not "advocate the duplication of live recordings for purposes other than free exchange. We do not condone unauthorized duplication for sale. We will not accept subscriptions or take advertizing [*sic*] from known bootleggers."[43]

More than just an alternative form of exchange, however, tape trading is decidedly anticommercial. For some collectors and traders, the appeal of tape trading derives from the belief that, as Lee Marshall has noted, "music is more authentic if it is untainted by music industry interests."[44] In contrast to the impersonal forms of exchange generally associated with the traditional marketplace, Katie Harvey has described how trading contributed to a "multi-faceted social system" that encouraged the formation of "relationships with other fans within the larger Dead Head scene and tape subculture."[45] Indeed, the belief that tape trading fostered a sense of community existed at the earliest stages of the practice. Harvey Lubar, a taper and trader based in New York City, remembers receiving many recordings in the early 1970s from Marty Weinberg, a taper known for his "legendary" collection of Dead tapes. Lubar recalls how, after Weinberg had shared over sixty hours of music with him and a friend, the only thing "Legendary Marty" (as he was known) "asked for in exchange was for us never to sell the tapes and to start lots of new people out in the same way he had helped us."[46]

As taping became an established practice by the early 1970s, the anticommercial ethos represented by trading would have resonated with many of the economic and cultural ideals that were still reverberating from the previous decade. Marshall notes that a strong "countercultural impulse" contributed to the rise and popularity of tape trading.[47] Of course, the countercultural impulse associated with taping and trading music of the Grateful Dead—the quintessential countercultural band—can be interpreted as a strategy on the part of early tapers to establish some sort of relationship with the group. Through the practice of trading (as opposed to the manufacture and selling of bootleg records), early tapers and traders aligned themselves with various artistic, cultural, and economic principles that had come to be associated with the Dead, principles that, in turn, reflected many of the antiestablishment ideals of the San Francisco counterculture of the 1960s.[48]

To be sure, members of the Grateful Dead organization took notice of the tapers, their products, and the various exchanges that were sprouting up throughout the country. In the "Mr. Tapes" article published in *Rolling Stone*, Les Kippel recounted how he and a friend passed an audience-made tape to drummer Bill Kreutzmann before a concert in New York City. "Ten minutes later," Kippel recalled, Kreutzmann came "running outside with Phil Lesh, looking for us. They gave us stage passes. We handed out over a hundred of our cards backstage, and the tapes really started coming in after that."[49] Emphasizing his very real relationship to the band, Kippel describes how, even as the band's crew continued to bust tapers, other people associated with the Dead were providing soundboard recordings to distribute among the various tape exchanges.

Despite all the rhetoric about how the tapes should be traded freely, Kippel admitted that he would ultimately like to "go legit" and to make money taping Grateful Dead shows. By late 1973, his wish may have seemed like a real possibility when, according to Kippel, tour manager Sam Cutler suggested that he could "make some money working with the Dead." "It seems that they have a lot of holes in their archives—somebody ripped off some tapes while they were in Oregon," Kippel explained. "There's certainly a demand for old stuff," he continued, "and the Dead are cut loose from Warner Bros. now, so the next move is theirs."[50]

Kippel's reference to an "archive" suggests that, by 1973, the Grateful Dead were already thinking about their recorded legacy and the commercial potential of live concert recordings. Indeed, by the time the article on Kippel appeared in *Rolling Stone* in October 1973, members of the Dead organization were fully aware of the nascent taping and trading scene. In November 1972, David Parker, a member of the Dead's office staff, wrote a note to Jon McIntire, the band's manager, concerning the many letters and inquiries that the organization had received from members of the various exchanges (including Kippel).[51] Regarding the actions of tapers and the practice of taping, Parker suggested that "we need to work out a policy on this sort of thing." Parker asked McIntire if the organization should "a) stomp, b) license, c) tacitly tolerate them?—or what?" Parker wrote, "If live tapes are that popular, should we look at this as an 'alternative method'? We've got a lot of those tapes, of good quality, which cost plenty to produce." For the time being, the band chose to "tacitly tolerate" the tapers, a policy that would persist (with some modifications) for the remainder of the Dead's career.

Kippel, on the other hand, was eager to work with the Dead selling live recordings. On behalf of his new organization, Dead Relics, Kippel submitted a business proposal to members of the Dead organization in March 1974.[52] In a twenty-five-page document, Kippel describes how Dead Relics and the Dead would work together to curate and distribute soundboard recordings of the band's concerts as part of a "Connoisseur's Club." As described in his proposal, "Dead Relics will be the name of a Company whose purpose it will be to obtain and distribute soundboard copies of concert tapes through the

Connoisseurs Club. The Company [Dead Relics] will operate the Connoisseur Club. Membership will be divided into two groups. Charter and Regular Members. There will also be a provision for Non-Members who wish to buy concert tapes."[53] Kippel's proposal outlines how select live recordings would be promoted and distributed via mail order and produced on cassette and 8-track formats. Despite the "superior" quality afforded by reel-to-reel tapes (the original format of the "tapes"), Kippel reasoned that, in addition to being cheaper to produce, "cassette and 8-track tapes are used by the public in car stereos, portable tape machines as well as home units."[54]

Kippel was only interested in distributing soundboard recordings through the club. "As any tape collector knows," he confidently asserted in his proposal, "it is better to have a soundboard tape than an audience tape of the same concert."[55] Kippel describes how "producing the actual tapes for the club members can be done in one of two methods. The first method would be for the Dead to release and send a copy of the Master to Dead Relics. Dead Relics, in turn, would reproduce the concert in Cassette and 8 Track form by using Mass Reproduction equipment such as the Ampex systems or other systems, or giving the tape to a company which will produce the tapes for the Club."[56]

Kippel must have realized there was almost no chance that the Dead would agree to "release and send a copy of the Master" tape to him for reproduction. As an alternative, Kippel suggested the following: "The other method would involve Dead Relics making a count of the orders, and letting the Dead reproduce the number of tapes ordered by the club. The Dead would be able to supervise the production of the tapes, assuring the Club of the best quality, without releasing the actual Master tape of the concert. The Dead in this system would have an exact count of the number of tapes ordered. If any royalties were to be expected, the Dead could add the price on each unit."[57]

Members of the Dead organization undoubtedly recognized that everything Kippel was proposing—from the production to the manufacturing, the marketing, and the distribution of the recordings—could already be accomplished by the record company. Kippel's proposal, therefore, provided the Dead with a solid business model that they could implement on their own and that, more important, would allow them to retain complete control over all aspects of producing and distributing the band's live concert recordings.

Although the Dead did not express any serious interest in working with Dead Relics, Kippel was quick to move on to other projects. He published the first volume of his influential fanzine, *Dead Relix*, in late 1974, around the time that the Dead announced they were taking an indeterminate "hiatus" from touring. As fans waited throughout 1975 and into 1976 for the band to return to the road, *Dead Relix* became enormously influential in connecting a growing community of people who were seeking out the Grateful Dead's live concert recordings, the original "Dead Relics."

Ground Records, *Steal Your Face* (1976), and the Demise of Grateful Dead Records

Nearly two years after corresponding with Les Kippel, members of the Dead organization considered forming a new label that would be devoted to releasing material from the band's archive of studio outtakes, "demos," and live recordings. The Dead created two record labels when they formed their company in 1973. One label, Grateful Dead Records, was co-owned by the band and record company president, Ron Rakow; Grateful Dead Records was reserved for official releases by the band. Solo records, band-related projects, and recordings by other artists were released on a second label, Round Records. Round Records was co-owned by Jerry Garcia and Rakow. In early 1976, Steve Brown, a member of the Dead's administrative staff (and a longtime fan), made provisional plans relating to a third label, tentatively called Ground Records.[58]

Among the extant materials relating to Ground Records is a list compiled by Brown identifying a number of possible releases. As reproduced in figure 2.2, numbers 1 and 2 refer to "Possible 'Archive' albums" composed of outtakes ("outs") from two solo albums by Jerry Garcia: *Garcia* from 1974 ("Rx 102" refers to the original catalog number of Garcia's second solo album) and *Reflections* ("Rx 107") from 1976.[59] Other proposed releases include "outs" ("jams") from the band's most recent studio album, *Blues for Allah* (identified as "G.D. 103"), as well as material from some of Garcia's projects, including an album he produced for a group called the Good Old Boys titled *Pistol Packin' Mama* ("P.P.M. Rx 109 outs") and material from the bluegrass "supergroup" Old & In the Way ("O.I.T.W. Rx 103 outs [live]").

Brown also considered releasing archival compilations devoted to specific themes. Figure 2.3, for example, includes a list of songs for a possible release titled "Railroad Blues." As seen in his proposed tracklist, Brown identifies songs that had already been released (including Robert Hunter's song "That Train" from his debut solo record, *Tales of the Great Rum Runners* ["Hunter Rx 101"]) as well as various studio outtakes and live performances by the Jerry Garcia Band, Old & In the Way, and the Grateful Dead. Interestingly, Brown singles out one live performance by the band in particular, an acoustic

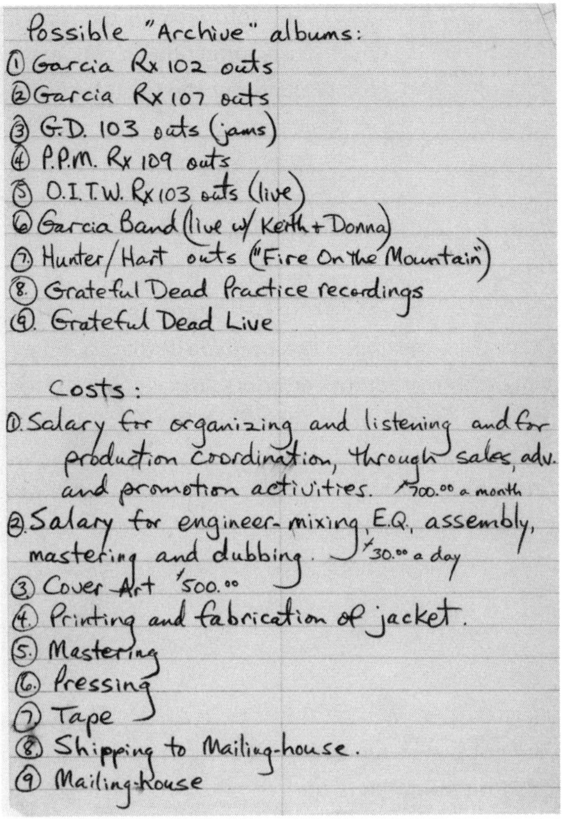

Possible "Archive" albums:
① Garcia Rx 102 outs
② Garcia Rx 107 outs
③ G.D. 103 outs (jams)
④ P.P.M. Rx 109 outs
⑤ O.I.T.W. Rx 103 outs (live)
⑥ Garcia Band (live w/ Keith + Donna)
⑦ Hunter/Hart outs ("Fire On The Mountain")
⑧ Grateful Dead Practice recordings
⑨ Grateful Dead Live

Costs:
① Salary for organizing and listening and for production coordination, through sales, adv. and promotion activities. $500.00 a month
② Salary for engineer- mixing, E.Q., assembly, mastering and dubbing. $30.00 a day
③ Cover Art $500.00
④ Printing and fabrication of jacket.
⑤ Mastering
⑥ Pressing
⑦ Tape
⑧ Shipping to Mailing-house.
⑨ Mailing-House

FIGURE 2.2. "Possible 'Archive' albums" and notes on production costs relating to Ground Records

version of "Big Railroad Blues" recorded at the Fillmore East in New York City on September 20, 1970.

Referring back to figure 2.2, it can also be seen that Brown and others considered the costs involved in establishing a new label, including preliminary figures relating to production and promotion, manufacturing, and distribution (albums released on Ground Records would have been sold directly by the band through mail orders). Having worked out many of the logistical and financial details of their proposed label, it is somewhat curious that recordings featuring the "Grateful Dead Live" are so low on the list of possible releases. Of course, given that there are only a few extant documents relating to Ground Records, it is possible that Brown and other members of the Dead were just beginning to consider what could be produced on the new archival label. But even as people throughout the organization came to recognize the growing appeal and interest among fans for the band's live recordings, it is

FIGURE 2.3. Song
list for "Railroad
Blues," a proposed
release on Ground
Records

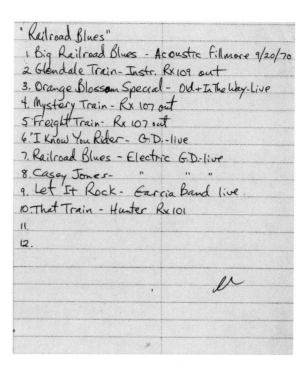

"Railroad Blues"
1. Big Railroad Blues - Acoustic Fillmore 9/20/70
2 Glendale Train- Instr. Rx 109 out
3. Orange Blossom Special - Old+In The Way-Live
4. Mystery Train - Rx 107 out
5 Freight Train - Rx 107 out
6. 'I Know You Rider - G.D.-live
7. Railroad Blues - Electric G.D.-live
8. Casey Jones -   "   "   "
9. Let It Rock - Garcia Band live.
10. That Train - Hunter Rx 101
11.
12.

noteworthy that Brown did not seem to consider releasing live performances
a priority as he made plans for Ground Records.

As Brown and others continued to explore the possibilities and opportunities offered by a new label, the Dead could no longer ignore the fact that
the record company was in serious financial trouble. To be sure, a number
of factors contributed to their dire economic circumstances by the middle of
the 1970s. After leaving Warner Bros., the band released three studio albums
on their new label: *Wake of the Flood* (1973), *The Grateful Dead from the
Mars Hotel* (1974), and *Blues for Allah* (1975). While each album sold a respectable number of copies, the money earned from record sales was not
enough to cover the organization's overhead.[60] At the same time, *The Grateful Dead Movie*, a longtime pet project of Jerry Garcia's, was seriously over
budget with no guarantee when, or if, it would ever be released.

Ultimately, however, the Dead's woeful financial situation was the fore-
seeable result of their decision to take a break from touring. Everyone in the
Grateful Dead organization understood, of course, that their greatest source
of income derived from live performances. The Dead had maintained a gru-
eling touring schedule since the 1960s and, by 1974, the band and people
throughout the organization had grown weary of the road. At the same time,

the cost of transporting, assembling, and maintaining the mammoth Wall of Sound had become incredibly expensive; as a result, the band was earning less money from touring. Following a series of "farewell" concerts at the Winterland in October 1974, the Dead enjoyed a hiatus from touring. Over the course of the next twenty months, the band only performed a handful of live concerts in and around San Francisco.

In an effort to keep their record company solvent, the Dead began to cut deals with other, more established record labels. In 1975, the band announced they had reached a deal with the United Artists Corporation (UA) that, according to band biographer Dennis McNally, was designed to "save the Grateful Dead Record Company from bankruptcy."[61] According to the deal, UA would relieve the Dead of all manufacturing, promotion, and distribution duties. In exchange, record company president Ron Rakow promised UA that the Dead would deliver a number of new releases, including a live album. By the spring of 1976, however, Rakow and the band had yet to deliver any new recordings.

In an effort to placate UA, Rakow asked Phil Lesh and Owsley Stanley to produce a live album of performances that had been recorded at the band's "farewell" concerts in October 1974. As the Dead's last concerts before their touring hiatus, the performances at the Winterland were also filmed and were being used as part of *The Grateful Dead Movie*. As Lesh and Bear began to work on the live album, however, they discovered a number of technical problems with the audio tracks. Despite their misgivings about the quality of the recordings, Rakow reportedly told Lesh to finish the project and that "fans will buy it anyway." "It's a wonder the record was ever finished," Lesh recalls. "The fact that it was released—against my better judgment—shows how desperate we were for product to take up the slack from the lack of touring income."[62]

The recordings were released in June 1976 on a double live album titled *Steal Your Face*. As Lesh and others probably anticipated, the record was panned by most fans and critics. In his review in *Rolling Stone*, critic Charley Walters was especially ruthless when he described the album as not "so much a collection of music" but just a "confirmation of the Dead's existence."[63] As the band's first live album on their own label (and their first official live release since 1973), Walters explained, "*Steal Your Face* could have been a musical statement." Unfortunately, he concludes, "it's only a memento."

In a review published in the recently formed Bay Area music magazine *BAM*, Blair Jackson challenged "even the staunchest Grateful Dead fan (and I rank myself way up there in 'staunchness') to tell me [that *Steal Your Face*] is a great record." "Blind love," he wrote, "just doesn't do it this time around."[64] Among his many criticisms, Jackson decried the form and organization of the record. "The order the songs are presented on the album," he remarks, "bears no resemblance to the order in which they were played in concert." The compilation is especially curious because, as Jackson notes, "for the first time on any live Dead album, there is no jam." Jackson's critique assumes, of course, that the band's live albums *should* adhere to the design of a "typical" Dead concert. But while albums such as *Live/Dead* and *Skull and Roses* were sequenced so as to resemble the general form of a concert, the same cannot be said of either *Europe '72* or *History of the Grateful Dead, Volume One*. Based on the band's official live releases, there probably should have been no expectation on the part of Jackson and other fans that *Steal Your Face* should be sequenced to resemble a concert.

As one of the band's "staunchest" fans, however, Jackson was judging *Steal Your Face* not only in relation to the Dead's commercial live albums but also in relation to the many unauthorized tapes that were now becoming increasingly available. Jackson noted, for example, that the performances he experienced at some of the original concerts, as well as what he has "heard subsequently on tapes of those concerts, differs dramatically from the sloppy material on this album." Jackson's opinion that freely available unauthorized recordings were of a better quality than the band's official release would have certainly been met with dismay by many members of the Dead organization. Ultimately, Jackson described *Steal Your Face* as an "inexcusable failure of a record from a band which undoubtedly has material 50 times better than this locked in vaults somewhere in Marin County."

Steal Your Face was the last album produced by the Grateful Dead Record Company. In June, after being fired by the band, Ron Rakow took $225,000 from the organization, and by the end of the summer, the record company was dissolved. Even as the band reckoned with the disappointing critical response to *Steal Your Face* and the turmoil surrounding the record company, the Grateful Dead resumed touring in June 1976. In an attempt to make as much money as quickly as possible, the version of the Grateful Dead that returned to the road in 1976 was a much leaner and efficient touring group. Whereas just a few years earlier the band had been playing stadiums and arenas, now the Dead were booking performances in midsize venues across the country. No longer burdened by the hassle and expense of touring with the Wall of Sound, Garcia confided to journalist Charles M. Young that, on their return to touring, the band had been intent on "using as little energy as possible and keeping everything simple." "The old Dead trip was getting to be a burden," Garcia explained, "so we sacked it and went on to new projects. We're having fun again."[65]

In the same article, Young also noted that the band's recent audiences, "which one might have expected to consist of aging hippies, instead are composed of young hippies."[66] Garcia suggested that the change in the age demographic of their audience could be a result of older fans having grown tired of the "hassle of buying tickets." What Garcia and other members of the Dead failed to recognize was how, during the band's touring hiatus, the practice of tape trading had forged an entirely new community of younger fans, fans who had absorbed the mythos of the band through the tapes (the Dead Relics) and who were now anxiously awaiting the chance to experience the band in a live concert setting.

At the same time, just as a new generation of fans were being turned on to the band through tapes and tape trading, the practice of taping continued to expand. Drawing on the technical and practical information concerning live concert recording as described in publications such as *Dead Relix*, Michael Getz and John Dwork observed that "by the time the band came out of retirement in June 1976, people were much more prepared to make decent tapes."[67] The practice of taping had become so prevalent at Dead concerts that, as veteran taper Barry Glassberg has noted, it is quite possible to locate an "audience tape of every show from June 1976 onward," a range of years that extends to 1995 (marked by the death of Jerry Garcia) and that includes nearly fourteen hundred concert performances.[68]

By the middle of the 1970s, many fans had learned to hear and conceive of tapes as more authentic recorded representations of the Grateful Dead's live performances, even in comparison to the band's official live albums (and not just *Steal Your Face*). In the years and decades that followed, the various aesthetic values, meanings, and technological developments that emerged alongside taping and trading would continue to exert a strong influence on the band and their evolving legacy of liveness.

The Grateful Dead (1980) (*Left to right*: Phil Lesh, Mickey Hart, Bill Kreutzmann, Bob Weir, Brent Mydland, Jerry Garcia)

A Time of *Reckoning*

NEW APPROACHES TO PRODUCING
AND MARKETING LIVENESS
(THE 1980S, PART 1)

The Grateful Dead signed a recording contract with Arista Records in October 1976. As the former president of Columbia Records, Clive Davis had been trying to sign the Dead since the early 1970s. As the current president of Arista, Davis believed that the group "could have signed with any of the majors based on their track record and reputation."[1] Despite Davis's high opinion of the Dead, Mickey Hart recalled how, following the demise of the Grateful Dead Record Company, the band did not have many suitors within the industry. "It wasn't like a whole lot of people wanted us," Hart explained.[2]

Having signed the Dead to his new label, Davis was determined to coax a studio album from the group that was "accessible and commercial."[3] To that end, he convinced the band to record with producers from outside of their immediate (albeit eminently qualified) circle of friends and acquaintances. Released in 1977, *Terrapin Station*, the band's debut album on Arista, was produced by Keith Olsen. At the time, Olsen was recognized throughout the industry for his work on *Fleetwood Mac*, the group's commercial breakthrough album from 1975. In 1978, the Grateful Dead released *Shakedown Street*, a studio recording produced by Lowell George, a singer, songwriter, and guitarist best known for his work with the band Little Feat. Following the departure of Donna Jean and Keith Godchaux in 1979, keyboardist Brent Mydland joined the band in time to appear on their next studio album, *Go to Heaven*. Released in 1980, *Go to Heaven* was produced by Gary Lyons, another respected producer who had worked on albums for Queen, Foreigner, and Alice Cooper. Including Jerry Garcia, Mickey Hart (who rejoined the band in 1976), Bill Kreutzmann, Phil Lesh, Brent Mydland, and Bob Weir, *Go to Heaven* features the lineup of the Grateful Dead that would perform together for the next decade.

Despite respectable sales, none of the band's studio albums achieved the critical accolades or the commercial success for which Davis was hoping. But while he and other label executives may have begun to question the commercial potential of the band, the members of the Dead were content to try something else. After delivering three studio albums in four years, Phil Lesh recalls that he and the band were ready to "make some live albums!"[4]

The band attempted to produce commercial live recordings a few years earlier. In September 1978, the Grateful Dead played three concerts at the base of the Great Pyramid in Egypt. All the concerts were recorded, but for various reasons none of the performances were deemed worthy of commercial release at the time, and the recordings were shelved. Following a steady stream of studio albums, fans would have to wait until the 1980s for the group to release new live records.

In commemoration of the band's fifteenth anniversary, Arista and the Dead released two double-record live albums in 1981: *Reckoning* and *Dead Set*. In this chapter I consider how the band's approach to engineering, producing, and mixing live recordings had evolved by the beginning of the 1980s. In the opinion of many fans and critics, some of the Grateful Dead's earliest commercial live recordings (notably *Live/Dead*) offered the best recorded approximation of the band's dynamic concerts. By the mid-1970s, however, tapes provided fans with an alternative sound and associated aesthetic of recorded liveness. In contrast to the sound and structure of the Dead's official live albums, tapes offered a unique listening perspective and, in the opinion of some fans, a more authentic recorded representation of the live concert experience. As they prepared to produce their first live albums since the release of the dismal *Steal Your Face*, the Grateful Dead and their crew adapted and modified their standard approach to recording so as to more closely approximate the sound of the tapes.

"The Dead on Broadway"

In June 1980, the Grateful Dead performed a pair of concerts at the University of Colorado in Boulder. Local promoters advertised the concerts as a "Fifteenth Anniversary Celebration," a historical occasion that, according to some accounts, the band overlooked at the time.[5] While members of the audience celebrated the remarkable history of the band, they also were looking forward to the future of the Grateful Dead. Before the band's second concert on June 8, the local announcer exclaimed, "I guess this is the beginning of the *second* fifteen years!"[6]

Following the concerts in Boulder, members of the Dead organization began to plan more events to commemorate the band's anniversary. Given the group's close connection to the Bay Area, the Dead and concert promoter Bill Graham announced a run of fifteen concerts over twenty days at the Warfield Theatre in San Francisco beginning in late September. Built in 1922, the Warfield was one of San Francisco's oldest theaters and had a capacity of approximately two thousand people. Beginning with a successful run of concerts by Bob Dylan in 1979, the Warfield (now under the direction of Graham) offered an intimate concert experience that was perfectly suited for the Dead's retrospective concerts. To further commemorate the occasion, the band recorded the concerts at the Warfield for a planned live album. The multitrack recordings were engineered and produced by many of the same people who had worked on the band's earlier live albums, including Dan Healy, Betty Cantor-Jackson, Bob Matthews, and Dennis "Wiz" Leonard.[7]

As part of their anniversary concerts at the Warfield, the Dead played three sets every night: an opening set of acoustic performances followed by two sets of electric performances. For some fans, the band's set of acoustic performances might have recalled the earliest incarnation of the Dead from 1964 when Garcia, Weir, and Ron "Pigpen" McKernan performed in a jug band called Mother McCree's Uptown Jug Champions.[8] As the Grateful Dead, the band had also featured a set of acoustic performances during many of their concerts in 1970, concerts that were often promoted as "An Evening with the Grateful Dead."[9] By the dawn of the 1980s, many of the band's concerts from 1970 were highly regarded by fans, including people who had attended the original performances as well as those who had only ever experienced the concerts on tapes. In terms of their structure, therefore, the concerts the band played in September and October 1980 served to historicize the group by invoking a version of the Dead from 1970, arguably the most commercially and critically successful year in their career (so far).

Even as preparations were underway for the Dead's upcoming concerts at the Warfield in September, Richard Loren, the band's manager, proposed another live recording project during a business meeting on August 6, 1980. Loren's proposal outlined a run of shows at the Uris Theatre (now the Gershwin Theatre) in New York City for a project titled "The Dead on Broadway."[10] For the band's first official live release on Arista, Loren suggested that the label could promote the album as a "15 Year Retrospective." Adding to the historicist impulse guiding his plan, Loren also proposed that the album would include "ten or twelve classics from [the] early Warner Bros. catalogue, including a few acoustic songs." While the record could be promoted as a career retrospective, members of the Dead organization recognized that an album featuring live versions of the band's early "hits" on Warner Bros. (and not their most recent songs on Arista) would have a much broader appeal and promised greater financial returns.

Like so many of their projects, Loren's proposal was designed to make the Dead as much money in as short a time as possible. Ideally, Loren hoped the project could cover the operating costs of the business organization for a few months and, if there was any money left over, begin to chip away at the band's growing debt. According to his proposal, the band would receive their standard album advance of $350,000 from Arista. From that amount, $150,000 would be deducted to cover the money that the label had advanced the band to record the concerts in Egypt in 1978. Of the remaining $200,000, $75,000 would be used to cover "union and recording costs" while performing in New York City. Loren anticipated delivering the album to Arista in December, at which point the band would receive the balance of $125,000. Following the anticipated release of the live album in the middle of January 1981, the band would then embark on a supporting tour in February.

A week after Loren presented his proposal to the band, he and other members of the Dead organization traveled to New York City and pitched the plan to Clive Davis. Davis approved the idea, but not before he and the band agreed on a few changes. As reflected in the amended contract the band signed with Arista in September 1980, the live performances that would be featured on the double album were to be drawn from concerts that would take place in Radio City Music Hall at the end of October.[11] Although the Dead would not be performing "on Broadway," the fact that Davis agreed to deduct a portion of the band's outstanding debt was, no doubt, more significant than the change of venue. The amended contract also stipulated that the forthcoming double album would count as the band's fourth official release (including the previous three studio albums). Following the release of the new live album, therefore, the Dead would owe one more record to Arista according to the terms of their original contract.

The amended contract with Arista is dated September 25, 1980, the same day that the Dead played their first anniversary concert at the Warfield Theatre in San Francisco. Between September 25 and October 31, the band played twenty-five concerts, including fifteen performances at the Warfield (between September 25 and October 14), two concerts on October 18 and 19 at the Saenger Performing Arts Center in New Orleans, and eight shows at Radio City Music Hall (between October 22 and 31). Given the smaller seating capacities of each venue and the high demand for tickets, all the concerts quickly sold out. The line of fans waiting for tickets outside of the Radio City Music Hall box office even attracted the attention of the national media. Remarking on the enduring Grateful Dead phenomenon and the commitment of the Deadheads, a piece published in *Newsweek* observed how "about 2,000 fans of the rock band waited for up to three days for the chance to get tickets," a scene that "brought back memories of the hall's great days of the 1940s and '50s."[12]

Shortly after the final performance in New York City on Halloween, the band and their crew began to compile and mix select recordings from their recent concerts. As production continued on their new live album, the band considered possible titles for the forthcoming release. Figure 3.1 reproduces a page of notes from a business meeting in December 1980. As the notes emphasize, everyone understood that "this new album cannot be another 'Grateful Dead Live' L.P. The title has been used too many times and will create a lot of print confusion—we definitely need a name for this record!!"[13] Even the proposed title of "Dead Alive" (or simply "Alive") was rejected because the phrase had "been used by the record [companies] in adverts alot already and has also headlined alot of G.D. newspaper stories, etc., etc."

Instead, the notes make clear that the Dead (and most certainly executives at Arista) were interested in a title that suggested the "retrospective aspect of this effort and/or the coast to coast S.F./N.Y. [connection]." Many of the notes reflect how well (or poorly) each of the proposed titles conveys the "retrospective aspect." In the opinion of some people, for instance, the title "Resurrection" would be a "good follow-up" to the band's previous studio album, *Go to Heaven.* "Resurrection" also "works good for [a] 'live' recording [and suggests] retrospection." Other people in the organization were not sold on "Resurrection" as a title, however, due to its "heavy religious connotations." Ultimately, the band decided on "Reckoning." Even though Garcia felt that the title lacked "warmth," everyone agreed that "Reckoning" did "suggest the retrospective trip!!"

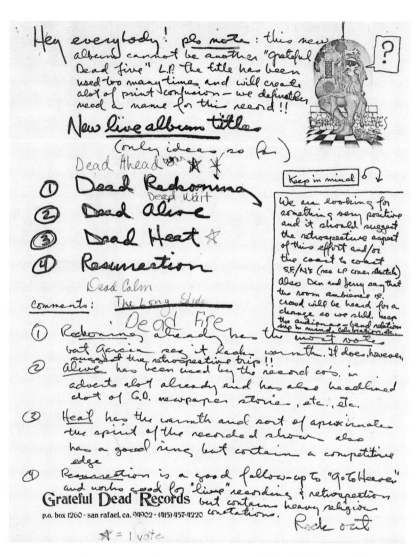

FIGURE 3.1. Notes from meeting regarding possible titles for live record (ca. December 1980)

Released in April 1981, Arista's ad campaign for the band's latest live double record gathered together as many clichés as possible, announcing, "The Dead Come Alive on an Historic *Reckoning*." Featuring photographs depicting various lineups of the Grateful Dead on the record sleeves, the packaging and design of *Reckoning* also participate in the historicist impulse of the album.[14] Whereas the Dead and Arista had agreed to a double album of performances recorded in New York City, *Reckoning* includes live performances from both Radio City Music Hall and the Warfield Theatre in San Francisco. Moreover, *Reckoning* is composed entirely of acoustic performances. A few months later, in August 1981, Arista and the band released *Dead Set*, another double-record live album featuring performances compiled from the group's electric sets at the Warfield Theatre and Radio City Music Hall.

As described earlier, prior to their concert at the Warfield on September 25, the Dead had not performed a live set of acoustic music in almost ten years. It should come as no surprise, therefore, that the band focused most of their attention on preparing for this segment of their upcoming shows. Over the course of nearly two dozen concerts at the Warfield and Radio City, the band played twenty-one songs as part of their acoustic sets. Two of those songs, "Sage and Spirit" and "Little Sadie," were played only once (at the final concert on October 31). Other songs were played multiple times but were not featured on *Reckoning*, including Marty Robbins's "El Paso," "Heaven Help the Fool," and "Iko Iko." The sixteen tracks that were selected for *Reckoning*, therefore, represent the remaining songs the band had prepared for their acoustic sets.[15] With the tracklist essentially predetermined, the act of compiling performances for the acoustic album would involve comparing and choosing between multiple versions of a rather limited number of songs. It was important, therefore, that the performances were up to the exacting standards of the Dead, especially because the band had decided they would not utilize overdubs when producing the recordings.

Each of the band's acoustic sets consisted of between seven and eleven songs. Featuring sixteen songs, therefore, *Reckoning* represents an expanded version of what audiences would have experienced at the concerts. Although the songs that appear on *Reckoning* were compiled from different concerts, the record is sequenced in a manner that would have been familiar to fans who had experienced the original concerts (in person and/or via the audience-made tapes that soon circulated). *Reckoning* opens with "Dire Wolf," a fan favorite from *Workingman's Dead* and a song that the band used to open many of their anniversary concerts. Similarly, *Reckoning* concludes with "Bird Song" followed by "Ripple." This same pair of songs concluded seven of the band's opening sets; "Ripple" was the last song performed on every acoustic set.

Like the form and design of some of their earliest live commercial albums, *Reckoning* is sequenced so as to suggest the structure of a "typical" show by the Dead, in this case, the band's acoustic sets from September and October 1980. Despite these formal similarities, however, *Reckoning* does not *sound* like any of the band's previous live albums. As described in chapter 1, the impression of liveness that had come to be associated with the band's official live releases was accompanied by what I described as the (relative) silencing of the audience. But whereas the presence of crowd noise had been minimized and downplayed when mixing earlier live albums (such as *Live/Dead*, *Skull and Roses*, and *Europe '72*), the band and their recording crew decided early in the preproduction process that the sounds of the audience would play a much more significant part in the final mixes of *Reckoning* and *Dead Set*. Indeed, the decision to include more crowd noise was considered by some people in the Dead organization to be an important feature of the forthcoming records. Referring to the boxed-off block of text on the right side of the image in figure 3.1, someone at the meeting noted that sound mixer "Dan [Healy] and Jerry [Garcia] say that the room ambience i.e. crowd will be heard for a change so we [should] keep the audience-band relationship in mind, collaboration, etc." when considering album titles.

The recording crew went to great lengths to ensure that even the sound quality of the audience tracks was up to the band's high standards. Engineer Don Pearson recalls how the crew used a variety of 16-track, 4-track, and 2-track machines when recording the band's anniversary concerts. In particular, Pearson describes how microphones connected to 4-track machines were positioned throughout the venue to capture the sounds of the audience, with "some [located] at the stage, some a third of the way out [in the audience], some halfway out, and some by the mixing board."[16] All the 4-track machines were synchronized via a SMPTE (timecode) track to the multitrack machines that were recording the band's performances. By syncing the various stage and room microphones, Pearson explains how, during postproduction, the recording crew "could take the multitrack tapes and then move the room mikes up and back and forward in time until there wasn't an echo. So you had all the presence of the mikes onstage and the ambience of the room, but the ambience was in time with the stage mikes. That's why those live shows have that sound, because we had the ability to move the room mikes backward and forward in time until it sounded acoustically the way we wanted it to."[17]

With its carefully balanced and coordinated blend of musical performances and crowd noise, *Reckoning* can be thought of as an "enhanced" soundboard recording. Unlike the nearly "audienceless" sound of the band's early live albums, *Reckoning* more closely approximates the sound of audience-produced tapes. The increased presence of the audience imparts an aura of sonic realism to *Reckoning* (and *Dead Set*) that is absent in the band's previous live albums. It would seem that, following the rise of taping and tape trading, the sound of the Dead's live albums had evolved to reflect the aesthetic of recorded liveness that had come to be associated with tapes. Whereas the band's earlier live albums were produced according to the prevailing aesthetics and technocultural logic of the recording studio, *Reckoning* marks the moment when the Dead explicitly acknowledged the unique sense of recorded liveness and the distinctive ambience of fan-produced tapes. As Pearson's account makes clear, however, a great deal of technological know-how and innovative production techniques were involved in crafting the more (or less) "realistic" sound of liveness featured on *Reckoning* and *Dead Set.*

The band's decision to not use overdubs on their latest live albums can be understood as yet another way that the sound and symbolism of the tapes had influenced the Dead's approach to live recording by the early 1980s. Whereas the band freely employed overdubs and would routinely "fix things in the mix" on their earlier commercial live records, the rise of taping and the spread of tapes were motivated, in part, by fans who desired a more authentic representation of the group's live performances. Even as they prepared to record their shows in San Francisco and New York for commercial release, the Dead knew that fans would also be taping the concerts. Furthermore, it was also certain that these fan-produced recordings would quickly begin to circulate among traders. Therefore, since some people would have already heard many of the performances that would eventually appear on *Reckoning* and *Dead Set*, the band understood that fans would notice if performances had been "sweetened," or "enhanced," during postproduction.

While just a few years earlier the Dead may have considered overdubbing to be a standard practice when producing an album (for both their studio and live recordings), the expanding practices of taping and trading contributed to the formation of an aesthetic that valued live recordings as realistic documents and not as studio productions. By boosting the presence of the audience in the mix and by eschewing overdubs, the Dead not only were responding to the aesthetic of recorded liveness that had developed around tapes but also were figuring out how that aesthetic could be reproduced and subsequently sold back to fans.

Even as the Dead sought to present a more "realistic" version of recorded liveness on their latest releases, many fans still believed that unofficial tapes provided a more authentic recorded representation of the live concert experience. As described in the previous chapter, the fact that they were produced and distributed outside of the established music industry lent a degree of authenticity to tapes that, for obvious reasons, distinguished them from the band's official live releases. Although a confluence of anticommercial sentiments and countercultural impulses provided much of the aesthetic justification for taping, trading, and collecting, many fans believed that noncommercial recordings offered a more accurate formal representation of the Dead's concerts. Like so many of the band's official live releases, *Reckoning* and *Dead Set* were compiled from a variety of performances that were recorded at different locations on multiple dates and then sequenced so as to resemble a "typical" concert. Although most of the live albums released by major labels during the rock era were compilations, taping and tape collecting had given rise to a greater demand among many fans of the Dead for complete recordings of individual concerts.

In June 1981, the band signed another, newly amended contract with Arista. Whereas the first amended contract from September 1980 stipulated that the Dead would release a live album recorded at Radio City Music Hall, the latest contract most likely reflects informal agreements between the band and the label that took place prior to the release of *Reckoning* in April. Drawn up approximately two months before the release of *Dead Set*, the new contract requires that the band deliver "two (2) separate albums consisting of two (2) LPs each which are recorded before a live audience as opposed to being recorded in a recording studio, provided each such double LP is recorded at *Warfield Theatre in San Francisco, California during September–October, 1980 and at* Radio City Music Hall in New York, New York during October, 1980."[18] The contract also acknowledges that "one such double LP shall consist of 'acoustic' performances" and the other LP "shall consist of 'electric' performances."

Given the many advances and allowances that had been provided to the band, the new contract indicated that the Dead still owed over $400,000 to Arista. Furthermore, the amended contract also stipulated that *Reckoning* and *Dead Set* would only count as one of the two long-playing records that the band still owed to Arista. Although the group delivered eight album sides as part of two double records in 1981, the Grateful Dead still owed one more album to Arista per the terms of the original contract.

Marketing Liveness at the Dawn of the Video Revolution

In addition to a live album (that then became two live albums), Richard Loren's proposal for the "Dead on Broadway" retrospective also included plans for a live video recording as well as live video and audio simulcasts. As described in the proposal, the Dead would "video color record the last four nights on Broadway for sale to video disc and cassette." While Loren acknowledged that the video "taping would not be an immediate money maker," it would cost very little to produce and could "be an enormous annuity later." Indeed, as Loren noted, if 100,000 videodiscs were sold over a few years, they could net over $200,000 "without having to leave home." Furthermore, Loren suggested that Arista could use footage from the video recordings to promote the new live album. Loren's proposal also included plans for a live video simulcast of the band's final concert performance. Loren estimated that, by simulcasting their concert in about a dozen 2,500-seat theaters in cities across the United States, the Dead "could conservatively earn $100,000."

On October 31, 1980, the Grateful Dead's final concert at Radio City Music Hall was simulcast live on local radio stations and in a handful of midsize movie theaters via closed-circuit TV. With listeners and viewers tuning in along the East Coast and throughout the country, the Dead enlisted comedians Al Franken and Tom Davis to provide entertainment before the concert and during set breaks. Franken and Davis, writers on *Saturday Night Live*, the irreverent late-night television show, were longtime fans of the Grateful Dead. As the "hosts" of the Halloween concert, they performed stand-up routines and introduced pretaped segments, many of which featured members of the band.

In a skit titled "Henry K: Bootlegger," for example, Davis conducts a backstage interview with a rather unexpected fan of the band: Henry Kissinger (played by Franken). As a committed Deadhead, Kissinger understands the historical significance of the band's anniversary concerts. Recalling the band's legendary "Evening with the Grateful Dead" concerts, Kissinger remarks that the "last time I saw the Dead play an acoustic set was [in] 1970 [at the] Fillmore East." Near the end of the interview, Davis discovers that Kissinger is hiding a microphone up his sleeve and has a tape deck hidden under his suit jacket. As Davis admonishes Kissinger for bootlegging the band's concert, drummer Bill Kreutzmann emerges from behind a road case, exclaiming, "Goddammit, Henry, give me that tape!" As Davis urges the concert audience to refrain from taping, Kreutzmann explains that he's going to "take this tape and I'm going to erase it right now!" Kissinger, meanwhile, stealthily inserts a blank cassette into the tape deck and assures Davis that he has learned an important lesson.

Almost a year later, in August 1981, some of these sketches appeared alongside live performances on *Live Dead!*, a special that was broadcast on the US cable TV channel Showtime. Directed by Len Dell'Amico, *Live Dead!* was produced to promote the release of *Dead Set*. Shortly after the special aired, *Billboard* reported that fans could also expect "subsequent releases scheduled for videodisk, videocassette and feature film configurations."[19] According to Dell'Amico, he and the band created two versions of a concert video, including the "70-minute version for Showtime" and a version that would be available for retail and that would feature "different songs and a different texture." While Dell'Amico noted that the forthcoming video release was intended for the "dyed-in-the-wool Grateful Dead fan," he also admitted, "We are certain that the fans will tape the Showtime special so that is why we are putting together something different for the other releases."[20]

By the middle of 1980, Richard Loren and other members of the extended Dead organization were seriously exploring how emerging video formats and technologies could be used alongside audio recordings in promoting the band. Following the premiere of MTV in August 1981, people throughout the music industry were turning their attention to the many artistic, promotional, and commercial opportunities offered by video. As part of a Talent Forum that was organized by *Billboard* magazine in September 1981, John Scher, a well-known concert promoter and head of Monarch Entertainment, moderated a panel titled "Exploring Other Areas to Maximize Profits While Using Music Industry Skills." Acknowledging the "challenges posed by a diminishing live concert market," Scher, who had promoted the Dead's concerts at Radio City Music Hall and helped produce their recent video performances, spoke about the importance of exploring multiple formats to avoid "killing off an act before it has reached its marketing potential."[21] Echoing comments made by Dell'Amico, Scher described how, when preparing video footage compiled from the Dead's live performances at Radio City Music Hall, he and the band "got enough footage for a one-hour special on cable, a two-hour videodisk, a 90-minute cassette and 45 minutes for the European market."[22]

The videocassette described by Scher was released by Warner Home Video in November 1981 as *Dead Ahead* and was the band's first commercial live concert video. Directed by Dell'Amico and featuring performances of twelve songs (as well as select skits by Franken and Davis), the original videocassette release of *Dead Ahead* is about ten minutes longer than the Showtime special (lasting nearly eighty minutes, the Showtime special featured ten performances). In terms of content, however, only a few performances appear on both the Showtime special and *Dead Ahead*: "On the Road Again," "Ripple," and "Good Lovin.'" By providing substantially different content across varying formats, Scher was putting into practice what he had preached at the Talent Forum a few months earlier.

While the video marketing strategies described by Scher could be applied to almost any musical act that faced the prospect of being "killed off," the overall success of such an approach depended, in large part, on a devoted fanbase, especially one with a seemingly insatiable appetite for all kinds of recordings. As he was developing his general marketing plans in response to the burgeoning video market (and the worsening live concert market), Scher seems to have envisioned the patterns of consumption and habits of collecting that had emerged among many Deadheads in the wake of taping and trading. As director Len Dell'Amico acknowledged, the fact that fans would almost certainly record (and then trade) the Showtime special meant that, by producing and manufacturing different versions of what was in essence the same commodity, Scher and the Dead could continue to make money on retail sales while trying to stay one step ahead of the video bootleggers, a prospect that became more difficult with the rise of portable video recording technologies.

Along with *Dead Ahead*, the Dead also released *The Grateful Dead Movie* on VHS and videodisc formats in 1981. After many delays, the film had finally been released in 1977 and was originally titled (once again) *The Grateful Dead*. Filmed and recorded at the Winterland in October 1974 as the Dead prepared to go on their touring hiatus, the movie opens with a remarkable animated sequence by Gary Gutierrez and features many dynamic performances by the band and intimate footage of the crew and fans. Four years after its initial release, *The Grateful Dead Movie* was among the first group of films released on RCA's SelectaVision brand of videodiscs. As reported in *Billboard* in October 1980, RCA was attracted to the Dead because, in the opinion of Seth Willenson, an executive at RCA, their "audience spans such a large age group," with Willenson noting that they "still have loyal fans from the '60s, and they're building up a whole new following as well."[23] As described by John Scher, the planned rerelease of *The Grateful Dead Movie* was part of an "all-encompassing developmental deal between [Scher's] company [Monarch Entertainment] and RCA SelectaVision." Scher remarked that the video production division of his company could provide RCA "with other concert programs on a regular basis" and suggested that footage from the Dead's performances at Radio City Music Hall might also be included as part of the deal.[24]

When RCA's inaugural list of SelectaVision titles was announced in March 1981, *The Grateful Dead Movie* was one of a handful of music titles that included Blondie's "video album" *Eat to the Beat*, the Rolling Stones in *Gimme Shelter*, and Elton John's concert documentary *To Russia . . . with Elton*. Despite Scher's commitment to RCA, the band did not release *Dead Ahead* or any of the concert footage recorded at Radio City Music Hall on the company's brand of videodisc. On the one hand, it is unlikely that the

Dead could have produced a film before March, the planned launch date of RCA's video players and associated brand of discs. By licensing the rights to *The Grateful Dead Movie* from Grateful Dead Productions (GDP), however, RCA was assured of immediate content with the promise of more material in the future.

On the other hand, however, it is doubtful that the band or Scher had any intention of ever releasing *Dead Ahead* on the videodisc technology that was being promoted by RCA. Designed much like phonograph records, RCA's capacitance electronic discs (CEDs) stored audio and video content in grooves that was read by a stylus. Even though CED videodiscs had been commercially available for some time, the rise of videotape recording and home playback systems beginning in the late 1970s, along with recent advances in laser optic technologies, meant that RCA's players and their accompanying brand of discs were practically obsolete the moment they appeared on the market in 1981.[25]

For an organization that had always prided itself on being at the forefront of the latest audio and video technologies, it should come as no surprise, therefore, that the Dead and Scher also made plans to release an expanded version of *Dead Ahead* on the newer laserdisc format. Utilizing laser optic technology that had been developed by the Philips and MCA corporations, *The Grateful Dead/Dead Ahead: Recorded Live Halloween, 1980* was released on Pioneer Artists laserdiscs in 1982. Like CED videodiscs, laserdiscs were double-sided and were capable of storing up to two hours (an hour on each side) of recorded content. Whereas the VHS version accommodated up to ninety minutes of content, the additional thirty minutes offered by the laserdisc format provided the band with an opportunity to produce yet another, even longer, version of *Dead Ahead*.

The song sequencing on the various formats of *Dead Ahead* preserves the form of the band's anniversary concerts. Acoustic performances of the songs "To Lay Me Down," "On the Road Again," and "Ripple" appear on both the VHS and laserdisc versions of *Dead Ahead*. The laserdisc version also includes a fourth acoustic performance, a moving rendition of "Bird Song" performed on October 31. Following the acoustic performances, the original VHS version of *Dead Ahead* continues with electric performances of "Don't Ease Me In," "Lost Sailor," "Saint of Circumstance," "Franklin's Tower," "Fire on the Mountain," "Not Fade Away," and "Good Lovin.'" An edited segment of percussion music performed by Bill Kreutzmann and Mickey Hart (often referred to simply as "Drums" or, as it appears on the VHS version, "Rhythm Devils") appears between "Franklin's Tower" and "Fire on the Mountain."

By contrast, the electric performances on the laserdisc begin with "Me and My Uncle" followed by "Mexicali Blues," "Ramble on Rose," and "Little Red Rooster." "Little Red Rooster" is the last song on side 1 of the laserdisc; side 2 features all of the electric performances that appear on the VHS version.

The Dead were clearly thinking in terms of the three-set format of their anniversary concerts when selecting and sequencing performances for the laserdisc release.[26] With the additional time available on the laserdisc format, the band created another "set" of electric performances. Appearing after the opening acoustic performances (and the "Henry K: Bootlegger" skit), the new set (beginning with "Me and My Uncle" to "Little Red Rooster") functions as the "first" electric set and lasts until the end of side 1. Side 2 begins with another Franken and Davis skit followed by the same electric performances that are featured on the VHS version. On the laserdisc format, these performances now function as a "second" electric set.

It was during the band's second sets, it will be recalled, that the Dead would typically engage in longer, more adventurous improvisations. To enhance that effect, the laserdisc version of *Dead Ahead* includes excerpts from an improvisation featuring the entire band. Often referred to as "Space," this portion of the video utilizes contemporary, state-of-the-art visual effects that add to the "trippiness" of the scene. With references to Pigpen and snippets of the song "Turn on Your Lovelight," the final song, "Good Lovin'," serves as a fitting encore to the video concert experience and the "retrospective trip" of the Dead's anniversary concerts.

The laserdisc version of *Dead Ahead* is also noteworthy in that, at the time, it was the most extensive representation of a single concert performance that the Grateful Dead had officially released. Except for the songs "To Lay Me Down" and "On the Road Again," which had been performed and recorded on October 30, the remaining fourteen musical performances on the laserdisc version of *Dead Ahead* are from the band's Halloween concert on the following night. Moreover, these electric performances appear in the same order (and appear in the same corresponding set) as they were performed during the concert.

By the end of 1982, the Dead appeared particularly interested in pursuing new opportunities offered by video. Before the rise of portable (and concealable) camcorders made it possible for fans to produce their own live video recordings of the band's concerts, the Dead seemed poised to develop a market for concert videos across multiple formats that, like their earliest live albums, would appeal to established Deadheads while also attracting new fans.

Instead, the band chose to focus on touring, a decision that was motivated, in large part, by a growing sense of fatigue, frustration with their record label, and rampant substance abuse throughout the organization. As described by Phil Lesh, by 1982, "it was a classic double-bind situation: stay locked into our vicious touring and recording schedule or ease up on touring, which we couldn't do [since] we didn't have any funds set aside to keep our people employed and our team together."[27] Following their return to the road in 1976, the Grateful Dead had maintained a relentless touring schedule that found them playing in various theaters, auditoriums, and arenas throughout the United States. As Lesh has pointed out, however, despite playing more concerts, the increased "earnings meant [nothing] to the individual band members; it was mostly numbers on paper, since the band drew what was basically a maintenance salary." "All the rest," Lesh explained, "went into the pot—for crew and management salaries, equipment expenses, etc.—to keep the trip going."[28]

Further Reckonings

Throughout the 1980s, the Dead chose to "keep the trip going" by doing what they had always done: tour. In the years immediately following the premiere of MTV in 1981, established performers such as Bruce Springsteen, Tina Turner, John Fogerty, and many others were successful in using the promotional power of music video to attract a new generation of fans, a strategy that, in turn, led to larger concert audiences and bigger venues. Unlike some of their "classic rock" contemporaries, however, the Grateful Dead continued to rely on word of mouth and the practices of taping and trading to maintain a stable critical mass of fans for their live performances. Following the release of *Dead Set* in 1981, the band did not release another commercial album—live or studio recording—until 1987. Despite not releasing any new commercial music for much of the decade, the Dead remained one of the highest-grossing touring acts.

Outside of the Dead organization, publications like *Relix* (formerly *Dead Relix*) and other fanzines such as *The Golden Road* (founded in 1984 by Blair Jackson and Regan McMahon) kept current Deadheads informed and attracted new "Heads." The band's audience continued to grow when the *Deadhead Hour* premiered in late 1984. Originally broadcast on KFOG-FM in San Francisco, within a few years, the *Deadhead Hour*—under the new name *The Grateful Dead Hour*—was syndicated on radio stations throughout the United States. Hosted by David Gans, *The Grateful Dead Hour* was devoted to all things Dead, including interviews and conversations with members of the Dead organization and musical performances drawn from the band's vault of live recordings.[29]

Meanwhile, the practice of concert taping continued to grow. By 1984, however, the increasingly belligerent behavior of some tapers toward other audience members (as well as toward some members of the Dead organization) forced the band to reconsider their position on taping. In a meeting held in September 1984, Bill Kreutzmann suggested that the entire taping situation "has gotten out of hand" and that it could not "be policed effectively."[30] At the same meeting, the organization considered various policies regarding taping: "1) Anything Goes 2) Close it down completely 3) [Allow] Taping only in [a designated] section 4) Make and sell our own tapes."

As one of his first duties as the band's publicist, Dennis McNally prepared a statement that would be included in the Grateful Dead's official newsletter to fans (the "Dead Heads" newsletter) detailing the current taping situation. Cognizant of the mutual respect between the Dead and their fans, the statement acknowledges that "we've always been loose about private, noncommercial Dead Head taping—'When we're done with it, you can have it,' Garcia once said. 'But lately,' says Billy Kreutzmann, 'I look out in the audience and see hassles, not enjoyment.'"[31] The band's statement also notes how "a sizeable part of the audience, including our own Dan Healy [the Dead's live sound mixer], is losing stage visibility due to overly tall mikestands [sic]." Furthermore, the statement continued, "people are beginning to videotape." "This is all creating a problem."

As a possible remedy, fans were informed that "at our upcoming Berkeley Community Theater shows we will be setting aside the area behind the soundboard for tapers—it will be OK to tape there, but nowhere else in the hall; get caught elsewhere and you are gone for the night. Videotaping is not OK at any time." True to their word, the Dead established a section in the audience reserved solely for tapers on October 27, 1984, the first night of a six-night run of concerts at the Berkeley Community Theater in Berkeley, California. As recorded in the minutes of a meeting from November 30, the "TAPERS SECTION was a success at BCT [Berkeley Community Theater]; this section will become a permanent part of our concerts until we decide otherwise."[32]

David Shenk and Steve Silberman have remarked that the establishment of the tapers section was "revolutionary" in that it fostered a unique relationship between the band and a "passionate and loyal constituency of tapers and traders."[33] While the decision to establish a tapers section exemplifies the remarkable sense of trust and goodwill that had developed between the band and their fans, people associated with the Dead also understood that they could not shut down the practice of taping altogether. By 1984, the band had not released new material in three years. In the absence of official releases from the band, tapers and traders continued to supply fans with the band's latest (unofficial) live recordings. During a period in which the band had decided to devote their attention to touring, there was no way that the Dead were going to cut off their main source of advertising: the tapes.

The band understood that they needed to address the taping situation with considerable tact so as not to alienate some of their most devoted fans. In an early draft of the statement, publicist Dennis McNally wrote how the Dead hoped that tapers would abide by the new procedures because the "idea of circulating through the [audience] pit with electromagnets seems rather . . . extreme."[34] McNally's suggestion that members of the road crew might use magnets to erase tapes if fans did not follow the rules was interpreted by at least one member of the organization as a "Threat!!" Not surprisingly, there is no mention of magnets in the official statement that appeared in the newsletter that was mailed to fans.

Occasionally the band would return to video as a way of reminding people who were not Deadheads that the Grateful Dead were still active. In the spring of 1985, for instance, the group and director Len Dell'Amico reunited to shoot footage of the band performing live in an empty auditorium in Marin County. At the time, the band and Dell'Amico were planning to produce a long-form video that would combine footage of these performances with computer animation to be sold and promoted as part of the band's twentieth anniversary.

Later that year, in August 1985, *The Grateful Dead Movie* was rereleased by Monterey Home Video. Finally available (commercially) on videotape, the rerelease features material that had been cut from the SelectaVision videodisc that was released in 1981. As seen in figure 3.2, the promotional campaign for the restored rerelease emphasized the band's reputation for liveness and the demand of fans for as much material as possible. Riffing on a well-known phrase, the ad noted, "There's Nothing Like a Grateful Dead Fan." Since fans will "do almost anything to see this legendary rock group perform," the ad suggests to retailers that "now you can capitalize on 'The Dead's' fanatical following with this incredible live performance on videocassette." In addition to the video release of *The Grateful Dead Movie*, fans also had a chance to see the second set of the band's New Year's Eve concert at the Oakland Coliseum, a performance that was simulcast live on the USA Network (and that was taped and copied by Deadheads all over the country).

By 1986, it appeared that the Grateful Dead would continue to rely on touring as a way to "keep the trip going." In July, the band joined Bob Dylan and Tom Petty for a handful of stadium concerts in Minnesota, Ohio, New

FIGURE 3.2. Advertisement for VHS release of *The Grateful Dead Movie*

York, and Washington, DC. Reporting on the upcoming concerts, journalist Jack McDonough found it remarkable that the "Bob Dylan/Tom Petty tour—by many accounts the concert event of the summer—will host as opener for . . . a band that has not released an album in five years."[35] While the Grateful Dead did not headline every concert, publicist Dennis McNally explained to McDonough that the band was "too big for arenas, but not big enough to play stadiums on our own." McNally estimated that the band grossed over $18 million by playing in arenas in 1985 and that "over the past two or three years, the only act to lead the Dead in ticket sales is [Bruce] Springsteen—and of course he does stadiums regularly." By co-headlining concert dates with Dylan and Petty, McNally and the Dead felt they had found a "compatible show."[36] Although the band still owed an album to Arista, McNally told McDonough, "I wouldn't expect to see [an album] anytime soon." "The Dead is a performing band. They need the juice they get from an audience," he explained.[37]

A few weeks after McNally's comments appeared in *Billboard*, Jerry Garcia became gravely ill. Years of substance abuse and an unhealthy lifestyle had finally caught up to Garcia, and shortly after the band's final concert alongside Dylan and Petty, he fell into a diabetic coma. Garcia's condition was very serious and it took the help of many physicians and therapists along with the support of friends and family as he recovered.

In the meantime, the Dead were forced to cancel their fall tour, and an entire organization that had sustained itself from gig to gig ground to a sudden halt. By October, however, Garcia was well enough to play a handful of concerts in small venues throughout California as part of his longtime project the Jerry Garcia Band and in duo performances with bassist John Kahn. In December, the Grateful Dead—including Garcia—returned to the stage with shows at the Oakland Coliseum and the Henry J. Kaiser Convention Center in Oakland. Even as Garcia continued to recover, the band planned a tour for the spring that would take them to the East Coast.

By the end of 1986, it was clear to everyone in the Dead organization that the business model they had been following for much of the decade, one that relied on touring to satisfy the musical interests of the band and support the financial obligations of their sprawling business organization, was no longer sustainable. In January 1987, before returning to the road, the band and a recording crew set up at Marin Veterans' Memorial Auditorium in San Rafael to record basic tracks for a new studio album. Following Garcia's health scare and the sense of uncertainty that engulfed the Dead organization, many people were hopeful that the band could produce something that was, in Clive Davis's words, both "accessible and commercial."

"That Quintessential
Spirit of the Band"

"TOUCH OF GREY," THE
"BETTY BOARDS," AND THE
REBIRTH OF THE DEAD
(THE 1980S, PART 2)

Shortly before the band signed to Arista Records, Steve Brown and other members of the Grateful Dead organization had been making plans to form a new record label. Inspired by the growing demand among fans for unreleased material, the newly proposed label, Ground Records, would be devoted to releasing archival recordings of the Grateful Dead and other Dead-related projects. As described in chapter 2, plans for the new label were put on hold when the band's record company, Grateful Dead Records, folded in the middle of 1976. As the band prepared to sign a new contract, however, some members of the Dead organization were still thinking about the prospect of producing and releasing material from their expanding vault of personal recordings.

The terms and conditions of the contract the Dead signed in 1976 reflect the band's desire to produce and market recordings on their own (as Grateful Dead Productions [GDP]) and the extent to which Arista sought to limit those opportunities.[1] As described in the contract, the Dead were permitted to release self-produced concert recordings provided that such recordings were of live performances that occurred *after* the band had signed to Arista. If the band chose to release such recordings (either on their own or through a third party), Arista retained the "right of first refusal." Even if Arista passed and the band chose to release the recordings, the terms and stipulations outlined in the contract, including the high royalty rates that would be collected by the label, rendered the entire enterprise commercially untenable for the Dead. At the same time, a separate paragraph in the contract explicitly prohibits the Dead from releasing recordings of live concerts that occurred *before* the commencement of the contract. Marked by an asterisk and appearing at the end of the twenty-six-page document, paragraph 36 affirms that the Dead "agree not to manufacture or distribute, directly or indirectly, or to license to any third party the rights to manufacture or distribute recordings owned or controlled by [the band] embodying performances of live personal appearances which were recorded . . . prior to the commencement of the Term."

When the Grateful Dead signed to Arista in 1976, label president Clive Davis hoped the band could produce a studio album that was "accessible and commercial."[2] In pursuit of a hit record, Davis, it would appear, was not especially interested in encouraging the Dead's side projects. Instead, during contract negotiations, Davis was committed to what he called "three vital issues." Specifically, he directed the band to record outside of San Francisco "to get a fresh perspective" and to work with outside producers. Moreover, he wanted the group to "commit to touring extensively again to reconnect with their fans and get recharged as a band."[3]

Following an extended break from touring that began in December 1974, the Dead and their crew returned to the road in June 1976. But even as the band began to settle into the familiar pattern of recording and touring (as directed by Davis), some members of GDP continued to prepare for the moment when they could manufacture and distribute the Dead's archival recordings. In particular, people throughout the organization began to pay greater attention to the production, quality, and preservation of the band's personal live recordings beginning in the mid-1970s. By the early 1980s, other people were revisiting the promotional and economic opportunities offered by what was being described as "Direct Mail Concert Tape Sales."

Planning Ahead (1976–1986)

As described in previous chapters, members of the Grateful Dead's live sound crew—notably Owsley "Bear" Stanley, Bill "Kidd" Candelario, Rex Jackson, and Dan Healy—had been recording the band's concerts since the

FIGURE 4.1. Betty Cantor-Jackson, Radio City Music Hall, October 1980

late 1960s. When the band returned to touring in June 1976, they were often accompanied by Betty Cantor (now Cantor-Jackson). As a producer and engineer on some of the band's most acclaimed live and studio recordings (including *Live/Dead* and *Workingman's Dead*), Cantor-Jackson was known for her discerning ear and intimate knowledge of the band's live sound. As part of the band's touring crew, she now drew a salary and was responsible for producing and engineering 2-track stereo recordings of the Dead's concerts (figure 4.1).[4]

From 1976 until approximately 1980, Cantor-Jackson recorded the band (as well as many of Jerry Garcia's side projects) on her Nagra IV-s, a professional-grade 2-track stereo tape recorder. Cantor-Jackson's recording setup, including the Nagra recorder and her dedicated mixers, was compact and portable and produced high-quality stereo recordings.[5] The addition of Cantor-Jackson to the touring crew suggests that, by 1976, members of the Dead organization recognized the potential commercial value of the band's personal 2-track live recordings and were committed to producing and archiving as many quality tapes as possible.

Following her production work on *Reckoning, Dead Set,* and the various video projects that appeared in the early 1980s (including *Dead Ahead*), Cantor-Jackson's position within the organization had become frayed; by 1982, she was no longer working with the Dead. After her departure, other members of the road crew (notably Dan Healy and Don Pearson) continued to record the band's shows using many of the latest technologies and formats.[6] By the end of 1982, for example, the band were recording their concerts using Sony's PCM (pulse code modulation), an adapter that converted and stored digital audio to a videotape format (the Dead used both Beta and VHS tapes). Alongside the many audiocassette and videocassette tapes that they were amassing, the Dead also recorded their concerts using 2-track stereo digital audio tape technology (DAT) beginning in 1987. In the early 1990s, the band recorded select concerts on ADAT, the multitrack version of DAT.

In addition to their self-produced live recordings, the Dead also began to accumulate tapes directly from select fans. Included among the organization's files relating to tapers and tape exchanges is a letter dated May 14, 1978, from "Matt" to Eileen Law, a longtime member of the Dead's administrative staff.[7] (Among her many responsibilities, Law oversaw the "Dead Heads" mailing list and was the Dead's first archivist.) In the letter, Matt enthuses that the "tour has been *great*! The band is playing in *peak* form. Really hot!" He tells Law that he had "no hassle in Hanover, NH, or Burlington, Vt. Tickets were held for us. The seats were *excellent*!" "On behalf of my friends and myself," he writes, "we'd like to thank you for the excellent tickets. We really appreciate it. Those shows were great!"

In exchange for the "excellent" tickets supplied by Law, Matt assures her that he "taped Hanover right next to the soundboard with primo Nakamichi microphones. Tremendous energy at that show. Probably *the best* 'Estimated Prophet' I've ever heard!" In addition to the Dead's concert on May 5 on the campus of Dartmouth College in Hanover, New Hampshire, Matt also attended concerts on May 6 in Burlington, Vermont; May 10 in New Haven, Connecticut; and May 11 in Springfield, Massachusetts. "Needless to say," he writes, "I have amazing 'master' tapes of all of these shows. The recordings came out *so excellent* this time around. I think due to the improved p.a.

[public address] sound." Matt assures Law that he will send "some of these tapes *soon*."

As they continued to accumulate tapes from a variety of sources, the Dead quickly amassed an extensive collection of live recordings. By 1976, the growing tape library was housed at Club Front, the band's rehearsal and recording space on Front Street in San Rafael, California. Among members of the Dead organization, the physical space in which the tapes were housed came to be known as the "vault." Betty Cantor-Jackson has noted how the vault quickly became a repository; "we built the Vault," she explains, "and started keeping everything in there."[8]

The vault was originally overseen by Willie Legate, whose memorable phrase "THERE IS NOTHING LIKE A GRATEFUL DEAD CONCERT" still reverberated throughout the culture of the Dead. As the band kept up their relentless touring schedule into the 1980s, tapes continued to pour into the vault and, within a short time, Legate began to run out of space to house the band's archival recordings. By 1984, he noted that the "upper vault is overflowing" but that there might be "some room in the lower vault." To address the issue, an ad hoc "Real Estate Committee" was formed to scout out possible new locations for the vault, including a "burned building on Lincoln [Avenue]" in San Rafael.[9]

As the contents of the vault continued to grow with each tour, the band also sought to add to their collection by locating and retrieving tapes that, for one reason or another, had gone missing. The band's personal recordings often circulated among members of the organization and, over the years, tapes were routinely loaned, borrowed, traded, or stolen. During the same meeting from 1984 in which Legate indicated they were running out of room in the vault, those in attendance also discussed a proposed legal settlement between GDP and Betty Cantor-Jackson. Cantor-Jackson, who had not worked with the Dead for a few years, was threatening to sue the organization over money she claimed was owed to her for work on multiple projects from the early 1980s. As indicated in the notes to the meeting, the band proposed a "nominal settlement amount ($1,500–$3,500)." Sue Stephens, Jerry Garcia's longtime assistant, also suggested that "whatever our agreement with Betty, it [should] stipulate her cooperation in the location of tapes, etc."

The minutes to the meeting indicate that some of Cantor-Jackson's personal tapes had been "rescued from unpaid storage" by people connected to the band. While no one seemed to be sure what was on the recovered tapes, someone suggested they may include recordings of the band's European tour in 1972. Of course, as the band continued to look toward the future, the recovery of original master tapes (especially multitrack recordings) could provide GDP with recordings that were previously unavailable and/or recordings whose audio and production qualities were superior to the tapes that already circulated among traders.

By the middle of the 1980s, Legate had served as the Dead's unofficial tape archivist for nearly a decade. As the archive expanded, he required assistance maintaining the many audio and video recordings. In April 1985, GDP approved payment of an hourly wage to Dick Latvala for his work assisting Legate in cataloging the contents of the vault. Latvala was a longtime Deadhead and had been collecting and trading tapes for years; his extensive knowledge of the Dead's history and their recorded legacy would prove crucial in the years to come.

As more people gained access to the vault, the band sought to ensure that the recordings would not be duplicated or otherwise go missing. As described in the minutes to a meeting from May 2, 1985, the Dead developed a "vault policy" whereby "in general, no copies [of tapes] are to be made—nothing leaves [the] building."[10] The band was so committed to keeping a watchful eye over their archive that, for a time, even Dick Latvala was not allowed in the vault except under the supervision of John Cutler, the band's manager.

While members of the organization continued to archive and preserve the band's live recorded legacy, the terms of the Grateful Dead's contract with Arista severely restricted the group from releasing live recordings on their own. Despite the conditions outlined in the contract, however, some people in the Dead organization were still considering the practical and logistical aspects of producing and releasing recordings from the vault.

In August 1982, Alan Trist (the manager of Ice Nine, the Dead's music publishing company) prepared a "preliminary rough outline" concerning "Direct Mail Concert Tape Sales."[11] Revisiting plans originally formulated in 1976 relating to Ground Records, Trist's proposal (addressed to the attention of drummer Bill Kreutzmann and bassist Phil Lesh) outlined how the Dead could release archival recordings, including studio outtakes, demonstration recordings, and live performances. Such materials, Trist noted, would be "selected from the vault" and sold directly via a "mail-order catalogue as part of a periodic newsletter [sent] to the Dead Head's list."

By selling recordings directly to fans via the group's official mailing list, Trist imagined how the organization "could entirely supplant record company albums and make more money." Furthermore, he continued, "such a method of marketing Grateful Dead music is most natural to the G.D.'s creative process." Given the "occurrence of new songs or the resurrection of old songs, new arrangements etc. 'popping up' from time to time in concerts," Trist recognized that the band's live tapes provided a more authentic recorded representation of the Dead, an image that is "less forced than the periodic compression of new material into an album." Along with complete concerts (including material recorded in Egypt in 1978), Trist envisioned other releases, including compilations of recordings selected by individual band members (a title called "Phil's choice" is mentioned), a collection of "Drum breaks," and a tantalizingly mysterious project referred to as "Bugs of Dada."

Despite the many artistic opportunities and financial advantages outlined in his proposal, Trist also acknowledged certain challenges to the plan. Assuming the position of "Devil's Advocate," he observed that, "although we might reach the same market as regular records do," by releasing recordings via mail order, "we would forfeit the chance to reach new markets through the power of record companies and the media." Trist also noted that, despite the band's acknowledged disinterest in making studio albums, such recordings do offer their own unique artistic appeal. "Intentional studio recording projects," he explained, "particularly of new material, can express a coherent 'concept' or aesthetic more fully than a concert." Trist imagined that, "as the concert-tape project" continued to take shape, perhaps the "set and concert design might begin to develop such coherence."

Trist understood the appeal of the group's live recordings among fans, noting that the Grateful Dead were the "only band where every concert is unique." Moreover, the Dead continued to provide plenty of unique live experiences for contemporary audiences. By 1982, for instance, the Grateful Dead were performing approximately seventy-five concerts a year. If the band maintained their current concert schedule, Trist estimated they could potentially fill forty thousand orders per year for a profit of $200,000. Furthermore, by keeping production "in-house," the organization could potentially earn more money while also ensuring that the recordings would not leave their possession. Trist noted that "any editing necessary could be done at Front Street" (the band's rehearsal and recording space) and that "cassette reproduction could *either* be farmed out to a commercial facility *or* done in-house, possibly by an acknowledged tape freak."

Even as Trist continued to examine the opportunities offered by "Direct Mail Concert Tape Sales" throughout the fall of 1982, the band still owed Arista one more record. Therefore, unless (or until) the band delivered their last contractually obligated album or otherwise came to some agreement with the label, there would be no way that Trist's plan could be implemented. To be sure, there were murmurs within the industry that the Dead were releasing a new album. In December 1982, *Cashbox* reported that a new record was due from the band sometime in February or March.[12] By the end of 1983, there was still no new official release from the Grateful Dead.

In February 1984, the band returned to the recording studio, but, in the words of Dennis McNally, the "sessions were a farcical waste of time."[13] McNally describes how the Dead were not particularly interested in recording and that their "ever-increasing popularity as performers . . . removed any economic incentive to record."[14] Meanwhile, fans continued to record and trade concert tapes, practices that remained the band's primary method of promotion. Such practices flourished, especially following the establishment of the tapers section in October 1984.

Although the band had not released any new official material in many years, the Grateful Dead maintained a tireless touring regimen that sustained the organization for most of the 1980s.[15] But as the group settled into a regular and predictable touring schedule, worsening drug and alcohol addictions among members of the band contributed to a level of creative and artistic inertia that permeated the entire organization. The Dead were abruptly roused from their collective malaise when Jerry Garcia fell into a diabetic coma in July 1986. As Garcia recovered, people throughout the organization recognized that they would need to change their ways if they wished to continue the "trip" they had been on for over two decades.

The Dead and/as Nostalgia: "Touch of Grey" and *In the Dark* (1987)

Even as Jerry Garcia continued to recover, the Grateful Dead gathered at Marin Veterans' Memorial Auditorium in San Rafael in January 1987. Two years earlier, the band and director Len Dell'Amico filmed performances in the empty auditorium for a long-form video that was planned for the Dead's twentieth anniversary. The venue was empty again in 1987 as the group began recording material for their forthcoming studio album. It had been almost seven years since the band released their last studio album (*Go to Heaven*) and six years since their last official release on Arista (the live recording *Dead Set*). Whereas the previous studio albums on Arista were produced by people from outside of the Dead's circle of friends and acquaintances, Jerry Garcia and John Cutler, an engineer on the band's sound crew, assumed production duties for the current sessions. The band recorded the basic tracks for multiple songs while playing live onstage in the empty auditorium. Following these live sessions, the band moved to their studio at Club Front, where they recorded vocal and instrumental overdubs and mixed the new record.

By the spring, there was a tremendous amount of excitement at the label as copies of the band's forthcoming record were being passed among Arista's executives. Clive Davis recalls that upon hearing the song "Touch of Grey," he thought, "Here was a song that had all the distinctive, unmistakable trademarks of the Dead sound, that quintessential spirit of the band, but at the same time had an irresistible hook and a lyric anyone could relate to."[16] The lyric from "Touch of Grey" to which Davis refers is the iconic line "I will get by, I will survive." To be sure, the song had been part of the band's live repertoire since the early 1980s. By 1987, however, it had assumed a much greater poignance among fans, both old and new.

"Touch of Grey" was the first song the Grateful Dead played when they returned to the stage following Garcia's illness. Tapes from the concert on December 15, 1986, at the Oakland Coliseum document the audience's joy at Garcia's return, especially during the song's chorus and the triumphant lyric "I will survive!"[17] As heard on the tapes, the crowd erupts toward the end of the song when the lyric changes from "I will survive" to "We will get by, we will survive!" More than just a song "about" Garcia ("I will survive!"), "Touch of Grey" embodied the determination of the Grateful Dead as a band and the perseverance of the Dead as a phenomenon. At the same time, the shift in the lyric to "We will survive!" acknowledges the unique relationship between the band and the community of Deadheads, a community that was set to become even bigger. As Davis noted, "Touch of Grey" was poised to become a "potential anthem for the band, for the Deadheads, for the baby boomers, maybe even for the MTV generation."[18]

"Touch of Grey" was selected as the first single from the Dead's forthcoming album, *In the Dark*. By the late 1980s, the term "single" had increasingly come to mean a song that was promoted on radio and as a music video. Of course, the Dead were no strangers to video production, and despite not having had much (if any) presence on MTV since the launch of the cable channel in 1981, they dove in headfirst. In early May, the band enlisted Gary Gutierrez to direct their video for "Touch of Grey."

Gutierrez had produced the dynamic animation sequence that opens *The Grateful Dead Movie* and was very familiar with the band, their iconography, and their fans. For the "Touch of Grey" music video, Gutierrez and his team re-created each of the band members as skeleton marionettes playing their instruments in front of a live audience. Much of the video was filmed following the band's performance on May 9 in Monterey, California, and includes members of the audience who had just experienced the concert. Throughout the video, the "live"/Dead duality is performed in multiple ways, from the skeletal marionettes performing in front of a "live" audience to the moment when the skeletons transform into the "living" members of the Grateful Dead. The periodic swells and bursts of crowd noise that appear on the audience soundtrack enhance the sense of liveness that the video seeks to (re-)create (albeit with tongue planted firmly in cheek).

Along with the videos to George Michael's "I Want Your Sex" and Wall of Voodoo's "Do It Again," MTV added "Touch of Grey" as a "Sneak Preview" video in the middle of June. A few weeks later, Arista placed a two-page advertisement in *Billboard* promoting the single, the album, and the Dead's upcoming tour dates, including concerts with Bob Dylan. The ad exclaimed, "It's Going to Be a Dead Summer!"[19]

Based in large part on the appeal of the video and widespread radio airplay, "Touch of Grey" became the band's first (and only) Top 10 hit when it peaked at number 9 on *Billboard*'s "Hot 100" chart on September 26. At one point, four songs from the new album—"Touch of Grey," "Hell in a Bucket," "West L.A. Fadeaway," and "When Push Comes to Shove"—appeared simultaneously on the "Album Rock Tracks" chart. *In the Dark* peaked at number 6 on the "Top Pop Albums" charts in August and was certified Gold (having sold over 500,000 copies) on September 4. Two weeks later, *In the Dark* had sold over a million copies and was certified Platinum. The success of *In the Dark* and "Touch of Grey" also contributed to an increase in sales of the band's back catalog. In early September, the band's first two releases on Arista, *Terrapin Station* (1977) and *Shakedown Street* (1978), also received Gold certifications.[20] In an attempt to capitalize on the band's recent successes, Warner Bros. also released reissues of the Dead's earliest albums on compact disc.

When the Grateful Dead released *Dead Set* in 1981, the long-playing album was still the dominant format. By 1987, however, profits from the sale of compact discs had surpassed those of LPs.[21] Given the recent trends in the industry, Arista's marketing campaign for *In the Dark* promoted compact discs alongside cassette tapes. As described by Jim Cawley, Arista's vice president of sales, the "game plan on this particular album was to try, as we did with the Whitney Houston album [*Whitney*], to put out just the right amount of records to every account."[22] In particular, Cawley noted how "Arista's marketing campaign for *In the Dark* calls for a heavy push behind the CD version" and that, "from the start, we noticed we were picking up strong demand for the CD—a lot of people were asking for it." Cawley pointed out that *In the Dark* had been "one of the fastest-moving CDs the label has released to date." By the end of August, Arista's commitment to the format had paid off as *In the Dark* was recognized by *Billboard* as the best-selling compact disc in the country (number 2 was *Whitney* by Whitney Houston).[23]

Arista continued to cultivate the market for cassette tapes, still the most popular contemporary format. The version of *In the Dark* that was produced on cassette included "My Brother Esau," a song that was not included on the compact disc release. As Arista no doubt realized, committed Deadheads would almost certainly seek out both formats.

While Arista worked to promote recent releases by the Dead, Whitney Houston, and others, the label announced the formation of a video division called 6 West Home Video. Arista entered the home video market with the release of two long-form videos, both of which featured the Grateful Dead. *Dead Ringers: The Making of the "Touch of Grey" Video and More* was directed by Justin Kreutzmann (son of drummer Bill Kreutzmann) and features interviews and behind-the-scenes footage documenting the filming and production of the band's breakthrough video. Arista also released *So Far*, a short film directed by Jerry Garcia and Len Dell'Amico. "Featuring a Seamless Blend of Music and Animation" (as described on the cover to the VHS and laserdisc releases), *So Far* combines computer graphics, found footage, and performances of the band rehearsing and playing live. (*So Far* includes performances that Dell'Amico and the band filmed at Marin Veterans' Memorial Auditorium in 1985.)

By the middle of December, *So Far* and *Dead Ringers* were number 1 and number 2, respectively, on the *Billboard* "Top Music Videocassettes" chart. Recounting the band's recent experiences with video, director Justin Kreutzmann described how *Dead Ringers* "opened up a lot of people who otherwise wouldn't have known there was a new Grateful Dead record out [as well as] a whole new group of people who didn't know there was a group called the Grateful Dead."[24] The band's increased exposure on radio also played a large part in their recent success. As one program director noted, the "audience reaction to the Grateful Dead [has been] astounding" and has been driven by people "who may not consider themselves Deadheads, but like other music by heritage artists and are suddenly discovering the Dead."[25]

Of course, referring to the band as "heritage artists" is a polite way of saying that the Dead were old. While the Grateful Dead had been making music for over twenty-two years, the band's latest renaissance and their growing appeal among younger audiences was tinged with a strong sense of nostalgia. In an exposé on the band published in *Rolling Stone*, Mikal Gilmore noted that "for much of the pop world, the Dead are an object of indifference and, just as often, downright ridicule."[26] For others, however, the Dead represented the "ferment and the romanticism of the 1960s" and "have long figured as a cultural icon, standing for ideals of humanity, benevolence, unity and even spirituality."[27] Considering the Dead's legacy and their increasingly youthful audience, lyricist Robert Hunter described "looking at an audience of nineteen- or twenty-year-old kids" and imagining that perhaps the Dead's "music is appealing to some sort of idealism in people." Still, Hunter wondered: "Can you have nostalgia for a time you didn't live in?"[28]

Of course you can because, as Dennis McNally has observed, "in the 1980s, idealism *was* nostalgic."[29] The year 1987 was the twentieth anniversary of the Summer of Love, and people throughout the United States were inundated with stories and reports on the "hippies," "free love," "psychedelic" drugs, and the social impact and political legacy of the countercultural movement that emerged from San Francisco in the mid-1960s. Writing in *Billboard* in July 1987, Paul Grein noted how "if you've been by a newsstand in the past few weeks, you know that this is the 20th anniversary of the Summer of Love." "What you may *not* know," he continued, "is that at least a dozen of the acts that dominated that summer are back" on the charts.[30]

Along with the Dead, Grein identified current chart successes by members of the Jefferson Airplane, Neil Young, Eric Clapton, Steve Winwood, and other "heritage artists." At the same time, albums by the Beatles and Jimi Hendrix were also enjoying commercial success after being reissued on compact disc. When *In the Dark* became the best-selling compact disc in the United States in August, Grein remarked that "this must be some sort of cultural signpost." As Grein wrote, "We can see the headline now: '60s Hippies Become '80s Yuppies."[31] Indeed, it was not just teenagers who were aiding in the resurrection of the Dead. The parents of many of those same teenagers, most of whom were baby boomers just beginning to settle into middle age, were also (re)discovering the band. Even as the group continued to reach new heights of success on the pop and album charts, the Dead rose as high as number 15 on the "Hot Adult Contemporary" chart alongside artists such as Kenny G, Dionne Warwick, and Dan Fogelberg.

For a generation of younger audiences who were coming of age during the Reagan years, the Grateful Dead provided a tangible and seemingly authentic connection to the increasingly romanticized image of San Francisco and the counterculture of the 1960s. Furthermore, some of those same fans recognized that many of the communal and artistic ideals that had come to be associated with the Summer of Love (especially as it had recently been depicted in the press) were being enacted and explored on a regular basis as part of the band's live performances.

Of course, audiences had been "getting hip" to the idea of the Grateful Dead and their reputation for liveness for more than two decades. Beginning in the mid-1960s, people were turned on to the Dead and their performances at dancehalls and ballrooms throughout San Francisco. By the early 1970s, the band had attracted an entirely new audience largely on the success of their studio albums *Workingman's Dead* and *American Beauty*. In 1987, a hit single and a popular music video introduced the Dead to a new generation of fans, many of whom were just beginning to learn about the band, their history, and their legacy of liveness.

The "Betty Boards"

An appreciation for the band's unique sense of liveness was also being rekindled among many of the group's established fans. While newer fans were still learning to navigate the discourse of liveness associated with the Grateful Dead, the attention of many established Deadheads was focused on a cache of tapes that had recently started to circulate among traders. As described at the time by John Dwork in *Dupree's Diamond News*, a well-known Dead fanzine, the newly surfaced batch of tapes "represents the largest and, so far, most important release of 'classic' Grateful Dead music at any one given time."[32] For "all you hardcore tapers," Dwork wrote, "your wildest dreams may just have come true!"

Including over 250 hours of music from dozens of concert recordings, the batch of tapes features "new pristeen [*sic*] soundboard copies of such all-time classics as the visionary '72 Veneta, Oregon show and the stellar second set from Cornell 1977." In the opinion of Dwork and other committed tape collectors, soundboard recordings of concerts of such stature "are unquestionably important 'gifts' which will surely have far-reaching, spiritual and social implications in the Dead Head community." At the same time, the availability of "high-quality (i.e. finally 'listenable') copies of such dated tunes as 'I'm a Hog for You Baby' and 'Oh Boy' from Manhattan Center [in April 1971] give a new and clearer idea of what it was all about way back when. And the promise of twelve Europe '72 shows, a tour which we are all lacking high quality sound boards of, is most promising." "But it doesn't end there," Dwork continued. "Another fifty-or-so hours of *pre-'74* soundboards are beginning to find their way into widespread circulation." Speaking on behalf of (and from the perspective of) tape collectors, Dwork concluded that "what's nicest about this find is that it releases us (at least for the meantime) from relying directly on the band for old tapes. As long as we don't abuse them (i.e. sell them), we should be able, as a whole, to have fairly easy access to them."[33]

Even as collectors began to feast their ears on these newly unearthed live recordings, the story behind the tapes proved to be just as remarkable and no doubt contributed to their mystical/mythical appeal among Deadheads. As described in *Dupree's Diamond News*, *The Golden Road*, and other Dead-related publications, the recently surfaced tapes were master soundboard recordings that had originally been produced by Betty Cantor-Jackson; given their provenance, the cache of reels came to be known among traders as "Betty Boards."[34] Before leaving the Dead organization, Cantor-Jackson gathered together much of her own equipment along with numerous recordings she had produced for the band from 1969 through the early 1980s. At some point, the collection of tapes (stored in road cases with "Grateful Dead" stenciled on the side) suffered water damage and were relocated to a storage facility. Cantor-Jackson became delinquent on her payments to the facility, and the contents of her storage locker—including hundreds of reels of original master recordings of the Grateful Dead, New Riders of the Purple Sage, the Jerry Garcia Band, and other bands and projects—were sold at auction.

The contents of the storage locker caught the attention of a handful of interested parties, and the lot of Cantor-Jackson's possessions was split among multiple buyers. Among the buyers was a group of people who worked diligently at cleaning and restoring the damaged recordings and who, over the course of several weeks, transferred the contents of the tapes to a digital format. By the spring of 1987, tapes that had been sourced from the digital transfers began to appear throughout the taping community, and the Betty Boards entered the lore of the Dead.

The story of the Betty Boards could be summarized simply as the discovery of a bunch of old tape recordings by an even older rock band. To fully appreciate the significance of many of the circumstances involving the Betty Boards, however, one must acknowledge just how deeply an ideology of liveness had come to dominate the critical and popular discourse surrounding the Grateful Dead. Using a language that would have been familiar to members of the taping and trading community, Dwork's references to performances such as "'72 Veneta, Oregon," "Cornell 1977," and the "Manhattan Center" suggest the degree to which specific concerts were already held in high regard by Deadheads. For fans familiar with the recordings (not to mention the stories) of such fabled concerts, the Betty Boards offered contemporary listeners a "new and clearer idea of what it was all about way back when."[35]

There was also a sense among many people within the community of collectors that there was something *different* about the sound of the Betty Boards. On the one hand, the sound quality of the tapes was unlike that of most other existing recordings of the band. Cantor-Jackson's soundboard recordings were often admired for their clarity and for the sense of space she was able to achieve in her mixes. "Until you hear things of this quality," Dwork remarked, "it is really quite impossible to appreciate the subtle nuances, the sometimes delightful interplay between band members."[36]

There was also something else, some ineffable quality, that distinguished the Betty Boards from the other tapes that commonly circulated among traders and collectors. Dwork tried to articulate this quality of the Betty Boards, suggesting that the tapes may have "far-reaching, spiritual and social implications in the Dead Head community." To be sure, themes of faith, devotion, and resurrection dominate the popular narrative of the Betty Boards, from the belief in the inherent power of Cantor-Jackson's tapes to how the recordings were "brought back to life" by a small group of devotees who then shared the sounds throughout the community of Deadheads.

When interpreted in such a "spiritual" manner, of course, the Betty Boards embody the popular notion of the tapes as "relics," an idea that extends back to Les Kippel ("Dead Relics"/*Dead Relix*) and other early tapers, traders, and collectors. Indeed, the story of the Betty Boards makes sense only within an established discourse and an associated rhetoric that ascribes meaning and power to live recordings. Recalling the work of Susan Stewart, relics—such as the many concert tapes that circulated among Deadheads—are forms of souvenirs. But whereas traditional souvenirs mark what Stewart calls the "transformation of materiality into meaning," relics, by contrast, embody the "transformation of meaning into materiality."[37] As the tapes began to circulate among older and newer fans by the summer of 1987, the Betty Boards (qua "relics") reaffirmed the idea(l) of liveness as a foundational tenet of the mythology of the Grateful Dead.

A New Era for the Dead at the End of the Decade

In the Dark was the last album that the Grateful Dead owed to Arista Records. Fresh off the success of their first Top 10 album, their first Top 10 single, and their commercial successes in video, the Grateful Dead held all the cards when it came time to renegotiate their record deal. According to the terms of the new contract the Dead signed with Arista in 1988, the band would supply three albums over five years.[38] In exchange, the Dead received an advance of $3 million for the immediate follow-up to *In the Dark* and would receive another $1 million on delivery of the two remaining albums. Flexing their recently acquired bargaining power, the band secured extremely favorable royalty rates, receiving $2.60 for every cassette/LP that was sold and $3.35 for every compact disc. The Dead were also granted the right to release recordings of the band and Bob Dylan from the summer of 1987, recordings that had been produced by members of the Dead organization. *Dylan & the Dead* was released on Columbia Records (Dylan's label) in 1989.

Significantly, the new contract also stipulated that the Dead could produce and distribute live recordings from the vault. According to the new contract, the Dead organization was permitted to manufacture "direct live recordings from concerts which do not contain overdubs and for which no special sound trucks or multi-track recording equipment were used, provided such records may only be sold directly by your merchandising entity and not more than 25,000 copies . . . of any particular record may be manufactured." While various members of the Dead organization had been exploring the possibility of releasing their own recordings for over a decade (beginning with Steve Brown and plans for Ground Records in 1976 and again, in 1982, by Alan Trist), it took a near-death experience, a smash single, and a breakthrough video to make the long-developing business plan a reality.

By 1988, the Dead were poised to finally reap the benefits of a career that had been meticulously documented on thousands of hours of audio and video recordings. Moreover, the aura of nostalgia that had come to envelop the band strongly suggested that fans (both new and old) would continue to seek out and collect the many inspired concert performances that had been documented and were stored in the Dead's vault. At the same time, more and more recordings were being added to the vault as the Dead and their crew continued to record the band's live performances. Don Pearson, a longtime sound engineer with the Dead, recalls how, while on tour, tapes of the band's concerts were routinely shipped back to the vault in San Rafael, where they would be cataloged by archivists Willy Legate and Dick Latvala.[39] In 1987, director Len Dell'Amico and his film crew began to provide visual content for the Dead's concerts. As Dell'Amico's crew continued to film the band's concerts (especially the Dead's enormously popular summer tours), the resulting video footage was also stored in the band's vault.[40]

Even before the release of *In the Dark*, the Grateful Dead were one of the highest-grossing live acts in the nation. Following the massive success of their latest studio recording, the Dead got even bigger. In September 1988, shortly after re-signing with Arista, the band played nine sold-out concerts at Madison Square Garden in New York City, a run of concerts that grossed an estimated $3 million. While the Dead's recent good fortunes were due to the success and appeal of "Touch of Grey" and *In the Dark*, the financial windfall provided by playing live meant that the band was in no hurry to return to the recording studio.

The band released their next studio album, *Built to Last*, in October 1989, nearly two years after "Touch of Grey" and *In the Dark* had stormed the charts. Featuring a photograph by Alton Kelly, the famed "psychedelic" artist whose designs had graced hundreds of concert posters at the height of the San Francisco scene in the 1960s, the cover of *Built to Last* shows the members of the Dead gathered around a house of cards. Drawing on the record's visual imagery, Arista mounted an aggressive promotional campaign for the new album, including a limited number of "Deluxe" editions of *Built to Last* called "Dead in a Deck." Available on cassette and CD formats, the "Dead in a Deck" packages included a booklet of photographs and a specially designed deck of Grateful Dead–themed playing cards. According to Sean Cawley, Arista's vice president of promotion, the design for the packaging grew out of a "desire to create something special for the fans," and "part of what makes this all so special," he noted, "is the limited nature of the product."[41] Within a few weeks "all 50,000 copies of 'Dead in a Deck' [had] been snapped up, with pleas for a second pressing pouring in. None is planned."[42]

Built to Last was well-received among fans and critics and was certified Gold a few months after its release. Although the album features a number of exceptional musical performances, *Built to Last* did not come close to matching the success of *In the Dark*. While some of the songs on *Built to Last* made their way into the band's live repertoire (including "Victim or the Crime," "Picasso Moon," and "We Can Run"), the Dead seemed less concerned about promoting the new record and were focused instead on honing their skills and strengths as live performing musicians. Indeed, when *Built to Last* was released on Halloween in 1989, most fans were attending to the band's recent concerts. From October 1989 through much of 1990, the Dead played what many fans consider to be some of their finest performances since the group had returned to the road following Garcia's health scare. For many people who followed the Dead, it might have appeared that the band would continue to thrive into the 1990s.

A few days after the Grateful Dead played the final concert of their 1990 summer tour, keyboardist Brent Mydland died of a drug overdose. Even while the band and their fans mourned the loss of Mydland, the group could not afford to cancel or postpone too many upcoming concert obligations. Following auditions in August, Vince Welnick, formerly of the legendary San Francisco art-rock band The Tubes, became the Grateful Dead's new keyboard player. Welnick played his first concert with the band in early September, less than two months after Mydland's death.

That same month, the band released *Without a Net*, a double live record compiled from performances recorded between October 1989 and April 1990. Produced by Phil Lesh and John Cutler, *Without a Net* includes more than two hours of music and was, at that time, the band's longest-running commercial live album release. Many of the songs featured on *Without a Net* had already appeared (in different versions) on the band's earlier live records. Arranged and sequenced like a standard Dead concert, the fourteen songs are distributed evenly across two compact discs (or cassettes) and are identified as part of either the "First Set" or the "Second Set."

In many ways, *Without a Net* hearkens back to the sound of the Dead's earliest live albums. Whereas the sounds of the audience permeate the mixes of *Reckoning* and *Dead Set*, *Without a Net* more closely resembles the sound of *Live/Dead*, *Skull and Roses*, and *Europe '72*, records whose sense of liveness, as I argued in chapter 1, came at the expense of crowd noise. To be sure, there are instances on *Without a Net* where Lesh and Cutler "boost" the sound of the crowd in the mix (for example, the roar following the lyric "It's gonna be a long, long, crazy, crazy night!" sung by Mydland during "Feel Like a Stranger"). For the most part, however, Lesh and Cutler include crowd noise between songs to impart a sense of continuity and to remind listeners that *Without a Net* is a live record. In place of crowd noise, Lesh and Cutler applied a generous amount of reverb to the final mix, an effect that evokes the cavernous stadiums and massive arenas in which the recordings were produced.

Although nobody knew it at the time, *Without a Net* was the last album the Grateful Dead would release on Arista Records. Just a few months later, in April 1991, the band released *One from the Vault*, the Dead's first officially released live archival recording. Appearing on Grateful Dead Records (their recently resurrected record label), produced by Grateful Dead Productions, and distributed via Grateful Dead Merchandising, *One from the Vault* marks the moment when the Dead assumed control over how their distinctive brand of recorded liveness would be marketed and promoted to fans.

The Grateful Dead (1992) (*Left to right*: Phil Lesh, Bob Weir, Bill Kreutzmann, Mickey Hart (obstructed), Jerry Garcia, Vince Welnick)

"The Live Feel
of a Tape"

*FROM THE VAULT, DICK'S PICKS,
AND THE LANGUAGE(S) OF LIVENESS*

By the early 1990s, a number of musical artists and groups, many of whom were associated with the era of "classic rock," were starting to explore the commercial market for unreleased recordings. In March 1991, Columbia Records released *The Bootleg Series Volumes 1–3 (Rare & Unreleased) 1961– 1991*, a retrospective box set of musical performances by Bob Dylan. The three-disc set was compiled from a variety of sources, including Columbia's extensive vault of unreleased demos, studio outtakes, and live recordings. Released shortly after Dylan received a Lifetime Achievement Award at the annual Grammy Awards ceremony, the box set was designed to appeal to both newer audiences and longtime fans, many of whom had been collecting and trading Dylan bootlegs for years. Featuring digitally remastered recordings of almost sixty songs along with an attractively produced booklet of liner notes, *The Bootleg Series Volumes 1–3* bears little resemblance to the minimalist design and rawer sound quality of the performances on *Great White Wonder*, the original Dylan bootleg that briefly shook up the record industry in 1969.

FIGURE 5.1.
Advertisement for
One from the Vault
(1991)

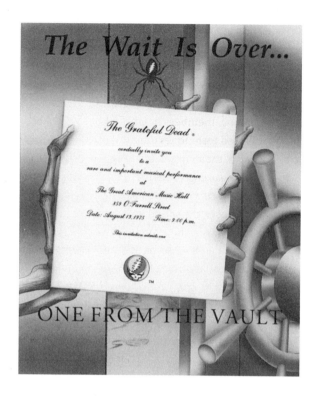

A few weeks after Columbia released the Dylan box set, Grateful Dead Productions (GDP) released *One from the Vault* (*OFTV*), the first officially released archival recording of the Grateful Dead (figure 5.1). Receiving significantly less media fanfare than Dylan's major-label release, *One from the Vault* sold well and rose as high as number 106 on the *Billboard* "Top Pop Albums" chart (where it was consistently misidentified as "One from the Vaults"). Whereas Columbia had mounted an aggressive media campaign and marketing strategy when promoting the new Dylan set, GDP adopted a more grassroots approach by promoting *OFTV* in independent record stores, direct to fans via the Dead Heads newsletter, and in print advertisements in the many Dead-related fanzines.[1] Of course, such an approach aligned with the band's long-standing "anticorporate" reputation. At the same time, the product that was being offered on *OFTV* was not intended for widespread commercial appeal but was produced and marketed, instead, to committed Deadheads. Indeed, for those fans who were just becoming familiar with the music and mythology of the Dead, *OFTV* might have aroused little attention. But for fans who were steeped in the legacy of liveness and the complex aesthetic ideologies that marked the band's live recordings, the release of *OFTV*

was a significant event. Featuring a complete performance of a concert from 1975, OFTV offered the first official glimpse inside the band's fabled vault.

As both the producers and distributors of their archival recordings, the Grateful Dead now had almost complete control over every aspect of their live recorded legacy. As they began to release recordings from the vault in the early 1990s, members of GDP employed many of the familiar strategies and established techniques they had used when producing, mixing, and mastering many of their commercial live records, including *Live/Dead*, *Skull and Roses*, and *Reckoning*. In many ways, the distinctive image of liveness that is presented on OFTV (as well as subsequent releases in the *From the Vault* series) reproduces the sound and aesthetic of the band's major-label live releases dating back to the late 1960s. Moreover, as I describe in what follows, the releases that appeared on the *From the Vault* series were aestheticized within a distinctive and highly rationalized "language of liveness" that emphasized the methods and tools used in the production of a recording and the technical expertise of the modern sound engineer.

"It's the Truth": Dan Healy, *From the Vault*, and a Rationalized Language of Liveness

One from the Vault features the complete performance of the Grateful Dead's concert at the Great American Music Hall in San Francisco on August 13, 1975. At the time, the band was in the midst of their touring hiatus, and the performance was one of only a few concerts the Dead staged that year. Attendance at the concert was by invitation, and the audience was composed primarily of music industry executives and radio programmers. For the few hundred people in attendance that evening, the Dead played some familiar tunes as well as all the songs from their forthcoming studio album, *Blues for Allah*. The concert was recorded on multitrack using a mobile studio owned and operated by Wally Heider Studios, a San Francisco–based company that was recognized as the industry leader in mobile recording.

In an effort to promote the Dead's latest studio album, portions of the concert were broadcast on select FM radio stations. Not surprisingly, FM-sourced recordings began to circulate among tape traders within weeks of the performance. At the same time, edited versions of the band's concert could be heard on the many bootleg LPs that appeared in record stores across the country.[2]

Given the recorded history of the original live performance, many committed Deadheads (and even casual collectors) already had high-quality

FIGURE 5.2. Dan Healy (ca. 1991)

recordings of the concert when OFTV was released in April 1991. In an interview broadcast on the *Grateful Dead Hour* radio show in February, Dan Healy, the Dead's longtime live sound mixer and the producer of OFTV, admitted that "it's probably one of the most collected of our tapes" (figure 5.2). Host David Gans likely spoke on behalf of many fans when he pointed out that the "tapers out there are going 'So why are you releasing this when we already have it, man?'" "Because," Healy replied, "it kicks butt."[3]

In an interview published a few months after OFTV was released, Healy offered a bit more insight concerning his criteria when selecting recordings. He explained to interviewer Toni A. Brown that OFTV was the first installment in what GDP imagined would be a regular series of compact disc releases. When selecting recordings for possible release in the series, Healy noted that performances were considered according to what he described as the "from-day-one concept" and the "most-noted-event concept."[4] Whereas Deadheads already had access to numerous recordings of concerts from the 1970s and later, live recordings from the 1960s (especially before 1969) were much rarer. By releasing the band's earliest recordings (the "from-day-one concept"), the *From the Vault* series could potentially introduce fans to a body of recordings and an entire era of the Dead that most contemporary audiences had never experienced.

Instead of selecting a recording that "had really poor audio quality from maybe an obscure earlier show," Healy chose to pursue the "most-noted-event" option for the debut release from the band's vault.[5] Healy understood that, among Deadheads, the concert—one of only a handful the Dead played in 1975—was already "cogent in event significance." He also knew that the original recordings of the concert were "cogent in quality." Healy recalled how "we had the presence of mind to bring a 16-track, which was the state-of-the-art technology in those days. So, we recorded the shows on 16-track. We also broadcast the show live over, I think, [San Francisco radio station] KSAN."[6]

While recordings of the complete concert did circulate within the taping community, many fans were familiar with performances that had originally appeared on bootleg records. Given the inherent time limitations of the con-temporary long-playing record, however, most bootleg albums omitted se-lect songs that were performed at the concert. Since many Deadheads only had access to tapes that had been sourced from the various bootleg albums of the concert (such as the well-known double record *Make Believe Ballroom*), Healy noted that many people "on the outside [never] got to really hear the whole thing."[7] For the band's first official vault release, Healy restored "U.S. Blues" and "Blues for Allah," two songs that were originally performed as encores but had been omitted from most bootleg albums.

In her interview with Healy, Brown acknowledges that the "availability of the Grateful Dead's live concert archives in soundboard quality" was a "dream come true" for many readers of *Relix*.[8] *Relix*, it will be recalled, was founded in 1974 by Les Kippel ("Mr. Tapes") as *Dead Relix*, one of the earliest fanzines devoted to the Dead and concert taping. For the audience of tapers, traders, and collectors who regularly read *Relix*, there was something bitter-sweet about the band releasing their own live recordings. "After two decades of sending out set lists and making taping contacts," Brown wrote, "tape col-lectors may soon have the material at their fingertips, and the entire taping scene as we know it may become obsolete."[9]

But even as Healy and GDP were beginning to unveil the contents of the Dead's live recorded legacy, Brown did not seem especially impressed by the sound quality of *OFTV*. In particular, she remarked that the "CD is very clean. It's almost crystalline, and that sort of takes away from the live feel of a tape."[10] Brown's remark appeared to strike a nerve with Healy. As someone who had spent years crafting the band's live sound and who was now producing the Dead's vault releases, Healy explained to Brown that the "Great American Music Hall is a very small place, so it doesn't give the impression of large audiences."[11] Healy also noted that, even though "two of the 16-tracks were [reserved for] microphones that were in the audience," the crowd that night "wasn't screaming and raving and flipping out like they typically [do] at a show." Instead, Healy explained that the original concert was "sort of a formal affair" and that the audience was composed primarily of "record company execs and the media." In Healy's opinion, these factors "are all things that contribute to the reality" of the recording. Despite Brown's misgivings, Healy considered OFTV an "honest" document of the concert.[12]

To be sure, Brown did not remark on the size of the venue or the makeup of the audience. Instead, her observation that OFTV sounded "very clean" ("almost crystalline") referred to a perceived lack of "liveness" on the compact disc release as compared with what she described as the "live feel of a tape." Despite the different formats, Healy explains to Brown that the recording "very much carries the characteristics of what it actually sounded like in that room. Again, it's a very small room, so I think if you're imagining that it should have a large, huge ambient sound, that is a misnomer because I would have had to synthetically create it to make it sound like that. It wasn't there."[13] Healy acknowledges that for "most bands, including ourselves, whenever they prepare live tapes for release, there's a lot of cosmetic stuff that goes on, [such as] replacing guitar parts and drum parts and vocal parts and so on and so forth." Regarding the production of OFTV, however, Healy asserts that he "didn't manipulate it" and "didn't doctor it." Healy assures Brown and the readers of *Relix* that OFTV utilizes "absolutely straight-on tour recording and tour mixing techniques." In Healy's estimation, the recordings that were produced at the Great American Music Hall embody the "essence of honesty."[14] "Whether it sounds big or not, like a large audience or not," he stresses, "it's the truth."[15]

For Healy, the qualities of "honesty" and "truth" that he ascribes to *One from The Vault* are embodied in the master multitrack recordings and, in his opinion, their ability to represent the distinctive sonic characteristics that made the original concert experience unique, including the musical performances, the features of the hall, the circumstances of the concert (including the restrained behavior of the audience), and the technical aspects of the recording process. Without a doubt, Brown and many other fans were excited to have access to a high-quality recording of a complete live performance from a notable moment in the history of the Dead. At the same time, however, Brown's remark that OFTV lacks the "live feel" of tapes and

Healy's vigorous defense of the "truth" and "honesty" of the multitrack recording reflect different (yet familiar) aesthetics of recorded liveness.

Although it may lack the "live feel" of the tapes, the distinctive sense of liveness that is imparted by *OFTV* was familiar to Brown and other fans. As a recorded document of liveness, *OFTV* reflects the general aesthetic and sound of most of the band's other official live releases. As a document of the events of August 13, 1975, *One from the Vault* is indelibly marked by the tools and practices of the modern recording studio. Indeed, much of the information included in the original CD liner notes draws attention not to the original performance but to the technical aspects of the recording itself.

In a lengthy passage devoted to "Technical Information" in the liner notes to *OFTV*, recording engineer Don Pearson describes in remarkable detail the processes by which the original tape recordings were digitally transferred and mastered for the compact disc release.[16] Pearson explains that the concert was originally "recorded on an Ampex MM-1100 sixteen track tape recorder" and that "there was no noise reduction or other signal processing used during this recording." He continues by describing how the original tapes were then "played on a Studer A820 tape reproducer and mixed on a Neve Series VR mixing console." (Pearson is also sure to note that the mix was monitored on a "pair of Meyer Sound HD-1 studio monitors.") "The stereo mix derived from these tapes," he continues, "was mastered onto a Sony PCM-1630 Digital Audio Processor. The PCM-1630 was fitted with an Apogee Filter Enhancement. The output from the PCM-1630 was recorded on a Sony DMR-4000 Digital Master Recorder using Ampex 467 Digital Audio Tape. A Sony DTA-2000 Digital Tape Analyzer was connected to monitor any errors created by the system." Finally (breathlessly), the "digital audio master tapes" were mastered using the "Sonic Solutions Digital Audio Editor."

Pearson's notes acknowledge that, strictly speaking, *One from the Vault* is not an entirely "true," or "honest," account of that evening. Instead, he describes how the Sonic Solutions editor was "used to assemble the songs into the final CD format, edit time between songs and to move the set break from between [the songs] 'Marbles' and 'Around and Around' to between 'Around and Around' and 'Sugaree.' These edits were necessary to achieve the proper time per CD as dictated by the CD format. . . . The final version was then transferred, digitally, back to the PCM-1630/DMR-4000 system to create the final tape from which this CD was mastered."

While the abundance of technical information included in his liner notes was probably comprehensible only to a handful of experienced producers, engineers, and sound technicians, Pearson assured everyone else—in much simpler terms—that "every effort has been taken to preserve the quality of the original recording and to provide superior sonic reproduction." Among those involved in the production of the *From the Vault* series, the quality of liveness was conceived in relation to a physical object, the "original recording," and not the live concert experience. The methodical manner by which Healy, Pearson, and others carefully transferred the master recordings served to preserve a sense of recorded liveness as it underwent "sonic reproduction."

A similar rationalized recording aesthetic also guided the next installment in the series. Released in 1992, *Two from the Vault* reflects the "from-day-one concept" and features performances that were recorded on 8-track at the Shrine Auditorium in Los Angeles in August 1968. As with OFTV, *Two from the Vault* features extensive liner notes concerning "Technical Information." In these notes, Healy and Pearson remark how, "when we first began making rough mixes of these tracks, we noticed the combined leakage of every instrument onto every track. This caused severe phase cancellation and time smear that reduced the time image to nothing."[17] As they note, "The challenge to bring back these tapes wasn't [in] reviving the sound of the instruments, but, rather correcting and restoring the immense time smear disparity."

Healy and Pearson recount a remarkable technological feat whereby they used Phil Lesh's "bass track for the time center, and compared this track to the others." "Thus," the notes continue, "we were able to measure the distance in time between the various microphones. Using this information, we then transferred the delay time measured by the analyzer, to TC1280 delay units. This along with careful mixing achieved a nearly perfect stereo image." While many readers were no doubt impressed by the knowledge, expertise, and commitment that Healy and Pearson brought to their work, the majority of fans just wanted to know one thing: What does it sound like? Healy and Pearson suggest that, when heard on the right equipment, the experience will be like "standing on the front center of the stage."

The excessively technical language of liveness employed by Healy and Pearson is representative of a discourse that accompanied what musicologist Paul Théberge has described as the "technological rationalization" of multitrack record production. Théberge notes how, beginning in the 1960s, the production of commercial popular music was "rationalized" vis-à-vis expanded capabilities of sound recording and audio technologies, an emerging aesthetic of recorded sound, and an established set of studio practices and modes of production. As detailed by Théberge, the rise of multitrack recording technology "helped to define rock aesthetics and has been instrumental in the reorganization of rock as a form of musical practice."[18] Ultimately, Théberge claims that "what becomes rationalized in multitrack studio production is music performance practice itself."[19]

The increasingly rationalized approach to recording as described by Théberge is reflected in the technical language and forms of speech that developed among performers, producers, and sound engineers. The language of liveness adopted by producer Dan Healy and engineer Don Pearson, for example, is thoroughly conditioned by the specialized discourse of the modern recording studio.[20] As is evident in the liner notes accompanying the earliest releases of the *From the Vault* series, the language and rhetoric employed by Healy and Pearson emphasize the forms of specialized labor and degrees of technological expertise required in preserving the unique characteristics of liveness associated with the original multitrack recordings. Of course, there is no question that a great deal of technical work and intellectual labor were involved in the production of the *From the Vault* releases. That being said, however, the exceedingly detailed liner notes dedicated to each recording's "Technical Information" underscore the fundamentally rational (not to mention thoroughly materialist) conception of liveness that guided the production of the releases in the *From the Vault* series.

Looking toward the future, Healy explained to Toni A. Brown that he was "hoping to do maybe four releases a year" or perhaps even "one release a month."[21] Healy admitted that he did not have "unlimited time to spend" on the series and that any work relating to the project "has to be done interspersed with my other Grateful Dead activities, namely live shows and stuff like that."[22] The fact that *Two from the Vault* would not be released for another year suggests that Healy was a bit overambitious when he spoke with Brown in 1991. Ultimately, Healy stressed that the "main goal [of the series] is to get the most significant shows out, to retain the honesty in audio quality and in performance, and to make it available packaged nicely, at a much lower price than the record industry would try to sell it at."[23]

For those people who assisted on the *From the Vault* series, the specialized production techniques, mixing skills, and editing tools associated with the modern recording studio were indispensable at being able to "retain the honesty in [the] audio quality" of the original multitrack recordings. While there was no doubt that Healy and Pearson were capable of producing recordings that satisfied their technical standards of liveness, their options were limited given how few multitrack recordings actually resided in the vault.

Figures 5.3 and 5.4 reproduce two sides of a document that Healy and Dick Latvala, the Dead's tape archivist, consulted as they prepared to release the

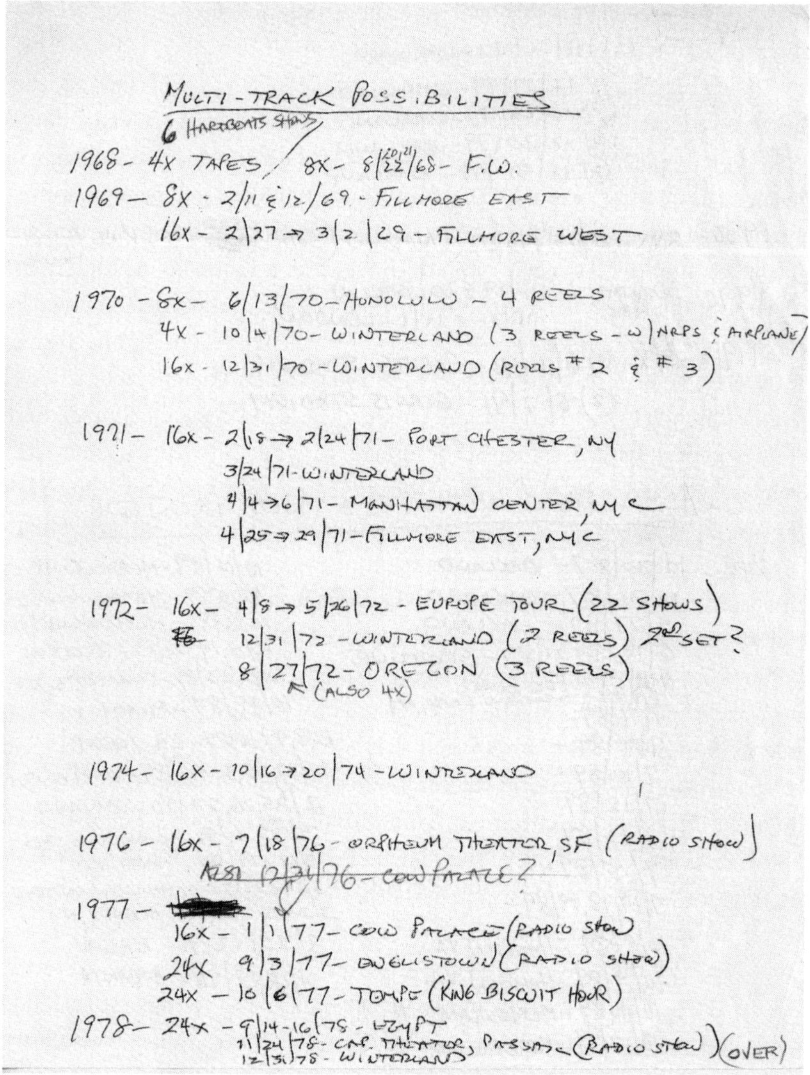

MULTI-TRACK POSSIBILITIES
6 HARTBEATS SHOWS
1968 - 4X TAPES / 8X - 8/20,21,22/68 - F.W.
1969 - 8X - 2/11 & 12/69 - FILLMORE EAST
16X - 2/27 → 3/2 - FILLMORE WEST
1970 - 8X - 6/13/70 - HONOLULU - 4 REELS
4X - 10/4/70 - WINTERLAND (3 REELS - w/NRPS & AIRPLANE)
16X - 12/31/70 - WINTERLAND (REELS #2 & #3)
1971 - 16X - 2/18 → 2/24/71 - PORT CHESTER, NY
3/24/71 - WINTERLAND
4/4 → 6/71 - MANHATTAN CENTER, NYC
4/25 → 29/71 - FILLMORE EAST, NYC
1972 - 16X - 4/8 → 5/26/72 - EUROPE TOUR (22 SHOWS)
12/31/72 - WINTERLAND (2 REELS) 2nd SET?
8/27/72 - OREGON (3 REELS) ← (ALSO 4X)
1974 - 16X - 10/16 → 20/74 - WINTERLAND
1976 - 16X - 7/18/76 - ORPHEUM THEATER, SF (RADIO SHOW)
~~ALSO 12/31/76 - COW PALACE?~~
1977 - 16X - 1/1/77 - COW PALACE (RADIO SHOW)
24X 9/3/77 - ENGLISHTOWN (RADIO SHOW)
24X - 10/6/77 - TEMPE (KING BISCUIT HOUR)
1978 - 24X - 9/14-16/78 - EGYPT
11/24/78 - CAP. THEATER, PASSAIC (RADIO SHOW)
12/31/78 - WINTERLAND (OVER)

FIGURE 5.3. List of available multitrack recordings in the vault (compiled by Dan Healy and Dick Latvala, ca. 1992)

third installment in the vault series.[24] Compiled sometime during the late summer or early fall of 1992, the list of "Multi-Track Possibilities" identifies most of the available 4-track ("4x"), 8-track ("8x"), and 16-track ("16x") recordings that were stored in the Dead's vault. As seen in figure 5.4, multitrack recordings from the late 1980s and early 1990s were fairly well-represented. In addition to the many 24-track ("24x") recordings made between 1987 and

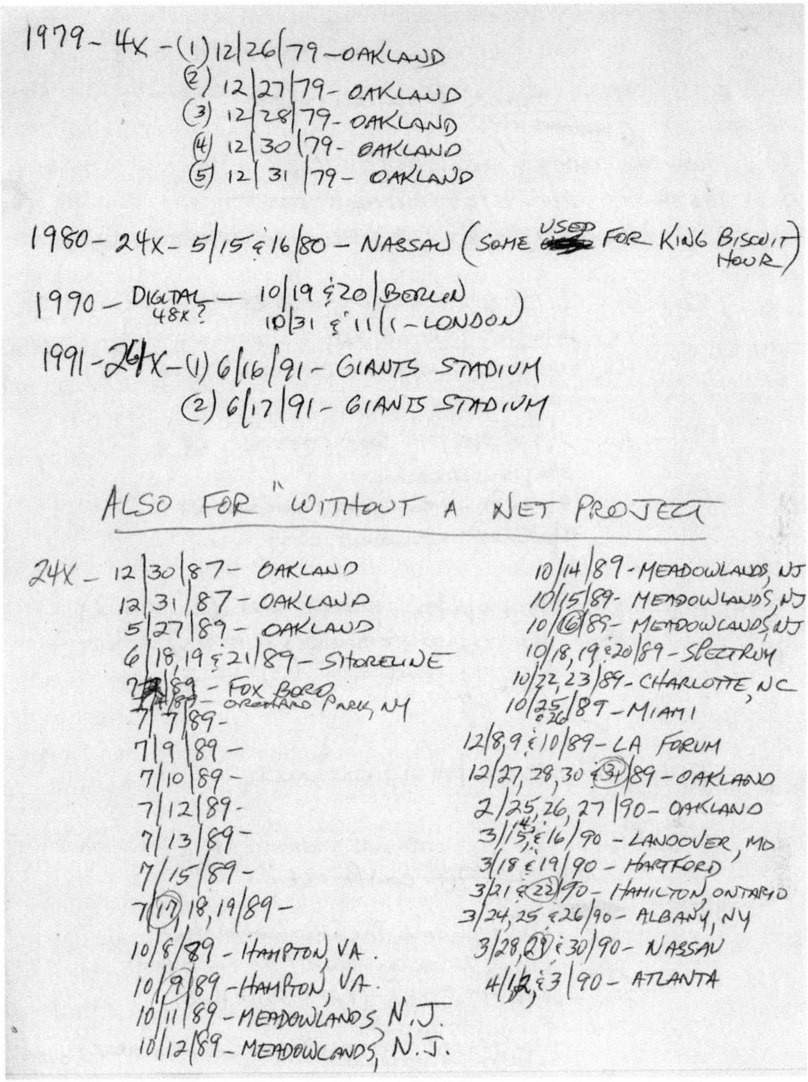

1979 – 4x – (1) 12/26/79 – OAKLAND
(2) 12/27/79 – OAKLAND
(3) 12/28/79 – OAKLAND
(4) 12/30/79 – OAKLAND
(5) 12/31/79 – OAKLAND

1980 – 24x – 5/15 & 16/80 – NASSAU (SOME USED FOR KING BISCUIT HOUR)

1990 – DIGITAL 48x? – 10/19 & 20/BERLIN
10/31 & 11/1 – LONDON

1991 – 24x – (1) 6/16/91 – GIANTS STADIUM
(2) 6/17/91 – GIANTS STADIUM

ALSO FOR "WITHOUT A NET" PROJECT

24x – 12/30/87 – OAKLAND
12/31/87 – OAKLAND
5/27/89 – OAKLAND
6/18, 19 & 21/89 – SHORELINE
7/2/89 – FOX BORO
7/4/89 – ORCHARD PARK, NY
7/7/89 –
7/9/89 –
7/10/89 –
7/12/89 –
7/13/89 –
7/15/89 –
7/17, 18, 19/89 –
10/8/89 – HAMPTON, VA.
10/9/89 – HAMPTON, VA.
10/11/89 – MEADOWLANDS, N.J.
10/12/89 – MEADOWLANDS, N.J.

10/14/89 – MEADOWLANDS, NJ
10/15/89 – MEADOWLANDS, NJ
10/16/89 – MEADOWLANDS, NJ
10/18, 19 & 20/89 – SPECTRUM
10/22, 23/89 – CHARLOTTE, NC
10/25 & 26/89 – MIAMI
12/8, 9 & 10/89 – LA FORUM
12/27, 28, 30 & 31/89 – OAKLAND
2/25, 26, 27/90 – OAKLAND
3/14, 15 & 16/90 – LANDOVER, MD
3/18 & 19/90 – HARTFORD
3/21 & 22/90 – HAMILTON, ONTARIO
3/24, 25 & 26/90 – ALBANY, NY
3/28, 29 & 30/90 – NASSAU
4/1, 2 & 3/90 – ATLANTA

FIGURE 5.4. List of available multitrack recordings in the vault (compiled by Dan Healy and Dick Latvala, ca. 1992)

1990 (some of which were used as part of the "Without a Net" project), the vault also contained 24-track recordings produced in June 1991 at Giants Stadium in East Rutherford, New Jersey, as well as 48-track ("48x") digital recordings made in Europe in the fall of 1990.

Although the band put on many excellent concert performances in the late 1980s and early 1990s, Healy and Latvala understood that most fans were more interested in recordings that documented earlier eras of the Dead. However, compared with the modest number of recordings from the band's more recent concerts, there were even fewer multitrack recordings from the 1960s and 1970s (see figure 5.3). Of the few early multitrack recordings that were housed in the vault, most were originally produced as the Dead prepared to release live albums. Select performances captured on 16-track from late February and early March 1969 were included on *Live/Dead*, while performances recorded in March and April 1971 appear on *Skull and Roses*. The vault also included multitrack recordings of all the concerts from the Dead's tour of Europe in 1972, the "farewell" shows at the Winterland in San Francisco from October 1974 (including recordings featured in the *Grateful Dead Movie* and *Steal Your Face*), and the three concerts the band played in Egypt in 1978.

While all the recorded performances identified on the list qualify as "Multi-Track Possibilities" for use in the *From the Vault* series, many of the recordings did not measure up to the technical requirements and performance standards that Healy and others required of an official release. Various technical imperfections, lackluster performances, or any number of other perceived deficiencies meant that there were fewer options available to Healy, especially if he was committed to releasing complete concert performances. It was during the production of the third installment in the *From the Vault* series that, in the opinion of archivist Dick Latvala, "it got a little difficult finding a good show." Latvala recalls how, by the end of 1992, "things stagnated" with Healy and the multitrack series.[25]

In addition to the multitrack recordings, the vault also contained numerous two-track stereo recordings (preserved in various formats) that documented performances spanning much of the band's career. Produced by members of the Dead's road crew, the earliest two-track recordings were ostensibly made for purposes of review. As examined in the previous chapter, even as the Dead spent less time reviewing their past concert performances, the practice of taping continued over the years as part of the band's ongoing archival project. While everyone agreed that numerous outstanding musical performances had been preserved on the band's massive trove of recordings, the two-track tapes could not be remixed or subjected to the same degree of technical control and sonic manipulation that was possible with the multitrack recordings. Given his commitment to multitrack recordings for the *From the Vault* series, therefore, the two-track recordings were of no use to Healy.

Although Healy expressed no interest in them, other people within the Dead organization knew that the two-track recordings in the band's vault were highly coveted among Deadheads. Throughout the history of Dead taping, tapes of the band's two-track soundboard recordings had occasionally "leaked" into the trading community; at other times, various members of the Dead's live sound crew would allow select tapers to patch into the mixing board. Indeed, the appeal of the band's two-track stereo soundboard recordings contributed to the excitement that rippled throughout the taping community when the first batch of Betty Boards surfaced in 1987. Among Deadheads, these soundboard recordings offered a sonic image of the Dead's live musical performances that existed somewhere between the band's meticulously mixed, professionally produced multitrack recordings and the "less-produced" (but often stellar) audio quality of many audience tapes. Copies of the band's soundboard recordings not only offered a unique image of recorded liveness but also represented a tangible link in a lineage of recordings that could ultimately be traced back to the original concert and to the Dead themselves (or, at the very least, members of their road crew).

As fans eagerly awaited the next installment in Healy's *From the Vault* series, tape archivist Dick Latvala and others began to work on a separate collection of vault releases. In 1993, GDP introduced a new series called, appropriately enough, *Dick's Picks*. Sourced from the band's two-track recordings, *Dick's Picks* functioned as the band's officially authorized version of the "tapes." Whereas releases featured in the *From the Vault* series were promoted according to a technical language of liveness that emphasized the "rationality" of the recording studio, the recorded performances released as part of the *Dick's Picks* series were shaped by a language of liveness that was spoken among the community of fans who collected and traded the Dead's unofficial live recordings.

"Occasional Weirdness Remains": Dick Latvala, *Dick's Picks*, and the Language of the Tapes

The story of how Dick Latvala became the tape archivist for the Grateful Dead could serve as a parable on the power of live recordings.[26] As a college student in the mid-1960s, Latvala attended many of the band's earliest shows in California. His interest in live recordings of the Dead developed in the early 1970s, shortly after he and his family moved to Hawaii. With limited opportunities to see the band perform while living in Hilo, Latvala was introduced to the nascent tape trading scene through an early fanzine called *Dead in Words*. Based in Chapel Hill, North Carolina, *Dead in Words* was one of the earliest zines devoted to the underground market for tapes and bootleg recordings of the Grateful Dead.

Latvala was subsequently introduced to the rapidly expanding taping community through *Dead Relix*. Eager at the prospect of acquiring even more live recordings, Latvala sent reels of blank tapes (and some of his finest marijuana) to the many exchanges that advertised in the pages of Les Kippel's fanzine. Not surprisingly, Latvala amassed many new friends as well as a substantial collection of tapes of the Grateful Dead. In a letter published in *Dead Relix* in 1975, Latvala explained that, as someone who was "deeply involved in obtaining and sending 'Underground' tapes of the Grateful Dead," he has "come to discover . . . how incredibly powerful these recordings actually are. I must assume that all of 'us' people [i.e., tape traders and collectors], who are involved in such an adventure, have had the same kinds of incredibly joyous and 'cleansing' experiences that I have been having with my family over here in paradise. We have, what one could call 'Dead-Ins' often, and these intense experiences of togetherness are the exact same as we have all repeatedly had seeing the Dead 'Live,' when we used to live in the Bay Area."[27]

Shortly after returning to California in 1979, Latvala struck up a friendship with Bill "Kidd" Candelario, a longtime member of the Dead's road crew. Introduced to the scene by Candelario, Latvala soon became a familiar figure around the band's offices on Front Street in San Rafael. Given his obsessive interest in tapes, Latvala gravitated toward the contents of the Dead's vault, and in 1985 he was hired to assist Willy Legate in archiving the band's library of live recordings. By 1991, Latvala was officially acknowledged as the Grateful Dead's "Tape Archivist" in the liner notes to *OFTV* (figure 5.5).

According to Latvala, it was Candelario who suggested the possibility of releasing recordings from the band's collection of two-track tapes. As Latvala explained to John Dwork, Candelario's "idea was to let me pick the three best two-track tapes, and we'd call it *Dick's Picks*."[28] One of the performances Latvala selected (and that would become the first release in the new series) was of a concert from December 19, 1973, at the Curtis Hixon Convention Hall in Tampa, Florida. Latvala maintained meticulous notes detailing the content, format, and condition of the many recordings that resided in the vault. Figure 5.6 reproduces a page from one of Latvala's notebooks that includes his notes on the tapes and the band's performance from Tampa in 1973.[29] The earliest layer of information (written in blue ink) identifies the date and location of the performance, the format of the original master recording ("2x"[2-track]-7½ ips [inches per second]"), and the number of tape reels. (Latvala also notes that the concert was originally recorded using a Nagra 2791 machine.)

Latvala also identifies the song lists for each reel. In many respects, the band's setlist is a fair representation of what concert audiences would have

FIGURE 5.5. Dick Latvala (ca. 1994)

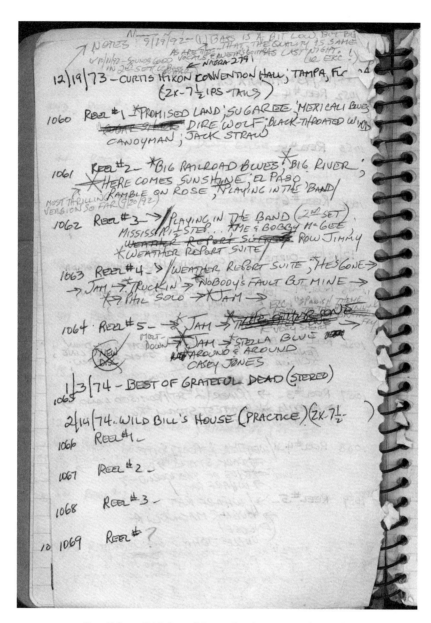

FIGURE 5.6. Detail from Dick Latvala's notebook entry on the vault recordings of the concert at Curtis Hixon Convention Hall, December 19, 1973

been hearing from the Dead at that time. From the perspective of Latvala and others working on the new series, the song lists on the reels reveal that there are incomplete performances. Note, for example, that the performance of the song "Playing in the Band" is spread across reels 2 and 3, "Weather Report Suite" extends across reels 3 and 4, and an instrumental "Jam" spans reels 4 and 5. As the tape ran out during the original performance, the band would have kept playing while a member of the road crew changed the reels. When preparing the recordings for commercial release, Latvala would need to decide what to do about the missing portions of music in these selections.

Another layer of notes (written in green ink) documents Latvala's opinions and impressions concerning the musical performances and the quality of the recordings. The earliest notes (dated 9/19/1992) were probably written shortly after the idea of the *Dick's Picks* series was first suggested by Candelario.[30] At the top of the page, Latvala notes that, although the "bass is a bit low" in the mix, the sound quality is excellent ("i.e. EXC!"). Another layer of notes (written in red ink) was probably written as Latvala and others were beginning to prepare the recordings for release. Appearing directly below the earliest notes, Latvala observes that, like the bass guitar, the "vocals & Weir's guitar" are low in the mix. The asterisks denote songs that Latvala and others had determined were worthy of being included on the planned double compact disc release. While some of these performances did not end up on *Volume One* of *Dick's Picks* (including "Promised Land" and Phil Lesh's bass solo), most of them did, including "Here Comes Sunshine" (the "most thrilling version so far (9/20/92)") and a massive jam that, in addition to an "EXC. 'Spanish Theme,'" also features a spacey, psychedelic "melt-down."

Echoing the effusive and evocative language that appears in Latvala's notes, Dennis McNally's promotional materials also employ a distinctive rhetoric that would have been familiar to most fans. Like Latvala, McNally, the Grateful Dead's publicist, was a tape connoisseur and was intimately familiar with the mythology of the vault and the "power of the tapes" among Deadheads.[31] McNally writes how "famous in song and story are the world's greatest repositories of hidden riches: There's Fort Knox, King Tut's Tomb, the Wreck of the Titanic . . . and, of course, the Grateful Dead Tape Vault." Referring to the *From the Vault* series, McNally notes how the "first two releases were the answers to a Deadhead's prayers: a pair of the very best shows from the band's stash of multitrack masters, impeccably mixed and mastered for optimum sound quality."

In contrast to the rationalized discourse that had been cultivated around the *From the Vault* series, McNally adopts a looser, more descriptive language that emphasizes the "roughness," as well as the "realness," of the recordings featured on *Dick's Picks*. The recordings on *Dick's Picks*, he stresses, are "not the relatively hi-tech multi-track items you've heard on the first two *Vault* releases." "No," he continues, "these come from somewhere deeper, darker—down in the cobwebbed catacombs, across the alligator-infested moat—that's where you'll find *Dick's Picks*." For those willing to brave the foreboding and treacherous recesses of the Dead's vault, the reward was authenticity. "This is the real, raw stuff," McNally explains. "Recorded direct to two-track, with no chance to 'fix it in the mix.' You hear it just like they played it—to borrow Phil Lesh's pet phrase, this is the Grateful Dead 'warts and all.'"

Indeed, McNally explicitly connects the "warts and all" quality of the two-track stereo recordings featured on *Dick's Picks* to the aesthetic that had developed around fan-produced tapes. McNally notes that Latvala has a "keen ear for a hot tape," a skill that he acquired after having "spent an alarming portion of his life wired to a tape deck, compulsively sifting through countless hours of Grateful Dead music, searching for those golden moments when the band unties the Gordian Knot, finds the Holy Grail, strums the Lost Chord." By highlighting Latvala's credentials as a tape aficionado, McNally invites Deadheads to listen to the *Dick's Picks* release in the same manner that they might listen to their favorite tapes.

Furthermore, the distinctive packaging of the earliest *Dick's Picks* releases reimagines the compact discs *as* tapes. The first six volumes in the series feature the same cover art: a reproduction of the iconic geometric figures and bold color scheme of the storage boxes associated with the Ampex brand of reel-to-reel tape (figure 5.7). At the same time, the individual compact discs were screen-printed to resemble the instantly recognizable design of a take-up reel (figure 5.8). Lacking an official title, each release is identified by the location and the date of the original concert. Figure 5.7 reproduces the cover to *Dick's Picks, Volume One: Tampa Florida 12/19/73*. The naming convention ("mm/dd/yy") reflects the established manner by which fans often cataloged their tapes and communicated with one another about specific live performances (i.e., "Twelve-Nineteen-Seventy-Three").

Another typographical convention that was common among tape collectors and traders involved the use of a rightward-pointing arrow to indicate a segue between songs. Of course, this convention was familiar to Latvala (refer to the suite of songs on reel 4 in figure 5.6) and was adopted in the printed tracklists that accompany each *Dick's Picks* release. As seen on the back cover of *Volume One*, for instance, almost all of "CD TWO" (the "second set") unfolds as a single, continuous musical performance (figure 5.9). Following

FIGURE 5.7. Front cover of *Dick's Picks, Volume One* (modeled on packaging of Ampex brand of tape)

FIGURE 5.8. CD artwork designed to resemble tape reel (*Dick's Picks, Volume One*)

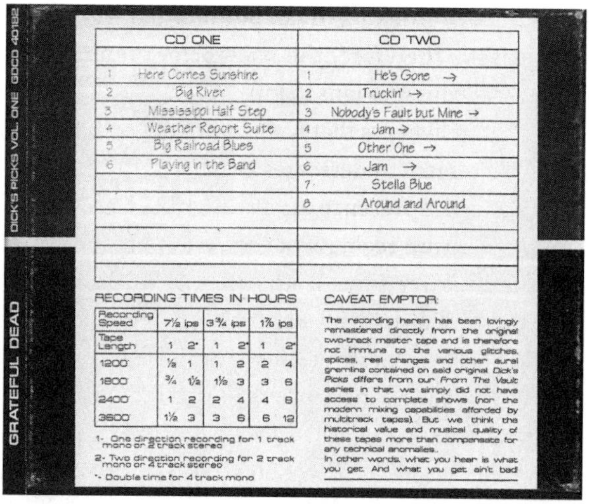

FIGURE 5.9. Back cover of *Dick's Picks, Volume One* (note naming/labeling conventions on "CD TWO")

"He's Gone," the band segues into "Truckin'" and then continues to explore a diverse terrain of songs and "jams" until, over fifty minutes later, they finally wrap up the extended improvisation with "Stella Blue." "Around and Around" serves as a fitting encore for the first volume of *Dick's Picks* (despite the fact that Garcia starts the song a half step low).

All the volumes in the *Dick's Picks* series include a unique "Caveat Emptor" statement that acknowledges the less-than-professional sound quality and (at times) uneven performances featured on each release. But even as the "buyer beware" statements inform and educate listeners as to the quality of each recording, they also assist in conditioning the consumer on *how* to listen to the band's two-track recordings. As seen in the lower right-hand corner of figure 5.9, the statement on the back cover of *Volume One* explains, "The recording herein has been lovingly remastered directly from the original two-track master tape and is therefore not immune to the various glitches, splices, reel changes, and other aural gremlins contained on said original." While the sound quality may be a bit "rougher" than what some listeners were accustomed to hearing on commercial recordings, the statement stresses, "We think the historical value and musical quality of these tapes more than compensate for any technical anomalies."

To be sure, any lingering "technical anomalies" also perform an important function within the familiar aesthetic of liveness that was being developed around the *Dick's Picks* series. Most Deadheads were very familiar with the various technical issues and imperfections that were described in the statement; indeed, such "aural gremlins" were often as much a part of the experience of listening to fan produced tapes as the recorded performances themselves. Therefore, the statement—along with the CD packaging and design—encourages fans to imagine the releases in the series according to an aesthetics of liveness that had come to be associated with "tapes." In particular, the statement underscores a sense of authenticity to the *Dick's Picks* series where even the presence of any number of "technical anomalies" contributes to the perceived realness of the recordings. The "Caveat Emptor" featured on *Volume Three* sums it up nicely, alerting listeners that, despite the best efforts of all those involved in restoring the band's tapes from May 22, 1977, "occasional weirdness remains." For those fans who crave the "real, raw stuff" and who want to experience the Grateful Dead "warts and all," you can't get much more authentic than *Dick's Picks*. As the "Caveat Emptor" statement on *Volume One* succinctly notes: "What you hear is what you get. And what you get ain't bad!"

By continuing to draw attention to the sound quality and production standards of the recordings, the *Dick's Picks* series communicates within its own rationalized discourse, albeit one that is peculiar to the aesthetic of liveness that had developed around tapes. Katie A. Harvey has described aspects of the unique language and cataloging methods employed by many tape collectors and traders, noting how, as "tapes surfaced and circulated, traders and collectors positioned them along the spectrum of quality and value":

> They organized them first according to date, venue, and city, using this standard information to associate the recording with the original live event. When the information was available, traders also identified the taper, the recording equipment, the distance from the master [recording], referred to as the "tape generation," and the lineage of the recording as it was transferred from one recorded medium to another, such as reel-to-reel to cassette. They also distinguished the nature of the recording by labeling tapes according to their source. Sources included vinyl bootlegs, radio broadcasts (labeled as FM), audience recordings (labeled as AUD), and the band's soundboard (labeled as SBD).[32]

As the namesake of the series, Dick Latvala certainly understood the archival mindset and curatorial tendencies of the modern tape collector. Even before he became the vault archivist for the Grateful Dead, Latvala (like many collectors) kept detailed notes documenting the sound quality and musical performances of the tapes in his own collection. Figure 5.10 reproduces Latvala's notes for a tape of a concert at the Boston Music Hall on December 2, 1973.[33] Recalling Harvey's description of the cataloging tendencies of tapers,

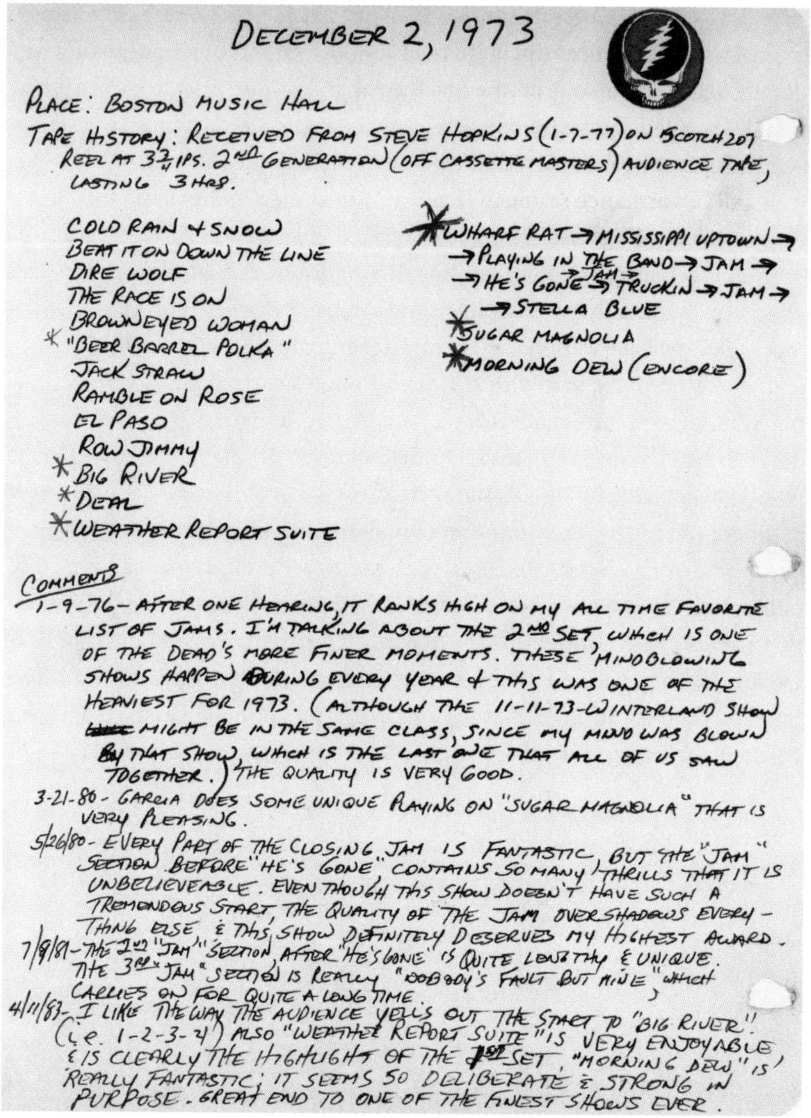

DECEMBER 2, 1973

PLACE: BOSTON MUSIC HALL

TAPE HISTORY: RECEIVED FROM STEVE HOPKINS (1-7-77) ON SCOTCH 207
REEL AT 3¾ IPS. 2ND GENERATION (OFF CASSETTE MASTERS) AUDIENCE TAPE,
LASTING 3 HRS.

COLD RAIN + SNOW
BEAT IT ON DOWN THE LINE
DIRE WOLF
THE RACE IS ON
BROWN EYED WOMAN
* "BEER BARREL POLKA"
JACK STRAW
RAMBLE ON ROSE
EL PASO
ROW JIMMY
* BIG RIVER
* DEAL
* WEATHER REPORT SUITE

* WHARF RAT → MISSISSIPPI UPTOWN →
→ PLAYING IN THE BAND → JAM →
→ HE'S GONE →JAM→ TRUCKIN → JAM →
→ STELLA BLUE
* SUGAR MAGNOLIA
* MORNING DEW (ENCORE)

COMMENTS

1-9-76 — AFTER ONE HEARING, IT RANKS HIGH ON MY ALL TIME FAVORITE
LIST OF JAMS. I'M TALKING ABOUT THE 2ND SET, WHICH IS ONE
OF THE DEAD'S MORE FINER MOMENTS. THESE MIND BLOWING
SHOWS HAPPEN DURING EVERY YEAR & THIS WAS ONE OF THE
HEAVIEST FOR 1973. (ALTHOUGH THE 11-11-73-WINTERLAND SHOW
MIGHT BE IN THE SAME CLASS, SINCE MY MIND WAS BLOWN
BY THAT SHOW, WHICH IS THE LAST ONE THAT ALL OF US SAW
TOGETHER.) THE QUALITY IS VERY GOOD.

3-21-80 - GARCIA DOES SOME UNIQUE PLAYING ON "SUGAR MAGNOLIA" THAT IS
VERY PLEASING.

5/26/80 - EVERY PART OF THE CLOSING JAM IS FANTASTIC, BUT THE "JAM"
SECTION BEFORE "HE'S GONE" CONTAINS SO MANY THRILLS THAT IT IS
UNBELIEVEABLE. EVEN THOUGH THIS SHOW DOESN'T HAVE SUCH A
TREMENDOUS START, THE QUALITY OF THE JAM OVERSHADOWS EVERY-
THING ELSE & THIS SHOW DEFINITELY DESERVES MY HIGHEST AWARD.

7/8/81 - THE 2ND "JAM" SECTION AFTER "HE'S GONE" IS QUITE LENGTHY & UNIQUE.
THE 3RD "JAM" SECTION IS REALLY "BOB BOY'S FAULT BUT MINE" WHICH
CARRIES ON FOR QUITE A LONG TIME.

4/11/83 - I LIKE THE WAY THE AUDIENCE YELLS OUT THE START TO "BIG RIVER"
(i.e. 1-2-3-4) ALSO "WEATHER REPORT SUITE" IS VERY ENJOYABLE
& IS CLEARLY THE HIGHLIGHT OF THE 1ST SET. "MORNING DEW" IS
REALLY FANTASTIC; IT SEEMS SO DELIBERATE & STRONG IN
PURPOSE. GREAT END TO ONE OF THE FINEST SHOWS EVER.

FIGURE 5.10. Dick Latvala's notes on concert at Boston Music Hall,
December 2, 1973

Latvala's entry includes detailed information regarding the "Tape History," including the source of the recording (he received the tape from a trader named
Steve Hopkins in January 1977), the brand of tape ("Scotch 207"), recording
speed ("3¾ ips [inches per second]"), lineage ("2nd generation"), the format of
the master recording ("cassette masters"), type of recording ("Audience Tape"),

and length ("3 hrs."). Latvala routinely used asterisks to identify exceptionally good song performances (including the band's impromptu rendition of "Beer Barrel Polka"). He also used the instantly recognizable image of a skull and thirteen-pointed lightning bolt (the "Steal Your Face" symbol) to indicate recordings that he considered to be especially noteworthy. Latvala liked this recorded performance so much that it was later remastered from the band's two-track recordings and released as *Dick's Picks, Volume Fourteen*.

Similar details relating to the "Tape History" appear in the liner notes and production credits that accompany every release in the *Dick's Picks* series. Of course, each release was digitally transferred from the two-track soundboard recordings that were stored in the band's vault. Following the general cataloging practices of tape collectors, many of the "Caveat Emptor" statements indicate the format of the master recording that was used in the production of the compact discs. Many of the earliest releases in the series were devoted to concerts from the 1970s that were originally recorded on reel-to-reel tape; *Volume Six* and *Volume Thirteen* document concerts from the 1980s that had been recorded on cassette tape. Each release also identifies the person within the Dead organization who produced the original recordings, including "Kidd" Candelario (volumes 1, 7, 12, and 14), Betty Cantor-Jackson (volumes 3, 5, 10, and 15), Dan Healy (volumes 6, 9, and 13), and Owsley "Bear" Stanley (volumes 4 and 11).

Although *Dick's Picks* was marketed and promoted to fans who were already "hip" to the rhetoric and the ideologized discourse of the tapes, the releases were still subject to the Dead's rigorous standards of musical performance, recording quality, and production. Even as Latvala diligently scoured the vault for possible releases, his picks were carefully scrutinized by, among others, sound engineer Jeffrey Norman and producer John Cutler, both of whom were longtime, trusted members of the Dead organization. Regarding the production process, Norman noted, "It's truly *Dick's Picks*, but it [involves] many people sort of narrowing this down. I approach it more on a technical side: 'Is the mix good enough? Is it sonically good enough?' John [Cutler] tries to cover all the creative bases, both performance and technical issues."[34] Ultimately, Norman notes, "We don't want to put anything out that's going to embarrass [the band] musically."[35] Norman also explains that there are certain "quality requirements on what can be sold as a commercial product." In the opinion of the Dead organization, it "has to be of a quality that really stands on its own. And I'm not even addressing performance issues here; I just mean the question of whether the tape sounds horrible and out of tune, or if the mix is so bad as to totally misrepresent the performance."[36]

Given the organization's high standards, the recordings featured as part of the *Dick's Picks* series were often subjected to extensive edits before being released to fans. As anyone with access to *Deadbase* (the published almanac of Grateful Dead concert setlists) could easily confirm, most of the early releases in the series did not chronicle complete concert performances. Instead, many songs and other improvised musical performances were edited from the recordings featured in *Volume One* and *Volume Three*, for example, while *Volume Two (Columbus, Ohio 10/31/71)* includes only material from the band's second set. Not unlike the Dead's earliest official live releases, *Volume Four* (released in 1996) is a compilation of performances recorded at two concerts at the Fillmore East in New York City in February 1970.

Despite the vast archive of two-track recordings in the vault, many of the tapes were deemed unusable because of unsatisfactory performances, missing and/or incomplete songs, problems with the mix, and a host of other "technical anomalies" and "aural gremlins." Although Latvala understood the desire among some fans for complete concert performances, he expressed his belief that, for "those who demand the whole show, I think that idea is what tape trading is all about. It's not the Dead's responsibility to adhere to those needs."[37] In fact, as he was sure to emphasize, "From [the band's] point of view they're taking a big chance [on the series], because they don't want to put out anything that's not just exactly right."[38] Regarding the edited early releases, Latvala explained, "This is the best that can be done as far as getting [the band] . . . to release this stuff. Listen, if this doesn't work, I seriously wonder if anything will ever come out of their vaults."[39]

While many hard-core tapers still hoped for complete concerts from the band's vault, the earliest edited performances and live compilations released as part of the *Dick's Picks* series sold very well and were extremely popular among Deadheads. As they looked ahead to future releases, therefore, Latvala and other members of the Dead organization began to seriously consider the opinions of fans. *Volume Three* (released in 1995) included a postcard that asked fans to identify concerts they would like to see released as part of the series; Latvala also conducted polls among fans on the WELL, an early online discussion forum that had become a virtual hub for serious tape collectors and tape traders.[40]

With the release of *Dick's Picks, Volume Five (Oakland Auditorium Arena 12/26/79)* in 1996, Latvala and company finally issued a complete live concert performance. In his accompanying press release, publicist Dennis McNally was sure to point out that *Volume Five* was the "first release in the series that presents a complete show from start to finish, and so the first to show how a

Dead show told the whole story—the nice gradual exposition, the plot getting more complex, the suspense building to a fever pitch, and the big, happy ending."[41] Despite the show's classical narrative design, however, McNally could not help but draw attention to various deficiencies in the execution of the musical story. "As on all the *Dick's Picks* releases," he explained, "you're hearing this stuff just as they played it, no overdubs, no cosmetic repairs, no studio trickery. There are, in other words, *mistakes*! But the Grateful Dead, on a good night, had a way of turning straw into gold, and what mistakes are here are indicative of the bracing recklessness that characterized the Dead at their best."

In just a few phrases, McNally summarizes the aesthetic of liveness that had motivated tapers and tape collectors since the early 1970s. He draws on the rhetoric of the tapes to underscore the authenticity and the "bracing recklessness" of the complete live concert documented on the compact discs of *Volume Five*. By the mid-1990s, it would seem that the Dead had successfully learned how the language of the tape(r)s could be used to promote their two-track recordings.

"Emotional Content versus Objective Reality": Latvala, Liveness, and the Limits of Language

At the same time that members of the Dead organization were becoming fluent in the ideological discourse of the tapes, Dick Latvala was also learning to speak an unfamiliar, more "technical," language of liveness. Speaking with John Dwork in 1994, Latvala described how, given his extensive knowledge and familiarity with the band's live recordings, he "felt that [he] had a lot of ideas of what was a good show and what wasn't before [he] got hired by the Grateful Dead."[42]

However, as Latvala began to work on the *Dick's Picks* series, he came to believe that the ideas and opinions he originally developed as a tape trader were not "very objective." "When I started," he explained, "I was so naïvely enthusiastic. Then I started getting a little more discriminating. But I still wasn't really noticing whether someone was low in the mix, or whether the drums were present enough. I'd never had to pick out stuff like that. I would just hear the emotional content of what was on the tape."[43] After having assisted on *Volume One* with engineer Jeffrey Norman, producer John Cutler, and bassist Phil Lesh, Latvala acknowledged that he was still learning how to distinguish "emotional content versus objective reality" when considering performances for release. But even as Latvala was "learning to be more objective" in his listening habits, he admitted that the technical insights and expertise he was acquiring "takes a lot of the passion away from the experience" of listening to tapes.[44]

Speaking with Dwork again in 1996, Latvala acknowledged that, over the "last couple of years," he has "learned a lot about sound [that] I had never considered before."[45] Given the listening habits he developed as a fan and the aesthetic of liveness that was familiar to him as a tape connoisseur, Latvala admits that he "never would have noticed whether [a recording] was stereo or mono a couple of years ago. If the music was out of tune, *that* didn't really click with me."[46] After having spent the past few years working on the *Dick's Picks* series, however, Latvala "learned to hear a little differently."[47] As for his recently acquired rationalized way of hearing, Latvala notes that he had "been trained by John Cutler, our sound wizard who is very technical."[48]

As he gradually gained fluency in the technical language that was being spoken by Cutler, Healy, and others, Latvala acknowledged that selecting shows for release on the *Dick's Picks* series had become more difficult. The act of "choosing what is and what's not a good show" was not as obvious as it had been when Latvala first started to think about the meaning and significance of the tapes while living in Hawaii in the mid-1970s.[49] At the same time, Latvala came to understand that most people within GDP had a very different relationship to the tapes. More specifically (and in stark contrast to the aesthetic ideology embraced by many fans), members of GDP—including members of the band—did not ascribe any special significance or meaning to the recordings. Speaking to Dwork shortly after the release of *Volume Four* in 1996, Latvala explained, "I doubt any of the band members currently alive have listened to the reissue of that show."[50]

Latvala reminded readers that the band had originally recorded their performances and "would go into the hotel room after the show or the next day and listen for purposes of doing a better job or something."[51] In their present form, the tapes were now critiqued and evaluated according to the requirements and expectations of a "product release by the Grateful Dead." Having "learned to hear a little differently," Latvala began to reconsider some of the "esoteric and sublime" qualities that he and other fans had often attributed to the tapes.[52] Referring to the compact discs released as part of the *Dick's Picks* series, Latvala emphasized that each is a "product that occurs in your own environment" and reminded readers that the recording "isn't a live show." "The live show is a phenomenon that only happens there," Latvala mused. "You aren't there when you're listening to it on the tape, no visuals, no people all around, just the bare bones. That's a different subject."[53]

As Latvala learned to navigate the distinct discursive practices and aesthetic ideologies of liveness that existed among the band and their fans, he came to understand that the people responsible for creating and releasing the music have a "different mindset than [those people] receiving it." "That's the difficulty in dealing with this release thing," he remarked. "The audience," Latvala recognized, "perceives it differently than the creators."[54] Over time, Latvala came to understand that the discursive tension among fans and the band over the meaning and significance of recorded liveness was an essential part of the general phenomenon of the Grateful Dead. As a longtime Deadhead who had recently learned to speak a kind of "rationalized" language of liveness, Latvala recognized that both perspectives work "together [to] make the explosion we call the Grateful Dead Experience." Latvala considered this to be an important insight. "There should be a book written about that," he noted, or "at least a chapter."[55]

Post-Dead

Jerry Garcia died in his sleep on August 9, 1995, in a drug treatment facility in Marin County, California. According to reports, he died of natural causes. As the news of Garcia's death spread throughout the media, fans from all over the world began to descend on San Francisco. Writing in *Rolling Stone*, journalist Alec Foege described how, by the afternoon of August 9, "hundreds of well-wishers had begun gathering at the northeast corner of Haight and Ashbury streets, the intersection irrevocably associated with the birth of the 1960s counterculture."[1] "That evening," Foege continues, "a crowd of nearly 2,000 mourners headed for the Polo Field—the site of a Dead performance at the Human Be-In 28 years ago—where they kneeled at a makeshift shrine and danced into the night to bootleg tapes of Grateful Dead concerts."[2]

As the crowd grew larger, a memorial was scheduled for August 13 at which time nearly twenty thousand people had gathered to celebrate the life and legacy of one of the most inventive musicians and iconic personalities of the second half of the twentieth century. Alongside eulogies and musical performances, a "concert-quality sound system blared tapes of vintage Dead shows." One mourner lamented, "I'm not going to be able to hear these crystal-clear tapes this loud ever again."[3]

Over the course of thirty years, the Grateful Dead had mourned the loss of other band members, notably Ron "Pigpen" McKernan, Keith Godchaux, and Brent Mydland. Given Garcia's stature as the de facto leader of the band (not to mention his reputation as the spiritual guru to millions of Deadheads around the world), his death also meant the end of the Grateful Dead. Although many of the surviving band members would continue (and have continued) to perform in a variety of configurations and as part of many musical projects, the Grateful Dead—as a touring and recording group—came to an end in 1995.

Following the death of Garcia, live recordings emerged as the primary documents by which the Grateful Dead's legacy of liveness would be preserved and historicized. By the mid-1990s, a growing repository of live recordings of the Grateful Dead were freely accessible on numerous sites scattered across the World Wide Web. For legions of Deadheads (and the Dead-curious), the internet offered a new digital forum for sharing live recordings of the Grateful Dead. Of course, the ease with which people could now access the band's many live recordings online epitomized the ideals (not to mention the idealism) that motivated the taping and trading community since the early 1970s. The rise of file sharing also meant that the various material objects traditionally associated with the practice of trading—tapes, cassettes, CDs, and so forth—were now superfluous. With enough memory and decent connection speeds, fans could quickly assemble a digital library of live concert recordings from every era in the long (and well-documented) recorded history of the Grateful Dead.

Given the nearly insatiable demand for concert recordings among Deadheads, people throughout the Dead organization recognized that the contents of the vault would be a significant source of future revenue. Despite the availability of the band's concert recordings in all corners of the internet, the Dead have managed to retain a sort of "official" control over their legacy of recorded liveness. Drawing on critical perspectives of Walter Benjamin, Susan Stewart, and others, I argue in this final chapter that, within the culture of the Dead, live recordings were valued not just for their contents and symbolic meaning(s) but also for their materiality. In what follows, I describe how the Dead and their business partners continue to rely on traditional (and increasingly outdated) forms of media—notably CDs, LPs, and DVDs—in promoting and marketing the band's still-evolving legacy of liveness.

The Persistence of Dead Things

The day after Jerry Garcia's memorial celebration in Golden Gate Park, members of the Dead organization met to discuss various "Nontour Operating Strategies."[4] As described in the notes to the meeting, funds collected from royalties, merchandising, and licensing were still considered "CONTINUING SOURCES OF INCOME." In fact, the notes indicate that (at least in the short term) the organization could expect to see income from these sources "increase dramatically."

Following the death of Garcia, however, "$20,000,000 in performance income plus merchandising from touring" was "gone." The notes describe an "IMMEDIATE CASH FLOW CRISIS" and warn of "MAJOR DOWNSIZING" as the organization would "need to reduce overhead dramatically and immediately: Salaries and other overhead to be reduced to minimum necessary to operate. May need to borrow or get advances just to pay operating expenses in the short-term. Employee layoffs seem unavoidable if there is no income from touring: all of GDTS [Grateful Dead Ticket Sales], many at GDP [Grateful Dead Productions, Inc.], some at GDM [Grateful Dead Merchandising]."

Given the organization's precarious financial situation, the band's vault recordings were identified as a "major asset to generate income in the future." In the minutes to a shareholders meeting that occurred on the same day, Phil Lesh expressed his desire "to start digging into the recent vault tapes as soon as possible."[5] Regarding the security of the vault, Hal Kant (the band's longtime legal counsel ["Legally Dead"]) and Cameron Sears (the band's manager at the time) "expressed concern that there are 4 keys to the vault." "Even though the people [with keys] are all trustworthy," everyone at the meeting agreed that a second lock would be added to the vault; it was also agreed that Sears would be the only person with a key for the new lock. Before the meeting adjourned, Sears "asked if we should put night watchpeople [*sic*] on [the vault] right away, and it was AGREED that we should."

By the end of the year, the second and third volumes of the *Dick's Picks* series were being sold direct to fans on compact disc via mail order. Subsequent installments in the series began to appear more frequently; starting in 1996, for example, three (and sometimes four) volumes were released each year. Even after the death of archivist Dick Latvala in 1999, the Dead continued to release new volumes in the series under the direction of David Lemieux, the band's new (and current) archivist. Between 1993 and 2005 (the year the series was retired), the Dead produced and distributed thirty-six volumes in the *Dick's Picks* series.[6]

In addition to the shareholders meeting, there was also a band meeting on August 14 during which attorney Hal Kant assured everyone that the "Arista contract is finished—period. That contract does not exist anymore."[7] During the meeting, Phil Lesh inquired about signing a deal with Bertelsmann Music Group (BMG), one of the largest music distributors and the parent company of Arista. Although the band did not owe any more records to Arista, the Dead signed a distribution deal with Arista/BMG in 1995. Even as the organization continued to produce recordings on its own (including those in the *Dick's Picks* series), the Dead began to release select archival recordings as part of a new deal with their former label.

Appearing in 1995, the double-disc release *Hundred Year Hall* includes select performances from the Dead's concert in Frankfurt, Germany, from April 26, 1972, and was available to record buyers throughout the world as part of Arista/BMG's vast distribution network. Featuring a show from the Dead's highly regarded tour of Europe in 1972, the compact disc release of *Hundred Year Hall* also served as a gauge in measuring the level of interest for the band's archival recordings among a wider group of consumers (i.e., not just people on the Deadhead mailing list). Both GDM and BMG were probably very pleased when *Hundred Year Hall* debuted at number 26 on *Billboard*'s album chart; just a little over a year after its release, the two-disc set had sold over 500,000 copies and was certified Gold. Over the next few years, the band continued to release a steady stream of archival live recordings as part of their distribution deal, including compact discs that were remastered from both multitrack and 2-track stereo recordings. *Dozin' at the Knick*, for instance, was released in 1996 and features performances recorded at the Knickerbocker Arena in Albany, New York, in March 1990, while *Fallout from the Phil Zone* (a double-disc compilation of live recordings selected by Phil Lesh) and *Live at the Fillmore East 2-11-69* were both released in 1997. In addition to these and other vault releases, Arista/BMG continued to distribute other Dead-related recordings, including compact disc releases of many of the band's studio albums (except for those that were originally released on Warner Bros.) and select solo releases.

As suggested by these and many other physical releases, the continued appeal of the Grateful Dead's live recordings among Deadheads is intimately connected to their materiality. Indeed, the enduring significance of the band's live recordings has been (and continues to be) shaped by what Nicholas Meriwether has described as the "complexity of the relationships between event, memory, and artifact."[8] The many compact discs, DVDs, and elaborate box sets that have been released since the death of Jerry Garcia function as the material remainders (and reminders) of the Grateful Dead's legacy of liveness. By continuing to emphasize and market physical releases, the Dead acknowledge that the tapes were valuable not only for what they contained (the aural proof of liveness) but also for what they came to symbolize as containers, that is, as material objects. It was not uncommon for many fans to decorate their tapes and tape cases with elaborate designs, artwork, and other personal touches. As Katie Harvey has recognized, the recordings that were collected and traded among Deadheads were just "one aspect of the material culture surrounding the band." "Among items such as T-shirts, band merchandise, ticket stubs, stickers, and newsletters," Harvey emphasizes how "the tapes functioned as sound objects that bound the scene together."[9]

Of course, such material "sound objects" became meaningful within the narratives of recorded liveness that shaped (and continue to sustain) the legacy of the Grateful Dead. Emphasizing both their spiritual significance and their materiality, live recordings have been called "Dead Relics" (Les Kippel) and "sacred talismans" (band publicist Dennis McNally).[10] David Shenk and Steve Silberman have described how "many collectors take good care of their tape libraries, and it is not uncommon for the racks of tapes to be the most visibly in-order area of a collector's living space." "The activity of hunting down obscure tapes, copying them, and logging them onto a list," they continue, "is a school of precision for many young tapers."[11]

The practices and obsessions associated with collecting and maintaining a library of Grateful Dead tapes recall a similar relationship with books as described by Walter Benjamin. In his essay "Unpacking My Library," Benjamin offers a whimsical examination "into the relationship of a book collector to his possessions."[12] Among many provocative and illuminating insights into the psychology of the collector, Benjamin acknowledges a strong historicist (not to mention historicizing) impulse associated with collecting. More specifically, he describes a peculiar "relationship to objects which does not emphasize their functional, utilitarian value—that is, their usefulness—but studies and loves them as the scene, the stage, of their fate." "For a true collector," Benjamin notes, "the whole background of an item adds up to a magic encyclopedia whose quintessence is the fate of his object."[13]

But just as the collector inherits the entirety of the (real and imagined) past that accompanies the object, the act of collecting further serves to historicize the objects. The imposition of historical narratives, forms of cataloging, and other methods of organization help one to make sense of the "chaos of memories" that drive the passions of the collector. Benjamin explains how, through the imposition of order on disorder, "the great physiognomists—

and collectors are the physiognomists of the world of objects—turn into interpreters of fate."[14] Among collectors, therefore, he suggests that "ownership is the most intimate relationship that one can have to objects. Not that they come alive in him; it is he who lives in them."[15]

Benjamin's acknowledgment of the "intimate relationship" that exists between a collector and their objects points to what Sherry Turkle has described as the "inseparability of thought and feeling in our relationship to things."[16] On the one hand, Turkle observes how "we find it familiar to consider objects as useful or aesthetic, as necessities or vain indulgences." "We are on less familiar ground," she notes, "when we consider objects as companions to our emotional lives or as provocations to thought." Referring to such "evocative objects," Turkle reminds the reader that "we think with the objects we love; we love the objects we think with."[17]

Recalling once again the thought of Susan Stewart, it is also possible to see how the "intimate relationship" described by Benjamin plays out in language, as when "we talk about the relation of language to experience or, more specifically, whenever we talk about the relation of narrative to its objects."[18] By conceiving of the Grateful Dead's live recordings as "souvenirs," I have considered how narratives of liveness animate the semiotic "transformation of materiality into meaning" described by Stewart. Such a transformation, however, does not diminish the "intimate relationship" that still persists among people and the physical, material qualities of such "sound objects." Indeed, despite global trends toward dematerialization, Elodie A. Roy has described how the "digitization of contents may fail to take into account the historical particularity and iconicity of the tangible musical artefact."[19] Moreover, Roy has emphasized how, among select audiences, the recorded sound object persists as a "visual, aural, and tactile entity, prompting various types of bodily memories and responses."[20]

By continuing to foster a demand for physical objects, however, the Dead may be accused of trafficking in what John Perry Barlow described as "bottles which have no macroscopically discrete or personally meaningful form."[21] As a boyhood friend of vocalist and guitarist Bob Weir, Barlow emerged as an invaluable songwriter for the Grateful Dead in the early 1970s. A longtime denizen on the WELL and other early online communities, Barlow was also a founding member of the Electronic Frontier Foundation (EFF), a nonprofit organization formed in 1990 devoted to "defending civil liberties in the digital world."[22] As he continued to work alongside the Grateful Dead in the early 1990s, Barlow also wrote a number of influential and prescient articles on various topics relating to digital culture and the gradual encroachment of cyberspace.

First published under the title "The Economy of Ideas" in *Wired* magazine in 1994, Barlow's essay "Selling Wine Without Bottles" examines the "riddle" posed by "digitized property." In particular, he observes that the "accumulated canon of copyright and patent law was developed to convey forms and methods of expression entirely different from the vaporous cargo it is now being asked to carry."[23] Traditionally, Barlow notes, the "rights of invention and authorship adhered to activities in the physical world. One didn't get paid for ideas but for the ability to deliver them into reality. For all practical purposes, the value was in the conveyance and not the thought conveyed. In other words, the bottle was protected, not the wine. Now, as information enters Cyberspace, the native home of the Mind, these bottles are vanishing. With the advent of digitization, it is now possible to replace all previous information storage forms with one meta-bottle: complex—and highly liquid—patterns of ones and zeros."[24]

Barlow predicts that most of the "physical/digital bottles to which we've become accustomed, floppy disks, CD-ROMs, and other discrete, shrink-wrappable bit-packages, will disappear as all computers jack into the global Net." "Once that has happened," he continues, "all the goods of the Information Age—all of the expressions once contained in books or film strips or records or newsletters—will exist either as pure thought or something very much like thought: voltage conditions darting around the Net at the speed of light, in conditions which one might behold in effect, as glowing pixels or transmitted sounds, but never touch or claim to 'own' in the old sense of the word."[25]

Given the radically changed circumstances that followed in the wake of the wired revolution, Barlow wonders how "if our property can be infinitely reproduced and instantaneously distributed all over the planet without cost, without our knowledge, without its even leaving our possession, how can we protect it? How are we going to get paid for the work we do with our minds?"[26]

Based on his experience, Barlow suggests that the "best thing you can do to raise the demand for your product is to give it away."[27] He notes, "in regard to my own soft product, rock and roll songs, there is no question that the band I write them for, the Grateful Dead, has increased its popularity enormously by giving them away." "We have been letting people tape our concerts since the early seventies," Barlow explains, "but instead of reducing the demand for our product, we are now the largest concert draw in America, a fact which is at least in part attributable to the popularity generated by those tapes." "True," Barlow admits, "I don't get any royalties on the millions of copies of my songs which have been extracted from concerts, but I see no reason to complain. The fact is, no one but the Grateful Dead can perform a Grateful Dead song, so if you want the experience and not its thin projection, you have to buy a ticket from us."[28]

Originally written in 1994, Barlow's essay on the production and distribution of intellectual property in an increasingly dematerialized marketplace is informed by an aesthetic of liveness whose ideological roots can be traced back to the 1920s and 1930s (if not earlier). As humanity was becoming familiar with life in cyberspace, Barlow (re)emphasizes the authentic (and authenticating) function of the live concert experience, a physical experience that can be provided by "no one but the Grateful Dead." In contrast to the concert, Barlow considers any and all subsequent forms of (re-)presentation (tapes, CDs, and "voltage conditions darting around the Net") as offering only a "thin projection" of the genuine, authentic live experience. "Listening to a Grateful Dead tape," Barlow explains, "is hardly the same experience as attending a Grateful Dead concert." Confessing his faith in the authenticity of the live concert experience, Barlow believes that the "closer one can get to the headwaters of an informational stream, the better his [sic] chances of finding an accurate picture of reality."[29]

As the so-called headwaters of the band's "informational stream," however, live concert performances by the Grateful Dead no longer functioned as an "accurate picture of reality" following the death of Jerry Garcia in August 1995. But while the Dead organization remained "obstinately physical" by continuing to produce and distribute vault recordings on a variety of physical formats, fans throughout the world had unlimited access to a growing library of live concert recordings that were freely available online as "vaporous cargo."

The Live Music Archive and the "Thanksgiving Day Massacre"

By the turn of the millennium, the internet site etree.org had emerged as a centralized database and repository of digital recordings of live music, including concert recordings of the Grateful Dead. As described by Matthew Vernon, one of the founders and developers of the Grateful Dead Internet Archive Project, the original goal of the project was to convert noncommercial recordings of the Grateful Dead to "lossless" digital file formats. "Between 2000 and 2003," Vernon explained, "our initial effort of digitizing music of the Grateful Dead expanded into collecting the complete 'circulating' opus . . . onto a single server."[30]

Over the next few years, Vernon and others continued to amass, convert, and upload live concert recordings of the Grateful Dead. In 2004, the files hosted by etree.org were backed up on the Internet Archive, the massive public online "digital library" that had been established in 1996. Between 2004 and 2005, fans had access to thousands of audience and soundboard recordings of the Grateful Dead, all of which could be streamed or downloaded on the Live Music Archive (LMA), a section of the Internet Archive dedicated to live concert recordings by a variety of performers and artists. With access to "nearly every extant Grateful Dead concert recording" and "downloadable files available at a click of a mouse," Gary Burnett has noted how, for collectors and traders who had grown accustomed to shipping and receiving physical recordings in the mail, "obtaining recordings of Grateful Dead shows was never easier."[31]

In a forum post on the LMA, Vernon explained that the recordings available on the archive "were not supplied by the Grateful Dead." Instead, he clarified that the "soundboard and audience recordings on the Archive [were] those that were being traded" freely among the trading community. Indeed, many of the recordings featured in the archive had been circulating as tapes and other physical formats for decades. However, the site also hosted a number of other soundboard recordings that had only started to surface following the death of Dick Latvala in 1999. As many of these soundboards made their way into the trading community, it became clear among fans and members of the Dead organization that Latvala had been making copies of the vault's contents, including the band's own soundboard recordings, and sharing them with people outside of the Dead organization. By the turn of the millennium, the majority of the live audio recordings contained in the Grateful Dead's vault—the same recordings that the Dead deemed a "major asset to generate income in the future"—were freely available online.

On November 22, 2005, Vernon and Brewster Kahle, the founder of the Internet Archive, posted a message to the discussion forum of the LMA. After consulting with representatives of the Dead, Vernon and Kahle informed users that, effective immediately, soundboard recordings of the Grateful Dead would no longer be hosted on the LMA.[32] While audience recordings would remain on the archive, they were now available only for streaming and could not be downloaded. Over the next few days, many people took to the discussion forum to express their anger, disappointment, and, for some, a sense of betrayal. Sensitive to the backlash that their decision had caused among fans and users of the LMA, members of the Dead offered a compromise. According to an amended policy that was announced on December 1, 2005, audience recordings would be available for streaming and could also be downloaded. Although soundboard recordings were restored to the site, they were available only for streaming and could not be downloaded.

The strong reactions of people following the events that unfolded on the LMA in late 2005 (a day that was dubbed the "Thanksgiving Day Massacre") underscore the extent to which live recordings continued to perform a number of symbolic and historical functions for both the Grateful Dead and their fans more than a decade after the death of Jerry Garcia.[33] For people unfamiliar with the band's complex legacy of liveness, the actions of the Dead can be understood as an attempt to retain control of a body of recordings that were originally produced by various members of the organization. However, among those people who were conversant in the discourse of liveness surrounding the Dead, the band's decision to suddenly restrict access to soundboards "ran headlong into a deep-seated Deadhead culture committed to the sharing and trading of live recordings."[34]

Chronicling the events that unfolded on the LMA in the *New York Times*, critic Jon Pareles elucidated many of the ideals associated with taping, trading, and collecting and how, for the "Grateful Dead, and the many bands that emulated them, there was a logic to the whole libertarian enterprise, as well as to the old hippie spirit." The "concert recordings," he explains, "were like memories, to be shared and savored, rather than products" to be bought and sold. Pareles even recalls a "generous suggestion that once the music was in the air, it belonged as much to listeners as to the band."[35]

Here Pareles recalls Jerry Garcia's remark that "when we're done with it, they can have it," a phrase that had been interpreted by many Deadheads to mean that noncommercial live recordings were freely available to everyone and everybody.[36] Pareles understood, of course, that Garcia's remark referred to the practice of taping and the production of live recordings by the band's fans. Regarding the band's own soundboard recordings, Pareles acknowledged that the "Dead do hold copyrights" and are "entitled to authorize or withhold permission to copy their work."[37] Despite the fact that the Dead had every right to restrict access to the soundboard recordings on the LMA, Pareles still admonished the band for, in essence, acting in bad faith. "Even if a Deadhead was not downloading dozens of concerts, the boundless opportunity to do so meant something," he noted. "There was a bond of trust between the band and its fans—one that is now strained."[38]

Like many fans, Pareles surmised that the band's decision to remove select recordings from the LMA was driven by financial considerations. He suggested that, since "Grateful Dead Merchandising . . . now sells downloads of the band's own concert recordings," they "didn't want free competition."[39] As Pareles notes, the Dead were just beginning to explore the market for digital downloads. In 2000, the Dead licensed songs to Amazon ("Casey Jones") and Barnes and Noble ("Uncle John's Band") for download; the band also made available four selections culled from the *Dick's Picks* series as part of an online promotion developed by Arista. Beginning in the spring of 2005, fans could download concert performances from the band's website as part of *The Grateful Dead Download Series*. Pareles acknowledged that, while the Dead may "sell some additional concert downloads in the short run," GDM's decision to limit access to recordings online "downgrades fans into the customers they were all along."[40]

The Rhino Years

In June 2006, shortly after the organization's clumsy forays and missteps in the digital realm, GDP announced a massive licensing deal with Rhino Entertainment, a deal that covered "everything from the band's vast archive of live recordings and its Web site to its merchandise and use of its likeness."[41] Known throughout the industry as a record label that specialized in reissues, Rhino had the experience, expertise, and (most important) the resources necessary for promoting the legacy of the Grateful Dead. Even before the two parties signed a ten-year licensing deal in 2006, Rhino and GDP had partnered to release material from the band's vault, including the Grateful Dead's New Year's Eve concert from 1978 (released in 2003 as *The Closing of Winterland*) and a concert recorded in Germany during the 1972 tour of Europe (*Rockin' the Rhein with the Grateful Dead*, released in 2004). Rhino and GDP also worked together on two lavishly produced retrospective box sets. Released on compact disc in 2001, *The Golden Road (1965–1973)* features expanded reissues of the albums the Grateful Dead recorded for Warner Bros. (Rhino's parent company) along with early singles, alternate mixes, studio outtakes, and many previously unreleased live performances. In 2004, Rhino and the Dead released another deluxe box set called *Beyond Description (1973–1989)* that includes expanded reissues of many of the albums originally released on Grateful Dead Records and Arista (the set does not include the live records *Steal Your Face* or *Without a Net*).

Some of the first live recordings to be released after the Dead signed with Rhino were sourced from the band's multitrack master tapes. Released in early 2007, the three-disc set *Live at the Cow Palace* features the Dead's complete concert from December 31, 1976, in Daly City, California. Attractively packaged with extensive liner notes and photographs, the performances featured on *Live at the Cow Palace* were originally recorded by Betty Cantor-Jackson and Bob Matthews. A few months later, Rhino and the Dead released

Three from the Vault, the latest installment in the *From the Vault* series (following a fifteen-year hiatus). Also sourced from multitrack recordings produced by Cantor-Jackson and Matthews, *Three from the Vault* documents the Dead's complete concert from February 19, 1971, at the Capitol Theatre in Port Chester, New York.

In 2008, the Dead and Rhino released performances that were recorded at the Great Pyramid in Giza, Egypt, in the fall of 1978. Recorded on 24-track, the performances that appear on *Rocking the Cradle: Egypt 1978* were originally produced for a commercial live album that the Dead planned to release on Arista in the 1970s.[42] Unlike the complete concerts documented on *Live at the Cow Palace* and *Three from the Vault*, *Rocking the Cradle* features performances compiled from two of the three concerts the Dead played in Egypt. As a compilation live recording, therefore, *Rocking the Cradle* more closely resembles the form and design of many of the Dead's official live releases, beginning with *Live/Dead* (1969) through *Without a Net* (1990). For fans whose aesthetic ideology of recorded liveness had been shaped by the sacred mythology of the "tapes" and who believed that a "live recording should accurately reflect the concert experience" (an attitude that Nicholas Meriwether has called the "Deadhead purist approach"), *Rocking the Cradle* might have been conceived as "an inexcusable exercise in heavy-handed editing."[43]

As Meriwether notes, the band's decision to not release an official live album documenting their time in Egypt contributed to the formation of what he calls a "dismissive critical consensus" concerning the original concerts and the quality of the band's performances, a consensus "perhaps more informed by the poor quality of the few, rare audience recordings in circulation."[44] In his opinion, however, the live recorded performances featured on *Rocking the Cradle* challenge this "dismissive critical consensus." Although they do not document a complete concert (and therefore do not satisfy the "Deadhead purist" aesthetic), Meriwether argues that the heavily edited performances compiled on *Rocking the Cradle* provide a "real benchmark, [and] definitive proof that the shows had some superb moments, and indeed, that the band had made enough good music to merit a multidisc release. By commercial standards, then, this clearly constitutes a successful set of shows."[45] Furthermore, Meriwether continues, the presumed "authority of the official release reaffirms the historicity of the events by laying to rest the canard that the band did not play well."[46]

In contrast to the existing audience recordings of the band's concerts in Egypt as well as the "largely unprocessed soundboards in circulation" (both of which he refers to as "less mediated sonic artifacts"), Meriwether argues that the band's edited and remastered recordings offer a more authentic representation of the original concert performances. Indeed, he suggests that, "while the level of Egypt's influence on each song varies, in places, we can say that indeed we hear the desert, we hear the pyramid, we hear Egypt."[47] While "no DVD or CD can recreate the effect of being there," Meriwether claims that the recordings "provide a stylized, idealized depiction of sound and image that captures views and nuances that no single participant could ever experience."[48] To be sure, such a "stylized, idealized depiction" is not *really* captured on the original multitrack recordings but is, instead, expertly produced and attractively packaged as part of the "rigorously edited and carefully planned official release."[49]

Alongside *Rocking the Cradle* and other remastered multitrack recordings, Rhino and GDP also released live performances sourced from the band's 2-track tapes. In 2007, GDP and Rhino debuted a series called *Road Trips*. Following in the aesthetic tradition of *Dick's Picks* (which had been discontinued in 2005), the compact discs released on the *Road Trips* series included an explanatory remark concerning the quality and condition of the original recordings. The *Road Trips* series was retired in 2011; since 2012, David Lemieux, the Dead's current archivist, has drawn upon the band's 2-track recordings as part of a series called *Dave's Picks*.

The Dead and Rhino have also collaborated on a number of limited edition box sets. In 2005, GDP produced and distributed *Fillmore West 1969: The Complete Recordings*, a ten-disc set documenting four full concerts from Bill Graham's Fillmore West in San Francisco. Originally recorded on 16-track, some of these recordings were previously released on *Live/Dead*. Among fans, the band's run of concerts at the Fillmore West from February to March 1969 are held in high regard; months before the box set was released, all ten thousand copies of *Fillmore West 1969* had been sold as preorders.

In 2011, GDP and Rhino released *Europe '72: The Complete Recordings*, a mammoth seventy-three-disc "mega–box set" featuring multitrack recordings of all twenty-two concerts from the Dead's famed 1972 tour. Packaged in an elaborate steamer case with a book of liner notes and other collectible items, all 7,200 copies of *Europe '72: The Complete Recordings* were sold as preorders. For fans who missed out on the limited edition set, archivist David Lemieux posted an announcement on the band's website explaining how, "after lengthy discussions, we've decided we don't want to deprive anyone of this music, some of the finest the Grateful Dead ever performed."[50] Therefore, Lemieux announced, "We're going to offer just the music, all 22 shows, more than 60 CDs, more than 70 hours of music, each show housed in its own packaging, for the same price as the boxed set." "Although perhaps not as cool as the boxed set," he continues, "the bottom line is that the most important aspect of *Europe '72: The Complete Recordings* is going to be made available to all, the music."[51]

Of course, if it really was about just "the music," fans might have been content to simply listen to recordings of many of these same concerts that were available for free on archive.org and other internet sites. But as Lemieux and others understand, many fans—including original Dead Freaks as well as latter-day Deadheads—are still drawn to material objects that remind them, in some way, of the legendary power of the tapes. The symbolism and meanings of the tapes described in the previous chapters were—for most of their existence—indelibly linked to physical objects. These objects—albums, tapes, cassettes, CDs, and so forth—were (and, for some people, continue to be) just as much a part of the experience of liveness as the sounds that were conveyed and the stories that were told and/or imagined. For decades, Deadheads manipulated "things" as they sought access to the distinctive forms of liveness offered by live recordings of the Grateful Dead. These various "things" became part of the experience, as listeners gazed at album artwork, read liner notes, and decorated tape cases and CD sleeves.

Indeed, the material qualities of the myriad "souvenirs" of liveness that continue to be purchased, collected, and traded by fans embody what Susan Stewart has described as a "transformation of meaning into materiality."[52] Whereas most contemporary listeners experience live recordings of the Grateful Dead in what John Perry Barlow characterized as "patterns of ones and zeros" that are "darting around the Net," a select few are fortunate ("cool") enough to have access to a more immersive and multisensorial experience of recorded liveness, a tactile experience that is provided by the many material sound objects that continue to be produced and marketed by the Dead.

Coda: Virtually Dead

There will come a time, however, when the contents of the Dead's vault are exhausted and there will be nothing left to release. In an interview published in 2012, archivist David Lemieux estimated that "ninety per cent of the vault [had] been circulated" among members of the trading community. Referring to the steady stream of vault releases from the Dead, Lemieux acknowledged that, although "this will end someday," there was still "enough good material in the vault to go at this rate for another twenty or thirty years, or, at a slower rate, for fifty years."[53]

The Grateful Dead re-signed with Rhino in 2017. As part of the Dead's new deal (a deal that extends to 2039), Lemieux described the organization's plans for future releases from the vault: "We know for sure that every year we're going to release four *Dave's Picks*, which are the three-CD complete live shows, quarterly. We know we're going to do one big box set each year, whether that's an eight-CD set or an 11-CD set, like the one we have coming up [*May 1977: Get Shown the Light*]. This gives us one other big thing to focus on every year."[54]

On the one hand, the predictable schedule of releases described by Lemieux was welcome news to those fans who still anticipated official recordings from the band's vault. On the other hand, each new release meant being one tape closer to the end of the vault. Faced with the inevitability of having complete access to all the band's extant live recordings as official releases, it is worth considering how (and if) the ideology of liveness might continue to shape the historiography of the Grateful Dead. As the material remains of liveness gradually become depleted, what will sustain the desire and satisfy the longing for some sense of the "authentic" Grateful Dead live experience?

Not surprisingly, Jerry Garcia had some thoughts. In an interview published in *Rolling Stone* in 1989, Garcia asked interviewer Fred Goodman, "Have you heard of this stuff called virtual reality?"[55] Garcia explained:

> There's a place here [in San Francisco] where they have something you put on your head. It's got like a pair of goggles on it, and the goggles are two little TV screens that give you a 3-D image. . . . When you put on the goggles, you are in this room. It's a completely fictitious room. But if you turn your head around, your view of the room is 360 degrees. . . . And you can pick up fictitious objects you can "see" in the room. You can see where it's heading: You're going to be able to put on this thing and be in a completely interactive environment. There is not going to be any story, but there's going to be the way you and it react. As they add sounds and improve the image, you're going to be able to walk around in that building, fly through the air, all that stuff. And it's going to take you to those places as convincingly as any other sensory input.[56]

In Garcia's opinion, the emerging technologies of virtual reality (VR) reflected the "remnants of the Sixties." "Nobody stopped thinking about those psychedelic experiences," Garcia explained. "Once you've been to some of those places, you think, 'How can I get back there again but make it a little easier on myself?'"

In 1989, Garcia's thoughts regarding VR may have struck the interviewer (and perhaps many readers) as the ramblings of an aging, drug-addled hippie.

Perhaps so, but that doesn't mean Garcia wasn't on to something. On August 14, 1995, members of the band and crew met to discuss the state of the Dead, consider downsizing, and share their thoughts about the future. As described in the notes to the meeting, Hal Kant, the longtime legal counsel for the organization, "asked about *virtual reality*."[57] Responding to Kant, manager Cameron Sears stated that the "technology is not really available yet." Sears noted, however, that the "most happening stuff" relating to VR technology was taking place in San Francisco; the minutes note that "there was general discussion about this."

By the second decade of the twenty-first century, the technologies and experiences that Garcia described in 1989 and that the band discussed in 1995 were available to anyone with access to a VR headset. In 2015, fans were offered a partial glimpse of the Grateful Dead as a live act once again when many of the surviving members—including Mickey Hart, Bill Kreutzmann, Phil Lesh, and Bob Weir—reunited for a limited run of live concert performances. On the occasion of the band's fiftieth anniversary, the group performed a handful of concerts in front of hundreds of thousands of fans in Santa Clara, California, and Chicago, Illinois. Many more fans tuned in to watch the concerts, billed as "Fare Thee Well: Celebrating Fifty Years of the Grateful Dead," on pay-per-view. For fans who desired a more interactive experience of the concerts, the Dead also arranged to have some of their performances filmed in virtual reality.

In 2016, a VR experience titled *Grateful Dead: Truckin'* premiered at the Tribeca Film Festival in New York City. Representing (perhaps) the next stage in the evolution of liveness, the twelve-minute film features a VR-captured performance of the song "Truckin'" as performed by the band during their concerts in Santa Clara. Writing in *Rolling Stone*, David Browne described the experience, noting how "after putting on your VR goggles, you'll find yourself standing almost directly in front of the stage, only a few feet away from Phil Lesh [and] Bob Weir. . . . (You can see, up close, the moment when Lesh looks at Weir for a nudge when it's time to launch into the bridge.)"[58] "Elsewhere," Browne continues, "the camera is positioned behind pianist Bruce Hornsby, and you see (and hear) things from his perspective; shift your head to the right and, hey, there's proud Deadhead [and NBA Hall of Fame member] Bill Walton standing near you!" Finally, Browne described how "when the band starts into the most recognizable part of "Truckin'"— the 'what a long strange trip it's been' line—you'll find yourself in the front rows of the crowd, right next to fans shooting the show on their cell phones and dancing away."

Elsewhere in the article, Cliff Plumer, the president of Jaunt Studios (the company that produced the film), exclaims that "there's nothing like Dead-heads and their fun and spirit," qualities that aren't "typically captured by traditional media." "With VR, you can look *anywhere*," Plumer explains. "If you weren't able to get a ticket or lived in a part of the world where you can't get access to these concerts, this is the next best thing."

The "next best thing." I've heard that before . . .

Conclusion

MEMENTO MORI

Shortly after agreeing to a new recording and merchandising deal in 2017, the Grateful Dead and Rhino Records released *May 1977: Get Shown the Light*, the latest box set of live recordings from the band's vault. The set includes eleven compact discs and extensive liner notes chronicling complete performances of four consecutive concerts from May 5 through May 9, 1977. Upon its initial release, *May 1977: Get Shown the Light* was available in a limited run of 15,000 copies; along with the compact discs and notes, the limited edition also included a copy of Peter Conners's book, *Cornell '77: The Music, the Myth, and the Magnificence of the Grateful Dead's Concert at Barton Hall.* Presented in an attractive case designed by the renowned graphic artist Masaki Koike, the set was nominated for a Grammy Award in 2017 in the category of "Best Boxed or Special Limited Edition Package."

Without a doubt, the centerpiece of the box set was the Dead's concert from May 8, 1977, at Cornell University in Ithaca, New York. As described in the introduction, a live recording of this concert was added to the National Recording Registry of the Library of Congress in 2011. At that time, a press release acknowledged that the "soundboard recording of this show [had] achieved almost mythic status among 'Deadhead' tape traders because of its excellent sound quality and early accessibility, as well as its musical performances."[1] Considered by many fans to be one of the best concerts the band ever played, six years later the Dead and Rhino were finally producing an official release "to celebrate the 40th Anniversary of that magical show."[2] The limited edition sold out quickly, and other formats were issued. In addition to an "All Music Edition" of the box set (featuring everything except Conners's book), the Dead and Rhino released the complete concert performance from Cornell separately on compact disc and long-playing record.

Given the "myth" and the "magnificence" (not to mention the "music") of a show like "5/8/77," it is worth considering what, exactly, was being commemorated with the release of *May 1977: Get Shown the Light*. In his liner notes, Nicholas Meriwether acknowledges the popular debate among Deadheads that Cornell is (or is not) the Dead's "best show." He also considers the band's performance from May 8 alongside the other concerts the group played that week. Like many fans, Meriwether hears something special about this run of concerts and suggests that these four shows offer "a good microcosm" of the band at that time.[3] Meriwether remarks there must have been "something about these four shows that dazzled" audiences and that "those lucky enough to hear [the concerts] would spread the word: get the tapes." "And as those [tapes] spread," he explains, "so did the legend of this remarkable week."[4]

As imagined by Meriwether, the tapes capture the events of that "remarkable week" and, in particular, the band's celebrated performance on 5/8/77. According to this way of thinking, the recordings document historic musical events and the many unique performances and dynamic qualities that could have been lost forever if not for the tapes. Of course, within a community that believed that (for better or for worse) "THERE IS NOTHING LIKE A GRATEFUL DEAD CONCERT," each live performance was already a self-fulfilling prophecy. Even if the band put on a less-than-stellar performance, the *potential* for significance was always latent in the event and in the environment. Within this scenario, therefore, the tapes are valued because of their ability to capture "lightning in a bottle" and to preserve those nights—perhaps even a night such as May 8, 1977—when the Dead put on an exceptional show.

It is also possible (and, in the case of 5/8/77, much more probable) that the unique characteristics and distinctive qualities of the recordings themselves contributed to the historicization of a particular moment, event, or experience. Understood this way, the tapes do not *tell* the story of 5/8/77; instead, the tapes *are* the story of 5/8/77. In the case of the Cornell concert, in particular, live recordings have played an important role in the mythmaking that developed around the Dead's show that evening, a myth that has generated a tremendous amount of personal meaning and a strong sense of historical significance among the Dead and their fans. Although marketed to commemorate the anniversary of a "magical" live show, *May 1977: Get Shown the Light* is perhaps better conceived as commemorating the history of a live recording.

Recordings of the show at Cornell began to circulate among traders shortly after the band played at Barton Hall. On June 5, 1977, less than a month after the concert, future vault archivist Dick Latvala received a copy of an audience tape from Jerry Moore (a longtime taper and the first editor in chief of *Dead Relix*). A short time later, Latvala jotted down some notes on the tape, commenting that, "after a few hearings, I remain pretty convinced that this is the best show I've yet heard from the 1977 tour."[5] Latvala returned to the tape in 1983, noting that "enough can't be said about this superb show. The 'Morning Dew' is, without any doubt, the most rousing [and] thrilling one ever. The quality is excellent, regardless what Rob Bertrando may say." (Along with Latvala, Jerry Moore, and Les Kippel, Rob Bertrando is another significant figure in the early taping and trading community.)

The real mythmaking surrounding the concert from May 8 began to gain momentum in the late 1980s. Writing in *Dupree's Diamond News* in 1987, John Dwork remarked that the "stellar second set from Cornell 1977" was among the group of Betty Boards that were beginning to trickle into the trading community.[6] For those Deadheads who were familiar with the Dead's concert at Cornell from the various audience tapes that had been circulating for years, the exceptional clarity of Betty Cantor-Jackson's two-track stereo soundboard recordings was a revelation. At the same time, the remarkable sound quality of Cantor-Jackson's recently unearthed recording attracted a new generation of fans who were just getting into the Grateful Dead following the recent success of "Touch of Grey." Recalling that time in the late 1980s, current Dead archivist (and "Legacy Manager") David Lemieux recalls how he and his friends had heard "most of the classic, canonical shows that circulated, but nothing could prepare us for the raw power and unfathomable energy of Cornell."[7]

Throughout the 1990s, the Dead's show at Cornell continued to grow in status and prestige among fans. With the release of the third volume of the *Dick's Picks* series in November 1995 (just a few months after the death of Jerry Garcia), Dick Latvala, now the Dead's tape archivist, included a postcard that encouraged fans to identify their "Top Ten Favorite Grateful Dead Shows." As the Dead began to plan for future releases in the series, Latvala and others tabulated the responses from returned postcards along with information compiled from surveys and polls conducted online. The Dead's concert from Cornell in May 1977 emerged as the overwhelming fan favorite, followed by the band's performance in Oregon on August 27, 1972 and a concert at Harpur College in Binghamton, New York, from May 2, 1970.

In an interview with John Dwork in *Dupree's Diamond News* a few months later, Latvala was asked to comment about these and other "classic" concerts by the Grateful Dead. In Dwork's opinion, these were "indisputable shows that are classics [and] that must be released."[8] Latvala assured him that a recording of the concert from May 2, 1970 would be released. (Acoustic and electric performances from this show were released as the eighth volume of *Dick's Picks* in 1997.) Regarding the other shows, Latvala reminded Dwork that fans already had access to exceptionally good recordings of the concert from August 27, 1972, and the Cornell concert. Despite its being the concert that was the most requested by fans, Latvala explained that there was "no way in the world" that the Cornell show would be officially released. "It's a Betty Board," he emphasized. "It's out; everybody already has perfect copies. Why waste everyone's time?"

Indeed, the pristine live recording of 5/8/77 that was so revered among fans was sourced from tapes that were originally produced by Betty Cantor-Jackson, tapes that had previously been stored in the band's vault. As many people throughout the trading community knew, though, the tapes of the Cornell concert were among the many reels that Cantor-Jackson took from the vault when she and the Dead organization parted ways in the early 1980s. After languishing in a storage locker, Cantor-Jackson's tapes were auctioned off to multiple buyers, some of whom worked diligently at restoring them and transferring the recordings to a digital format. Cantor-Jackson's sound-board recording of the Dead's concert at Cornell was among the earliest of the so-called Betty Boards to spread throughout the trading community in the spring of 1987. By the mid-1990s, when Latvala was being interviewed by Dwork, Cantor-Jackson's original master tapes were still in the possession of a private party and therefore did not reside in the band's vault. Responding to Dwork, Latvala was gently reminding Deadheads that they already had (free) access to what was, for all intents and purposes, the "official" soundboard recording of 5/8/77.

Marketed as the fortieth anniversary of a "magical show," *May 1977: Get Shown the Light* commemorates the aura and mystique of a concert that, in many ways, was made meaningful by the tapes. There is no denying that the distinctive sonic qualities and sparkling clarity of the Betty Boards were crucial factors that contributed to the popularization and historicization of concerts such as May 8. On the one hand, the box set commemorates the legacy of a specific live recording of a unique concert. On the other hand, the Betty Boards also disclosed more performances that were subsequently identified as being of historical significance, including the other shows in the box set as well as, in Lemieux's estimation, shows in "Boston and Beacon [Theatre in New York] June '76! Binghamton '77! April 1978!"[9] In fact, the box set celebrates all of the Betty Boards for, as Lemieux reveals, Cantor-Jackson's original master tapes had finally been returned to the vault. More than just a commemoration of May 8, *May 1977: Get Shown the Light* celebrates the reinterment of tape recordings that had been missing from the Dead's vault for over thirty years.

Lemieux explains that, without access to the original recordings, the Dead were unable to "share these wonderful concerts in an official capacity." But now that Cantor-Jackson's master tapes were back in the vault, Lemieux boasts that "we're able to present this music to you in the best quality that you'll ever hear it, with every note transferred from the original analog master tapes, using Plangent Process and mastered in HDCD."[10] (The Plangent Process refers to a technology designed to reduce aspects of "wow and flutter" in analog tape transfers.)[11] Echoing the rationalized language of liveness employed by Lemieux, the description on the page for preordering the box set emphasizes that the digital "transfers from the master tapes were produced by Plangent Processes, further ensuring that this is the best, most authentic that Cornell . . . has ever sounded."[12]

"Most authentic."

In many ways, that phrase sums up the story I have been telling throughout the book. For over half a century, the Grateful Dead and their fans have forged a complex relationship that has been shaped and sustained by a desire for (and a belief in) the "most authentic" recorded representation of a live musical performance. Writing in the *Village Voice* in 1967, for example, journalist Richard Goldstein exclaimed that the Dead "sound like live thunder," an impression he experienced not at a concert but as part of an "evening at the Fillmore listening to tapes."[13] Although the future did not turn out the way he predicted, critic and guitarist Lenny Kaye declared in 1969 that "if you'd like to visit a place where rock is likely to be in about five years, you might think of giving *Live/Dead* a listen or two."[14] In 1975, Dick Latvala sent a letter to *Dead Relix*, Les Kippel's influential fanzine, in which he described how the "intense experiences of togetherness" that he and his family share while listening to tapes "are the exact same as we have all repeatedly had [when] seeing the Dead 'Live.'"[15] More than a decade later, John Dwork, the publisher of another respected fanzine, *Dupree's Diamond News*, remarked that the newly surfaced Betty Boards were "unquestionably important 'gifts' which will surely have far-reaching, spiritual and social implications in the Dead Head community."[16]

Of course, claims regarding the alleged "power" of the Grateful Dead's live recordings only make sense within an aesthetic discourse that already assumes that recordings are capable of providing a sense of the energy or excitement of the original concert performance. One must believe, in other words, that live recordings are the "next best thing" to being there. To be sure, this is an idea that has been promoted to record buyers for decades. Recall how, in 1963, prospective buyers were assured that "the producers and engineers have completely captured the James Brown personality, the James Brown sound, the James Brown feel" on *"Live" at the Apollo*.[17] In 1956, audiences were invited to imagine the scene when the "platinum-blonde girl in a black dress" started to dance during "Diminuendo and Crescendo in Blue" as heard on *Ellington at Newport*. As commercial live recordings became more common (and lucrative) in the 1950s, fans and critics acknowledged the ability of live recordings to enhance memories and shape recollections. Speaking of Jess Stacy's piano solo on "Sing, Sing, Sing" during Benny Goodman's concert at Carnegie Hall in 1938, critic Barry Ulanov remarked how "in recorded retrospect, those delicate measures stand way out" even though, as he admits, "those of us who were there that night didn't realize it."[18]

Of course, the belief that live recordings are even capable of capturing or imparting a sense of the "aura" or some other distinctive quality of a concert only makes sense within an aesthetic ideology that imagines live performances as the "authentic" manner for experiencing music. As I described in the introduction, an ideology of musical liveness was vigorously promoted in the United States as part of a public relations campaign that was carried out by the American Federation of Musicians at the dawn of the Great Depression. In an effort to "sell the public the value of manual music as contrasted with mechanical music," the AFM's campaign was instrumental in forming an idealized understanding of live musical performance in the collective imagination of people throughout the country.[19]

Of course, the very idea that music performed "live" represents a more authentic (indeed, the "most authentic") manner of experiencing music only makes sense within a musico-cultural milieu where concepts such as "real" and "authentic" carry any ideological meaning. Quite obviously, the idea of an authentic experience of music would have made no sense prior to the invention of sound recording and reproduction technologies. Given that, prior to 1877, sound had only ever been experienced as an ephemeral quality, it is not surprising that the earliest accounts of these new technologies emphasized their fundamental humanity and their remarkable ability to faithfully replicate and reproduce essential qualities of not just sound but the sources of those sounds as well.

On November 17, 1877, the journal *Scientific American* published a letter by Edward H. Johnson, an inventor and business associate of Thomas

Edison. In his letter, Johnson (identified as an "Electrician") describes the function and design of an "apparatus" recently developed by Edison, an apparatus capable of "recording the human voice" so that "at any subsequent time it might be automatically re-delivered with all the vocal characteristics of the original speaker accurately reproduced."[20] "A speech delivered into the mouthpiece of this apparatus," Johnson wrote, "may fifty years hence—long after the original speaker is dead—be reproduced audibly to an audience with sufficient fidelity to make the voice easily recognizable by those who were familiar with the original."

In their introduction to Johnson's letter, the editors of *Scientific American* marveled at the possibility that "our great grandchildren or posterity centuries hence [may] hear us as plainly as if we were present. Speech has become, as it were, immortal."[21] The editors are clearly overwhelmed at the prospects offered by Edison's new apparatus, the earliest phonograph. "It has been said that Science is never sensational; that it is intellectual not emotional; but certainly nothing that can be conceived would be more likely to create the profoundest of sensations than once more to hear the familiar voices of the dead."

For more than sixty years, live recordings featuring the familiar voices (and music) of the Grateful Dead have played a part in some of the "profoundest of sensations" for Deadheads throughout the world. As imagined and idealized by both the band and their fans, live recordings—including official and unofficial releases, soundboards and audience recordings, multitracks and 2-tracks, compilations and complete shows available as albums, open reel tapes, cassettes, 8-track, DAT, and CDs (not to mention films, videodiscs, laserdiscs, VHS and BETA tapes, DVDs, and "patterns of ones and zeros")—have shaped and will continue to shape the general history, the personal stories, and the evolving mythology of the Grateful Dead.

Notes

INTRODUCTION

1   From the description of the National Recording Registry on the Library of Congress site: "Frequently Asked Questions," Library of Congress, https://www.loc.gov/programs/national-recording-preservation-board/recording-registry/frequently-asked-questions/#:~:text=What%20is%20the%20National%20Recording,by%20the%20Library%20of%20Congress (accessed March 31, 2023).

2   From the original press release dated 2011. A revised and updated version is available: "Recordings by Donna Summer, Prince and Dolly Parton Named to the National Recording Registry: Additions Mark 10th Anniversary of Registry," Library of Congress, May 24, 2012, https://www.loc.gov/item/prn-12-107/.

3   See the many recordings of this concert on the Internet Archive site: https://archive.org/search.php?query=date:1977-05-08&and[]=mediatype%3A%22etree%22&and[]=collection%3A%22etree%22&and[]=collection%3A%22Grateful Dead%22 (accessed March 31, 2023).

4   Getz and Dwork, *Deadhead's Taping Compendium*, 2:153–56.

5   Getz and Dwork, *Deadhead's Taping Compendium*, 2:153 (emphasis in original). Dwork refers to another celebrated live recording of the Dead ("2/13/70"), a concert at the Fillmore East in New York City.

6   Getz and Dwork, *Deadhead's Taping Compendium*, 2:153. Dwork refers to "Morning Dew," a song that had been a regular part of the band's live shows since 1967.

Information concerning the band's setlists, performance and recording history, and a host of other historical details and reviews can be found in *Deadbase*, a reference manual/encyclopedia that was first published in 1987 and has been updated multiple times. See Scott, Nixon, and Dolgushkin, *Deadbase 50*.

7　Conners, *Cornell '77*, 38.

8　The essay is reprinted in Brendel, *Music Sounded Out*, 200.

9　Gracyk, *Rhythm and Noise*, 81.

10　Gracyk, *Rhythm and Noise*, 88.

11　Gracyk, *Rhythm and Noise*, 88.

12　Gracyk, *Rhythm and Noise*, 88. On the technologically enhanced representations and experiences produced by commercial live recordings, see Wurtzler, "She Sang Live, But The Microphone Was Turned Off," 94–95.

13　Gracyk, *Rhythm and Noise*, 81.

14　Gracyk, *Rhythm and Noise*, 1.

15　Gracyk, *Rhythm and Noise*, 79.

16　Lydia Goehr offers a nuanced examination of this aesthetic tradition in *Imaginary Museum of Musical Works*.

17　Gracyk, *Rhythm and Noise*, 81.

18　Stephen Davies, for instance, develops a generalized ontology of "studio" and "live" recordings in his *Musical Works and Performances*; see especially chapter 7. Lee B. Brown also offers a critique of Gracyk in his "Phonography, Rock Records, and the Ontology of Recorded Music."

19　Bangs, "[Review] *Get Yer Ya-Ya's Out*, the Rolling Stones, London (NPS-5)." All subsequent citations are to this source.

20　Ulanov, "[Review] BG: 1938," 29. All subsequent citations are to this source.

21　Archetti, "In the Popular Vein," 254.

22　On the midcentury quarrel between the "ancients and the moderns" (as represented in the transformation from swing to bebop), see Gendron, "Moldy Figs and Modernists."

23　Levin, "Mix Reviews the Goodman Carnegie LP," 14.

24　Tackley, *Benny Goodman's Famous 1938 Carnegie Hall Jazz Concert*, 174.

25　Tackley, *Benny Goodman's Famous 1938 Carnegie Hall Jazz Concert*, 186.

26　Flory, "Liveness and the Grateful Dead," 124 (emphasis added).

27　Flory, "Liveness and the Grateful Dead," 123.

28　Peters, "Helmholtz, Edison, and Sound History," 177.

29　Auslander, *Liveness*, 61. As part of a generalized theory of liveness, Paul Sanden has referred to this as a "traditional" form of liveness. See Sanden, *Liveness in Modern Music*, 20.

30　Elsewhere, Philip Auslander ("Live from Cyberspace") notes that, in Britain, the earliest uses of the word "live" to refer to a nonrecorded musical performance date from 1934. Auslander locates the emergence of a contemporary understanding of liveness, therefore, as a response to the rise of recorded music heard on radio. In particular, he asserts that the "possibility of identifying certain performances as live came into being with the advent of recording technologies; the need to make that identification arose as an affective response specifically to radio, a communications technology that put the clear opposition of the live and the recorded into a state of crisis" (Auslander, "Live from Cyberspace," 17). Contra Auslander, I argue that the "need to make that identification" first developed in the United States in the 1920s as musicians were forced to confront the professional crisis posed by the introduction of synchronized sound in theaters.

31 Thornton, *Club Cultures*, 34ff.
32 Thornton, *Club Cultures*, 42.
33 Thornton, *Club Cultures*, 42.
34 Thornton, *Club Cultures*, 42.
35 Thornton, *Club Cultures*, 42.
36 Thornton, *Club Cultures*, 42.
37 "7,000 of 25,000 Theater Musicians Held Jobless," 1.
38 Just a year earlier Weber was a bit more optimistic, remarking that, as "to canned music ever substituting adequately for the real performance, we are not alarmed" ("Interview with Joseph N. Weber," 228).
39 "7,000 of 25,000 Theater Musicians Held Jobless," 3.
40 "7,000 of 25,000 Theater Musicians Held Jobless," 1.
41 "Robot as an Entertainer," 5.
42 For a more comprehensive account of the AFM's response to the rise of synchronized sound in theaters, see Kraft, *Stage to Studio*, 33–58. See also Kelley, "Without a Song."
43 See Sousa, "Menace of Mechanical Music," 113–22. Patrick Warfield examines the personal, professional, and political motivations that underlie Sousa's celebrated essay in his "John Philip Sousa and 'The Menace of Mechanical Music.'"
44 "Serenade Mechanistic," 11.
45 "Robot Sings of Love," 3 (emphasis in original).
46 "My Next Imita-a-ashun," 3.
47 The image of the Muse appears in many of Helguera's illustrations as a generic representation of "True Music," a symbol of "True Art," and a guardian of "Musical Culture."
48 "Is Art to Have a Tyrant?," 3.
49 "Robot as an Entertainer," 5.
50 "Music? A Picture No *Robot* Can Paint!," 18.
51 "O Fairest Flower!," 16.
52 Some advertisements also evince a degree of "Europe-envy" that is reflective, perhaps, of underlying feelings of cultural inferiority and artistic inadequacy on the part of the AFM. In an ad titled "Is the Robot Fooling You," for instance, readers are told how "The *music-wise* Continentals object violently to mechanical music (in the theatre)." "What, then, if Europeans thus prove their 'music-wisdom,' are we North Americans supposed to be, that we are asked to accept mechanical music—and mechanical music only—in the theatre? *Music-stupid*, perhaps?" ("Is the Robot Fooling You?," 2 [emphasis in original]).
53 Middleton, *Studying Popular Music*, 94 (emphasis in original).
54 Benjamin, *Work of Art*, 24.
55 Sterne, *Audible Past*, 220.
56 Weber, "Canned Music," 124.
57 Weber, "Canned Music," 123.
58 Weber, "Canned Music," 126.

59 Weber, "Canned Music," 125.

60 Weber, "Canned Music," 126.

61 See Kraft, *Stage to Studio*, 107ff. On the impact and legacy of the recording bans initiated by Petrillo, see Anderson, "'Buried under the Fecundity of His Own Creations.'"

62 Williams, "Mr. Petrillo's Hopeless War," 291.

63 Williams, "Mr. Petrillo's Hopeless War," 291.

64 Williams, "Mr. Petrillo's Hopeless War," 292.

65 Smith, "What's Petrillo Up To?," 92.

66 Smith, "What's Petrillo Up To?," 93.

67 Smith, "What's Petrillo Up To?," 95.

68 On the tensions and complexities of an ideology of liveness involving television, see Feuer, "Concept of Live Television," 12–22.

69 Research Company of America, *National Crisis for Live Music and Musicians*.

70 Zak, *I Don't Sound Like Nobody*, 31. See also Zak's remarks on authenticity and recordings in *Poetics of Rock*, 17ff.

71 On the emergence of a phonographic sensibility, see Eisenberg, *Recording Angel*.

72 From George Avakian's liner notes to Duke Ellington, *Ellington at Newport*. All subsequent citations are to this source.

73 For more on the history and legacy of Ellington's concert, see Morton, *Backstory in Blue*. Morton considers how the historical significance of the concert was aided by the commercial success and critical reception of the live recording (Morton, *Backstory in Blue*, 201ff.).

74 "Pop Spotlight," 25.

75 Dewar, "Music as Written: Boston," 18.

76 From Hal Neely's liner notes to James Brown, *The James Brown Show*. All subsequent citations are to this source.

77 Recall that Neely's reference to "the actual 40 minutes" is repeated ("or so") in *Billboard*'s "Pop Spotlight." The entire album is just over thirty minutes in duration.

78 Auslander, *Liveness*, 60.

79 Keightley, "Live Album," 620. Similarly, Landon Palmer has observed how live recordings "display the power of live performance as the originating source of a recorded object, offering an encapsulation of the immediacy and presence associated with the live experience through the capacities of recording technologies" (Palmer, "Portable Recording Studio," 54–55).

80 It should come as no surprise, perhaps, that many of the enduring myths involving popular music (especially rock), live performance, and live recordings were developed and refined during the heyday of the American advertising industry. Jon Stratton briefly considers the commercial and ideological contradictions inherent in live records in "Capitalism and Romantic Ideology in the Record Business," 153–54.

81 I am referring to Louis Althusser's well-known essay "Ideology and Ideological State Apparatuses," reproduced in *Lenin and Philosophy and Other Essays*, 85–126.

82 My views on ideology have been shaped by the work of Barbara J. Fields. See especially her essay "Slavery, Race, and Ideology in the United States of America," in Fields and Fields, *Racecraft*, 111–48. Conceiving of ideology as a "language of consciousness" by which systems of belief and social formations are consistently re-created and reinscribed, Fields stresses that ideology is not any sort of "material entity, [or] a thing of any sort, that you can hand down like an old garment, pass on like a germ, spread like a rumor, or impose like a code of dress or etiquette. Nor is it a collection of disassociated beliefs—'attitudes' is the favored jargon among American social scientists and the historians they have mesmerized—that you can extract from their context and measure by current or retrospective survey research. . . . Nor is it a Frankenstein's monster that takes on a life of its own."

Instead, Fields continues, "people deduce and verify their ideology in daily life" (Fields, "Slavery, Race, and Ideology in the United States of America," 135).

CHAPTER 1

1   Goldstein, "Flourishing Underground," 5.
2   Goldstein, "Flourishing Underground," 5.
3   Goldstein, "Flourishing Underground," 34.
4   Goldstein, "Flourishing Underground," 34.
5   Goldstein, "Flourishing Underground," 34.
6   Goldstein, "Flourishing Underground," 34.
7   Goldstein, "Flourishing Underground," 34.
8   Gleason, "Dead Like Live Thunder," 31. See also Gleason's discussion of the contemporary dance scene in his book *The Jefferson Airplane and the San Francisco Sound*, 3ff.
9   Gleason, "Dead Like Live Thunder," 31.
10 Journalist Tom Wolfe provided some of the earliest accounts of the band performing as part of the Acid Tests in *The Electric Kool-Aid Acid Test* (1968). Representative excerpts from Wolfe's book are reproduced in Dodd and Spaulding, *Grateful Dead Reader*, 5–7.
11 Gleason, "Dead Like Live Thunder," 31.
12 For more on the band's improvisational practices, see Kaler, "How the Grateful Dead Learned to Jam"; Malvinni, *Grateful Dead and the Art of Rock Improvisation*. See also Olsson, *Listening for the Secret*, along with many of the essays in Tuedio and Spector, *Grateful Dead in Concert*.
13 From an interview with Garcia from 1967 originally published in Gleason, *The Jefferson Airplane and the San Francisco Sound*, 308–309.
14 Sculatti, "San Francisco Bay Rock," 25.
15 Sculatti, "San Francisco Bay Rock," 25. Along with "In the Midnight Hour," "Everybody Needs Somebody to Love" was another popular record for Pickett.
16 Sculatti, "San Francisco Bay Rock," 25.
17 Butler, "Clash of the Timbres," 279.

18 Goldstein, "Flourishing Underground," 5.

19 Goldstein, "Flourishing Underground," 5.

20 Goldstein, "Flourishing Underground," 34. Of course, Goldstein is referring to the Haight-Ashbury district, the symbolic crossroads of the San Francisco countercultural scene. Between 1965 and 1968, members of the Dead occupied a house at 710 Ashbury Street.

21 Reflecting the enduring rivalry between the two cities, band biographer Dennis McNally has remarked that the "sound of ["The Golden Road"], recorded in San Francisco, was vastly superior to the sound of the material [the Dead] recorded in Los Angeles" (McNally, *Long Strange Trip*, 182).

22 From an interview originally conducted in February or early March 1967 by Randy Groenke and Mike Cramer and later published as "One Afternoon, Long Ago . . . : A Previously Unpublished Interview with Jerry Garcia, 1967," 27.

23 Available at "Grateful Dead Live at KMPX Radio Show on 1967-04-01," Internet Archive, April 1, 1967, https://archive.org/details/gd67-04-xx.prefm. vernon.9261.sbeok.shnf/gd67-04-XXd1t03.shn. Tom Donahue is often recognized as one of the pioneering figures of FM and "free form" radio programming beginning in the late 1960s. Shaugn O'Donnell considers the recordings selected by Garcia and Lesh during their appearance on Donahue's radio program in "American Chaos," 58–70.

24 Williams, "Golden Road," 8.

25 Williams, "Golden Road," 8 (emphasis in original). Regarding the version of "Viola Lee Blues" on *The Grateful Dead*, bassist Phil Lesh has noted that the "recording *almost* captures in ten minutes what used to take thirty or more" in live performances. See Lesh, *Searching for the Sound*, 99 (emphasis in original).

26 Goldstein, "Albumin," 19.

27 Smith's letter (along with the band's colorful response) is reproduced in Steve Silberman's liner notes to Grateful Dead, *Anthem of the Sun: 50th Anniversary Deluxe Edition*, 11.

28 On Healy's early experiences working in recording studios and his responsibilities as the Dead's live sound mixer, see "The Sound Ideas of Dan Healy."

29 Leigh, "Live Sound of the Grateful Dead," 19.

30 Leigh, "Live Sound of the Grateful Dead," 19.

31 Lesh, *Searching for the Sound*, 129.

32 For a unique perspective on segues within the band's live practices, see Holt, "Crowned Anarchy."

33 In what follows I will be referring to the mix that appears on the original release of *Anthem of the Sun* from 1968. In 1971, the band and Warner Bros. re-released the album with a significantly different mix. Both mixes are included on Grateful Dead, *Anthem of the Sun: 50th Anniversary Deluxe Edition*.

34 For more details on the making of *Anthem of the Sun*, see Lesh, *Searching for the Sound*, 125ff.; Jackson, *Grateful Dead Gear*, 60ff. See also the discussions and demonstrations by Lesh and Healy in *The Grateful Dead: Anthem to Beauty*.

35 Lesh and Constanten shared an affinity for music and composers of the postwar avant-garde. On Lesh's avant-garde proclivities, see *Searching for*

the Sound; Wood, "Musical Imagination of Phil Lesh." See also Constanten, *Between Rock and Hard Places.*

36 "The Grateful Dead, *Anthem of the Sun*," 4.

37 Miller, "[Review] *Anthem of the Sun*, The Grateful Dead (Warner Brothers WS 1749)," 28. All subsequent citations are to this source.

38 Gracyk, *Rhythm and Noise*, 81.

39 Gracyk, *Rhythm and Noise*, 82.

40 Gracyk, *Rhythm and Noise*, 82.

41 From an interview with Garcia included in *The Grateful Dead: Anthem to Beauty.*

42 Lesh, *Searching for the Sound*, 130.

43 The 8-track recordings that were produced at the Shrine Auditorium were used in the production of *Two from the Vault* released in 1992. See the discussion in chapter 5.

44 See Jackson, *Grateful Dead Gear*, 74ff.

45 McNally, *Long Strange Trip*, 283.

46 McNally, *Long, Strange Trip*, 301.

47 Christgau, "Grateful Dead Are Rising Again," D22.

48 Lydon, "Grateful Dead," 18.

49 Lydon, "Grateful Dead," 22.

50 Gleason, "[Review] 'Live/Dead' (Warner Bros. 1830)," 63. Gleason also commends the album as "attractively programmed and mixed."

51 Kaye, "[Review] *Live Dead*, the Grateful Dead," 44.

52 Williams, "[Review] Grateful Dead: 'Live Dead' (Warner Bros.)," 28. No doubt influenced by the reception of *Live/Dead*, the Grateful Dead played their first shows in England in May 1970.

53 The band tries to smooth over this break in the musical continuity as the fade-out on the end of side 1 ("Dark Star") is answered by an overlapping fade-in on side 2 (beginning with "St. Stephen").

54 Kaye, "[Review] *Live Dead*, the Grateful Dead," 44.

55 black shadow, "[Review] *Live/Dead* (Grateful Dead)," 14.

56 Information on tracking is presented in Jackson, *Grateful Dead Gear*, 80–81. Stage microphones do pick up some crowd noise; refer especially to the performance of "Turn on Your Lovelight."

57 In the analysis that follows, I will be referring to the original LP release of Grateful Dead, *Live/Dead* (2WS 1830 Warner Bros. Records, 1969).

58 black shadow, "[Review] *Live/Dead* (Grateful Dead)," 14. My examination of "Dark Star" ends approximately where Graeme M. Boone begins his analysis of the same recorded performance. See his "Tonal and Expressive Ambiguity in 'Dark Star,'" 171–210. Written by Robert Hunter and first played live in 1968, "Dark Star" quickly became one of the band's most enduring vehicles for live improvisation and an audience favorite. For an extended discussion of the song, see Malvinni, *Grateful Dead and the Art of Rock Improvisation*, especially chapters 3 and 4. Compared with the original LP release, some reissues of *Live/Dead* feature an even longer prelude leading into "Dark Star." For

a comparison of the different mixes of "Dark Star" on the various releases of *Live/Dead*, see "Dark Star: A Tale of Four Mixes," *Grateful Dead Guide*, January 11, 2017, http://deadessays.blogspot.com/2017/01/dark-star-tale-of-four-mixes.html.

59 In addition to his work with the Dead at this time, Jerry Garcia also played pedal steel in the country rock band New Riders of the Purple Sage. Garcia and Mickey Hart appear on the New Riders' eponymous debut album released in 1971.

60 For more on Alembic, see Jackson, *Grateful Dead Gear*, 85–91.

61 Matthews quoted in Jackson, *Grateful Dead Gear*, 100.

62 Gilmore, "New Dawn of the Grateful Dead," 55.

63 Zwerling, "[Review] *Workingman's Dead*, Grateful Dead," 32.

64 Kreutzmann with Eisen, *Deal*, 137.

65 After refusing to issue the album under the title that the band had suggested ("Skullfuck"), Warner Bros. released the album as *Grateful Dead*. Not to be confused with the band's debut studio album (*The Grateful Dead*), the popular title (*Skull and Roses*) refers to the distinctive cover art designed by Alton Kelley and Stanley Mouse.

66 Kreutzmann with Eisen, *Deal*, 142.

67 Kreutzmann with Eisen, *Deal*, 142.

68 Kreutzmann with Eisen, *Deal*, 142.

69 Unlike *Live/Dead*, *Skull and Roses* was not pressed to accommodate automatic sequencing.

70 In what follows, I am referring to the mix of the original LP release of Grateful Dead, *Grateful Dead* (2WS 1935 Warner Bros. Records, 1971).

71 Jackson, *Grateful Dead Gear*, 119. See also Betty Cantor's recollections on the recording process for *Europe '72* in Getz and Dwork, *Deadhead's Taping Compendium*, 2:7.

72 For a detailed account of the various overdubs, alterations, and edits made in postproduction, see Seachrist, "*Europe '72*."

73 In what follows, I am considering the original LP release of Grateful Dead, *Europe '72* (3 WX 2668 Warner Bros. Records, 1972).

74 From a promotional letter dated October 25, 1972, included in Grateful Dead Records: Business Records. MS 332, ser. 2, box 12, folder 9 ("#3WX 2668 *Europe '72*"), Special Collections and Archives, University Library, University of California, Santa Cruz.

75 Kaye, "[Review] Grateful Dead, *Grateful Dead*," 56.

76 Kaye, "[Review] Grateful Dead, *Grateful Dead*," 55.

77 Kaye, "[Review] Grateful Dead, *Grateful Dead*," 56.

78 Kaye, "[Review] Grateful Dead, *Grateful Dead*," 56.

79 Snyder-Scumpy, "[Review] *Europe '72*," 73.

80 Snyder-Scumpy, "[Review] *Europe '72*," 73.

81 Snyder-Scumpy, "[Review] *Europe '72*," 74.

82 For more on his philosophy of sound, see the interview with Bear in Getz and Dwork, *Deadhead's Taping Compendium*, 1:38–45. See also Greenfield, *Bear*.

In addition to his work with the Dead, Bear also produced recordings for a number of other artists and groups, including the Allman Brothers Band, Tim Buckley, Doc and Merle Watson, and Johnny Cash. Bear's sound-board recordings—what he referred to as "sonic journals"—are part of an archive that is maintained by the Owsley Stanley Foundation, a nonprofit organization dedicated to preserving Bear's extensive collection of original analog tapes. For more information (including commercially available recordings), see the website of the Owsley Stanley Foundation, https://owsleystanleyfoundation.org/ (accessed September 10, 2022).

CHAPTER 2

1   Although the group had not released a studio album under the name Grateful Dead since *American Beauty* (1970), many band members appeared on recordings that were marketed by Warner Bros. as solo projects, including Jerry Garcia's *Garcia* (1972), Mickey Hart's *Rolling Thunder* (1972), and Bob Weir's *Ace* (1972).
2   Crowe, "Grateful Dead Flee Big Business," 26.
3   Crowe, "Grateful Dead Flee Big Business," 26. For a contemporary overview of the band's expanding business organization (including the publishing division, road crew, fan club, and a travel agency), see Perry, "New Life for the Dead."
4   Crowe, "Grateful Dead Flee Big Business," 26.
5   Dead Heads Newsletter, June 1973, Grateful Dead Records: Business Records. MS 332, ser. 2, box 107, folder 19 ("Dead Heads Newsletter [May] June 1973"), Special Collections and Archives, University Library, University of California, Santa Cruz.
6   Perry, "Alembic."
7   Dead Heads Newsletter, December 1974, Grateful Dead Records: Business Records. MS 332, ser. 2, box 108, folders 1–2 ("Dead Heads Newsletter, December 1974"), Special Collections and Archives, University Library, University of California, Santa Cruz. For a more detailed examination of the Wall of Sound, see Reeder, "Co-evolution of Improvised Rock and Live Sound," esp. 285ff.
8   From an interview with Weir, keyboardist Keith Godchaux, vocalist Donna Jean Godchaux, and manager Jon McIntire originally broadcast on WAER-FM (Syracuse, New York), September 17, 1973, accessed September 15, 2022, https://www.gdao.org/items/show/378883.
9   McNally, *Long Strange Trip*, 385.
10 Shenk and Silberman, *Skeleton Key*, 280.
11 Getz and Dwork, *Deadhead's Taping Compendium*, 1:xi (emphasis in original).
12 This exchange can be heard before the performance of "Sugar Magnolia" at "Grateful Dead Live at Winterland Arena on 1970-12-31," Internet Archive, December 31, 1970, https://archive.org/details/gd70-12-31.sbd-fm.7283.sbeok.shnf/gd70-12-31d1to9.shn.
13 For more on the emerging bootleg industry at the dawn of the rock era, see Cummings, *Democracy of Sound*, 95ff. See also Heylin, *Bootleg!*, esp. 32ff.

14 Heylin, *Bootleg!*, 49.

15 Marcus, "Bootleg LP's," 38.

16 Marcus, "Bootleg LP's," 38.

17 For a contemporary account of these releases, see Fong-Torres, "Not-So-Good Old Dead Records," 12. Nicholas Meriwether examines the circumstances surrounding the release of *Vintage Dead* and *Historic Dead* in Getz and Dwork, *Deadhead's Taping Compendium*, 1:114–16.

18 From Cohen's liner notes included on Grateful Dead, *Vintage Dead* (SUN-5001 Sunflower, 1970). All subsequent citations are to this source.

19 Here Cohen is citing a quote from Garcia that appears in Leigh, "Live Sound of the Grateful Dead," 19.

20 Reich and Wenner, "Jerry Garcia," 32 (emphasis in original). The complete unabridged interview appears in Garcia, Reich, and Wenner, *Garcia*.

21 See the many stories recounted in Getz and Dwork, *Deadhead's Taping Compendium*, 1:33ff.

22 The exchange can be heard at "Grateful Dead Live at Temple University on 1970-05-16," Internet Archive, May 16, 1970, https://archive.org/details/gd70-05-16.aud.weiner.14769.sbeok.shnf/gd70-05-16t06.shn.

23 The exchange can be heard following the performance of "Bertha" at "Grateful Dead Live at Hollywood Palladium on 1971-08-06," Internet Archive, August 6, 1971, https://archive.org/details/gd71-08-06.aud.bertrando.yerys.129.sbeok.shnf/gd08-06-71d1t01.shn.

24 Katzenjammer, "Grateful Dead Pig Backlash," 15 (emphasis in original). All subsequent citations are to this source. Katzenjammer is referring to a bootleg recording of a concert from October 4, 1970 that was broadcast on radio stations in San Francisco. Recordings of the radio broadcasts were used in the production of this well-known bootleg record. For more on the history of this recording, see "Tag Archives: Grateful Dead Winterland 1970-10-04 Bootlegs," The Amazing Kornyfone Label, July 15, 2018, https://theamazingkornyfonelabel.wordpress.com/tag/grateful-dead-winterland-1970-10-04-bootlegs/.

25 The phrase "Dead Freak" emerged in the late 1960s to refer to the band's fans. In the liner notes accompanying *Skull and Roses*, for example, the band urged "DEAD FREAKS [to] UNITE." The phrase "Dead Heads" also appears in these notes. By the mid-1970s, the phrase "Dead Head" (or "Deadhead") had infiltrated popular culture and was commonly used to refer to the group's loyal fans.

26 Rosen, "Mr. 'Tapes' of Brooklyn," 22.

27 Getz and Dwork provide an informative overview of the early community of tapers and traders in *Deadhead's Taping Compendium*, 1:19–37. For more background, see Nash, "Grateful Tapers"; Cummings, *Democracy of Sound*, 156ff.

28 Kippel, "History of Taping through the Eyes of One Deadhead," 122.

29 In the earliest days of trading, it was quite possible that, within the relatively small community of collectors, a tape received in a trade had been recorded directly from the original master recording or from a tape that was one or two "generations" removed from the master. Before the advent of digital

recording technologies, tapes whose "genealogies" could be traced more directly to the original master recordings were valued for their sound quality and for their imagined spatiotemporal proximity to the originating event (i.e., the concert). For more on the significance of tape genealogies and generations among traders and collectors, see Harvey, "Embalming the Dead," 100ff.

30 Stewart, *On Longing*, 135.

31 Stewart, *On Longing*, 135.

32 Stewart, *On Longing*, 135.

33 Stewart, *On Longing*, 135.

34 Stewart, *On Longing*, 135.

35 Stewart, *On Longing*, 150.

36 Marshall, "For and against the Record Industry," 60.

37 Marshall, "For and against the Record Industry," 69.

38 Marshall, "For and against the Record Industry," 70.

39 Neumann and Simpson, "Smuggled Sound," 333. Neumann and Simpson also draw on Stewart's critical interpretation of the souvenir when considering the proximity of the bootleg to the "authentic"/"authenticating" live event.

40 The Grateful Dead were known for playing very long concerts. At the same time, they were notorious for taking a long time between songs as they tuned, adjusted levels and knobs, and decided what song to play next (and then taking the time to remember/relearn that song). To preserve precious tape, some tapers would stop recording between songs. As a result, it is not uncommon that, among many audience recordings, the openings of some songs are missing as tapers scrambled to turn on their tape machines when the band finally decided to resume playing. To be certain, most (if not all) of what had been recorded between songs was edited from the majority of audience and soundboard recordings that subsequently circulated among traders.

41 Marshall, "For and against the Record Industry," 66. Drawing on the sociological work of Marcel Mauss and Bronislaw Malinowski, Katie Harvey considers the place of tapes within an economy of the "gift." See Harvey, "Embalming the Dead," especially 89ff.

42 Daniel Cavicchi makes a similar observation regarding the community of tapers and collectors devoted to Bruce Springsteen in *Tramps Like Us*, 75.

43 Text included on the mailing label to *Dead Relix* 1, no. 1 (November/December 1974).

44 Marshall, "For and against the Record Industry," 66. Nadya Zimmerman considers the band's ambiguous relation to idea(l)s of anticommercialism in "Consuming Nature."

45 Harvey, "Embalming the Dead," 91.

46 Getz and Dwork, *The Deadhead's Taping Compendium*, 1:22.

47 Marshall, "For and against the Record Industry," 65.

48 In this regard, I am considering the tapers as products of the "psychedelic America" examined in Jarnow, *Heads*. In particular, see Jarnow's account of Kippel and other early tapers in *Heads*, 67ff.

49 Rosen, "Mr. 'Tapes' of Brooklyn," 22.

50 Rosen, "Mr. 'Tapes' of Brooklyn," 22.

51 The following quotes are drawn from a note written by David Parker to Jon McIntire dated November 29, 1972, included in Grateful Dead Records: Business Records. MS 332, ser. 2, box 106, folder 3 ("Business: Free Underground Tape Exchange: 1972–1988"), Special Collections and Archives, University Library, University of California, Santa Cruz.

52 A copy of Kippel's proposal is included in Grateful Dead Records: Business Records. MS 332, ser. 2, box 106, folder 3 ("Business: Free Underground Tape Exchange: 1972–1988"), Special Collections and Archives, University Library, University of California, Santa Cruz. In the following notes, I will refer to this document as the Dead Relics Proposal.

53 Dead Relics Proposal, 7.

54 Dead Relics Proposal, 13.

55 Dead Relics Proposal, 15.

56 Dead Relics Proposal, 19.

57 Dead Relics Proposal, 19.

58 By 1976, the Dead had consolidated their business operations under the name Grateful Dead Productions (GDP). Before Brown became an employee of GDP, he was already respected among tapers and tape collectors for having recorded one of the band's most celebrated early concerts, a performance on a flatbed truck in front of thousands of people crammed into Haight Street in San Francisco on March 3, 1968.

59 The handwritten documents reproduced in figures 2.2 and 2.3 are included in the Steve Brown Papers, MS 338, box 2, folder 1 ("Archive Releases: Notes"), Special Collections and Archives, University Library, University of California, Santa Cruz. Garcia's second solo release is sometimes referred to as "Compliments" or "Compliments of Garcia."

60 The organization's earnings from record sales were also significantly affected by the appearance of counterfeit copies of Wake of the Flood. See McNally, Long Strange Trip, 460.

61 McNally, Long Strange Trip, 481.

62 Lesh, Searching for the Sound, 223.

63 Walters, "[Review] Steal Your Face, Grateful Dead," 60.

64 Jackson, "Record Review: Steal Your Face," 5. All subsequent citations are to this source.

65 Young, "Awakening of the Dead," 11–12.

66 Young, "Awakening of the Dead," 12.

67 Getz and Dwork, Deadhead's Taping Compendium, 1:37.

68 Getz and Dwork, Deadhead's Taping Compendium, 1:37.

CHAPTER 3

1 Davis with DeCurtis, Soundtrack of My Life, 244–45. In an earlier memoir, Davis describes meeting with members of the Dead in 1972 in an effort to lure the band from Warner Bros. to Columbia Records. As Davis quickly realized,

the Dead were not entirely serious about signing with Columbia but instead were using him to learn more about the recording industry as they prepared to form their own label. See Davis with Willwerth, *Clive*, 186–88.

2   Hart quoted in McNally, *Long Strange Trip*, 495.

3   Davis with DeCurtis, *Soundtrack of My Life*, 245.

4   Lesh, *Searching for the Sound*, 251.

5   See McNally, *Long Strange Trip*, 531ff. Refer also to the "Bonus" episode of "The Good Ol' Grateful Deadcast" titled "Dead Behind/Dead Ahead," Dead .net, accessed September 16, 2022, https://www.dead.net/deadcast/bonus -dead-behind-dead-ahead.

6   "Grateful Dead Live at Folsom Field, U. of Colorado on 1980-06-08," Internet Archive, June 8, 1980, https://archive.org/details/gd80-06-08.eaton. tome.7193.sbefail.shnf/gd80-06-08d1t01.shn.

7   For an informative discussion on how the concerts from September and October were engineered and recorded, see the interview with Don Pearson in Getz and Dwork, *Deadhead's Taping Compendium*, 2:19ff. Pearson was an engineer on these recordings, and, while this was the first time he had assisted on a live recording, he would continue to work as a member of the Dead's sound crew for many years.

8   Gary Lambert considers the Dead's acoustic sets in relation to their "deep folk roots." See his liner notes included with Grateful Dead, *Reckoning*. For a more extensive examination of the influence of folk traditions and related styles on the music and songwriting of the Dead, see Carr, "Black Muddy River."

9   Writing in *Rolling Stone* in 1970, Michael Lydon described how the band had "created a unique musical experience" with their recent concerts, an experience "which they call, rather formally, An Evening with the Grateful Dead." See Lydon, "An Evening with the Grateful Dead," 23.

10 Grateful Dead Records: Business Records. MS 332, ser. 2, box 137, folder 14 ("Business Meeting Minutes 1977, 1980"), Special Collections and Archives, University Library, University of California, Santa Cruz. All subsequent citations are to this source.

    Loren may have come up with the idea of the Dead playing "on Broadway" shortly after the band's concerts in Colorado. As detailed in documents provided by Betty Cantor-Jackson in 1982, Loren approached her in June 1980 about recording "three to seven days at a theatre on Broadway in New York." Grateful Dead Records: Business Records. MS 332, ser. 2, box 133, folder 15 ("Business: Legal: GD Productions—Pending + Proposals 1981–1983"), Special Collections and Archives, University Library, University of California, Santa Cruz.

11 The amended contract with Arista is included in Grateful Dead Records: Business Records. MS 332, ser. 2, box 133, folder 11 ("Business: Legal: Arista Record Contract 1976–1988"), Special Collections and Archives, University Library, University of California, Santa Cruz. Along with economic considerations, the change of venue can be attributed to a "turf war" between concert promoters John Scher (who represented the Dead) and Ron Delsener (who booked the Uris Theatre). See Scher's angry letter to Delsener dated September 15, 1980, in

Grateful Dead Records: Show Files. MS 332, ser. 3, box 9, folder 9 ("Radio City Music Hall, New York, NY, Oct. 22–31, 1980 - Productions"), Special Collections and Archives, University Library, University of California, Santa Cruz.

12   "Survivors: Grateful Fans Camp Out for Tickets," 9.

13   From notes included in Grateful Dead Records: Business Records. MS 332, ser. 2, box 137, folder 14 ("Business Meeting Minutes 1977, 1980"), Special Collections and Archives, University Library, University of California, Santa Cruz. These notes may have been written by Rock Scully, another manager for the band.

Although there is no date listed, this document appears to be from a meeting that probably took place in early or mid-December. On December 8, the musician and songwriter John Lennon was shot and killed in New York City. As seen in the upper right-hand corner of figure 3.1, the phrase "Lennon Lives" is written underneath the Skeleton Jester, an image the band had adopted as a logo for their record company.

14   Curiously, Tom Constanten, Donna Jean Godchaux, and Keith Godchaux do not appear in any of the photographs.

15   Live performances of "El Paso," "Heaven Help the Fool," "Iko Iko," "Little Sadie," and "Sage and Spirit" are included as "Bonus Material" on the expanded reissue of *Reckoning* released in 2006.

16   Quoted in Getz and Dwork, *Deadhead's Taping Compendium*, 2:20.

17   Getz and Dwork, *Deadhead's Taping Compendium*, 2:20–21.

18   Grateful Dead Records: Business Records. MS 332, ser. 2, box 133, folder 11 ("Business: Legal: Arista Record Contract 1976–1988"), Special Collections and Archives, University Library, University of California, Santa Cruz (emphasis in original). All subsequent citations are to this source.

19   Darling, "Music Monitor," 30.

20   Darling, "Music Monitor," 30.

21   Wadsley, "Video Possibilities Are Mulled," 38.

22   Wadsley, "Video Possibilities Are Mulled," 38.

23   Kopp, "Grateful Dead in Concert Due on RCA Videodisk," 56.

24   Kopp, "Grateful Dead in Concert Due on RCA Videodisk," 56.

25   For an early overview of RCA's videodisc technology and competing formats and systems, see Schuyten, "RCA Videodisks Due in 1981." Adding to RCA's concerns about its unique videodisc technology, Steve Knoll reported in early 1981 that there currently were no pressing facilities for the SelectaVision system (see Knoll, "Majors Face 'Pressing' Problem"). A photocopy of Knoll's article appears among the extant materials relating to the various video projects the Dead were producing at the time. Included on the photocopy is a note to "Send [to] J. Scher." Grateful Dead Records: Business Records. MS 332, ser. 2, box 31, folder 17 ("Business: Radio City Music Hall Video—Showtime Broadcast 1981"), Special Collections and Archives, University Library, University of California, Santa Cruz.

26   Multiple sheets with proposed song sequences and timings are included among the extant materials relating to these various video projects. See

Grateful Dead Records: Business Records. MS 332, ser. 2, box 31, folder 14 ("Business: Radio City Music Hall Video—Editing 1980/1982"), Special Collections and Archives, University Library, University of California, Santa Cruz.

27 Lesh, *Searching for the Sound*, 259.

28 Lesh, *Searching for the Sound*, 259–60.

29 For more details, see the entry on *The Grateful Dead Hour* in Schenk and Silberman, *Skeleton Key*, 122–24.

30 Business Meeting Minutes, September 5, 1984, Grateful Dead Records: Business Records. MS 332, ser. 2, box 137, folder 15 ("Business: Meeting Minutes—notes by Garcia 1981, 1983–1986, n.d."), Special Collections and Archives, University Library, University of California, Santa Cruz. All subsequent citations are to this source.

31 Grateful Dead Records: Business Records. MS 332, ser. 2, box 137, folder 17 ("Business: Office: Meeting Minutes 1984 October–December"), Special Collections and Archives, University Library, University of California, Santa Cruz (emphasis in original). All subsequent citations are to this source.

32 Business Meeting Minutes, November 30, 1984, Grateful Dead Records: Business Records. MS 332, ser. 2, box 137, folder 15 ("Business: Office: Meeting Minutes—notes by Garcia 1981, 1983–1986, n.d."), Special Collections and Archives, University Library, University of California, Santa Cruz.

33 Schenk and Silberman, *Skeleton Key*, 278.

34 Business Meeting Minutes, September 17, 1984, Grateful Dead Records: Business Records. MS 332, ser. 2, box 137, folder 16 ("Business: Office: Meeting Minutes 1984 June–September"), Special Collections and Archives, University Library, University of California, Santa Cruz.

35 McDonough, "The Dead Are Anything But," 22.

36 McDonough, "The Dead Are Anything But," 22.

37 McDonough, "The Dead Are Anything But," 25.

CHAPTER 4

1 Grateful Dead Records: Business Records. MS 332, ser. 2, box 133, folder 11 ("Business: Legal: Arista Record Contract 1976–1988"), Special Collections and Archives, University Library, University of California, Santa Cruz. All subsequent citations are to this source.

2 Davis with DeCurtis, *Soundtrack of My Life*, 245.

3 Davis with DeCurtis, *Soundtrack of My Life*, 245.

4 For an informative and entertaining account of the many crew members responsible for recording the Dead's concerts, refer to the "Bonus" episode of "The Good Ol' Grateful Deadcast" titled "Inside the Vault," accessed September 17, 2022, https://www.dead.net/deadcast/bonus-inside-vault.

5 For more on Cantor-Jackson and the many roles she performed in crafting and capturing the band's recorded legacy, see the interview in Getz and Dwork, *Deadhead's Taping Compendium*, 2:5–18. See also the chapter devoted to Cantor-Jackson in Harvey, "Embalming the Dead," 122ff.

6　On the various formats that the crew used to record the band's concerts, see the interview with Dick Latvala in Getz and Dwork, *Deadhead's Taping Compendium*, 1:45–51. See also the interview with Don Pearson in Getz and Dwork, *Deadhead's Taping Compendium*, 2:19–27. The Dead's longtime sound engineer Jeffrey Norman also details the many formats in Getz and Dwork, *Deadhead's Taping Compendium*, 3:3–11.

7　Grateful Dead Records: Business Records. MS 332, ser. 2, box 106, folder 3 ("Business: Free Underground Tape Exchange 1972–1988"), Special Collections and Archives, University Library, University of California, Santa Cruz (emphases in original). All subsequent citations are to this source.

8　Getz and Dwork, *Deadhead's Taping Compendium*, 2:18.

9　Business Meeting Minutes, August 3, 1984, Grateful Dead Records: Business Records. MS 332, ser. 2, box 137, folder 15 ("Business: Meeting Minutes—notes by Garcia 1981, 1983–1986, n.d."), Special Collections and Archives, University Library, University of California, Santa Cruz. All subsequent citations are to this source.

10　Business Meeting Minutes, May 2, 1985, Grateful Dead Records: Business Records. MS 332, ser. 2, box 137, folder 15 ("Business: Meeting Minutes—notes by Garcia 1981, 1983–1986, n.d."), Special Collections and Archives, University Library, University of California, Santa Cruz. All subsequent citations are to this source.

11　These documents are contained in Grateful Dead Records: Business Records. MS 332, ser. 2, box 133, folder 15 ("Business: Legal: GD Productions—Pending + Proposals (1981–1983)"), Special Collections and Archives, University Library, University of California, Santa Cruz. All subsequent citations are to this source.

12　Ressner, "Stellar Slate of LPs Set for Release," 20.

13　McNally, *Long Strange Trip*, 548.

14　McNally, *Long Strange Trip*, 548–49.

15　Arista rereleased *Reckoning* in 1984. Without any new material to promote, however, Arista (in a not-so-subtle dig at the Dead) issued the rerelease under the title *For the Faithful*.

16　Davis with DeCurtis, *Soundtrack of My Life*, 248–49.

17　"Grateful Dead Live at Oakland-Alameda County Coliseum on 1986-12-15," Internet Archive, December 15, 1986, https://archive.org/details/gd86-12-15. nakcm101-dwonk.25263.sbeok.flacf/gd1986-12-15-dwonk-d1t01.flac.

18　Davis with DeCurtis, *Soundtrack of My Life*, 249.

19　"Grateful Dead, *In the Dark*," 12–13.

20　See Grein, "Whitney, Barry Share Multiplatinum," 6, 98.

21　See Morris, "CDs Sail Past LPs in $ Volume," 1, 84. As described in Morris's article, a 1986 survey by the National Association of Recording Merchandisers (NARM) predicted the "continuing market growth of the CD and a concurrent precipitous decline for the vinyl configuration" (1).

22　"Dead Is Alive," 23.

23　See the chart for "Top Compact Disks" in *Billboard*, August 29, 1987, 66.

24　Bessman, "Dead's Popularity Nudges Arista's Home Vid Launch," 50.

25 Freeman, "Outa' the Box," 10.

26 Gilmore, "New Dawn of the Grateful Dead," 50.

27 Gilmore, "New Dawn of the Grateful Dead," 50, 49.

28 Gilmore, "New Dawn of the Grateful Dead," 50.

29 McNally, *Long Strange Trip*, 564 (emphasis in original).

30 Grein, "On Charts, It's Summer of Love Again," 6 (emphasis in original).

31 Grein, "'La Bamba' Gives Valens His 1st No. 1 Hit," 6.

32 Dwork, "Seek and Ye Shall Find," 6. All subsequent citations are to this source.

33 Dwork's remark about having to "rely upon the band for old tapes" may have been a reference to recordings of previously unreleased live performances that were sometimes featured on the *Dead Head Hour* radio program. Although host David Gans did not work for the Dead, he had access to the vault and would often play archival recordings on the rechristened *Grateful Dead Hour*. Not surprisingly, many Deadheads routinely taped the weekly radio program. By the late 1980s, Gans's radio show, along with print publications such as *Relix*, *The Golden Road*, and *Dupree's Diamond News*, were important resources linking the community of tapers and tape traders.

34 Although details were still murky at the time, Dwork briefly describes the story behind the tapes in "Seek and Ye Shall Find," 6. See also Cantor-Jackson's remarks in Getz and Dwork, *Deadhead's Taping Compendium*, 2:16ff. For a more extensive account of the the Betty Boards, see Getz and Dwork, *Deadhead's Taping Compendium*, 3:33–41. See also Harvey, "Embalming the Dead," 129ff.; Paumgarten, "Deadhead." The story of the "discovery" of the Betty Boards in 1987 closely resembles the scenario involving the tapes that had "been rescued from unpaid storage" as discussed during a band meeting from 1984. Details of the Betty Boards, it would appear, are still murky.

35 Dwork, "Seek and Ye Shall Find," 6.

36 Dwork, "Seek and Ye Shall Find," 6.

37 Stewart, *On Longing*, 140. Referring to relics as "souvenirs of the dead," Stewart notes how "if the function of the souvenir proper is to create a continuous and personal narrative of the past, the function of such souvenirs of death [i.e., relics] is to disrupt and disclaim that continuity." Pertinent to the materialist story of liveness I have been telling, Stewart suggests that relics "are not so much a nostalgic celebration of the past as they are an erasure of the significance of history" (140).

38 Grateful Dead Records: Business Records. MS 332, ser. 2, box 134, folder 8 ("Business: Legal: New Record Contract Notes [Arista] 1988"), Special Collections and Archives, University Library, University of California, Santa Cruz. All subsequent citations are to this source.

39 See the interview with Pearson in Getz and Dwork, *Deadhead's Taping Compendium*, 2:24.

40 See Muhlberg, "Grateful Web Interview with Len Dell'Amico."

41 Flick, "Arista Execs Rise for the Dead," 26.

42 Flick, "Arista Execs Rise for the Dead," 26.

CHAPTER 5

1   Mayfield, "Over the Counter," 93.

2   For more on the concert and the history of the recordings, see Nicholas Meriwether's entry on August 13, 1975, in Getz and Dwork, *Deadhead's Taping Compendium*, 2:83–86. Even before the release of OFTV, Meriwether notes that "this performance was a seminal tape" among the band's fans (Getz and Dwork, *Deadhead's Taping Compendium*, 2:83). For more on the recorded history of the concert, see the blog post "August 13, 1975: Great American Music Hall, 859 O'Farrell Street, San Francisco, CA (FM IX)," *Lost Live Dead*, August 7, 2014, http://lostlivedead.blogspot.com/2014/08/august-13-1975-great-american-music.html.

3   The complete episode is available at "Grateful Dead Hour No. 130," Dead.net, January 22, 2009, https://www.dead.net/features/gd-radio-hour/grateful-dead-hour-no-130.The exchange begins at approximately 34:04. A transcript of the interview is available at "February 1991 Interview with Dan Healy," Cloud Surfing, accessed March 13, 2002, https://cloudsurfing.gdhour.com/archives/1451.

4   Brown, "Dan Healy, from the Vaults to the Pyramids," 18.

5   Brown, "Dan Healy, from the Vaults to the Pyramids," 18.

6   Brown, "Dan Healy, from the Vaults to the Pyramids," 18.

7   Brown, "Dan Healy, from the Vaults to the Pyramids," 18.

8   Brown, "Dan Healy, from the Vaults to the Pyramids," 17.

9   Brown, "Dan Healy, from the Vaults to the Pyramids," 17.

10 Brown, "Dan Healy, from the Vaults to the Pyramids," 19.

11 Brown, "Dan Healy, from the Vaults to the Pyramids," 19.

12 Brown, "Dan Healy, from the Vaults to the Pyramids," 19.

13 Brown, "Dan Healy, from the Vaults to the Pyramids," 19.

14 Brown, "Dan Healy, from the Vaults to the Pyramids," 19.

15 Brown, "Dan Healy, from the Vaults to the Pyramids," 19.

16 The following quotations are drawn from Pearson's liner notes included in Grateful Dead, *One from the Vault*.

17 The following quotations are drawn from the liner notes included in Grateful Dead, *Two from the Vault*.

18 Théberge, "'Sound' of Music," 99.

19 Théberge, "'Sound' of Music," 99.

20 In "Speaking of Sound," Thomas Porcello considers the functions and forms of language in the modern, "professionalized," recording studio.

21 Brown, "Dan Healy, from the Vaults to the Pyramids," 19.

22 Brown, "Dan Healy, from the Vaults to the Pyramids," 19.

23 Brown, "Dan Healy, from the Vaults to the Pyramids," 19.

24 Handwritten sheet ("Multi-Track Possibilities") included in Dick Latvala Papers, MS 333, box 15 ("Dead.Net, Dead.Net Central: shelf lists, notebooks 1978–1979, Dick's Picks files"), Special Collections and Archives, University Library, University of California, Santa Cruz. All subsequent citations are to this document.

25 Dwork, "DDN Interviews Dick Latvala," 11.

26 Jesse Jarnow considers Latvala within the culture and milieu of the Grateful Dead in *Heads*, 107–13.

27 From a letter that originally appeared in *Dead Relix* 2, no. 5 (September–October 1975): 1. Excerpts from Latvala's letter appear in Brown, Abraham, and Munson, *Relix, the Book*, 7.

28 Dwork, "DDN Interviews Dick Latvala," 11.

29 From a notebook identified as "Shelf List #1, 7" Reels" included as part of the Dick Latvala Papers, MS 333, box 15 ("Dead.Net, Dead.Net Central: shelf lists, notebooks 1978–1979, Dick's Picks files"), Special Collections and Archives, University Library, University of California, Santa Cruz.

30 The date of the earliest note (September 19, 1992) is approximately one month after Jerry Garcia suffered another significant health crisis. Recalling similar circumstances from 1986, the band was forced to cancel their fall tour while Garcia recovered.

31 The following quotes are drawn from Dennis McNally's press release for *Dick's Picks, Volume One*. Grateful Dead Records: Business Records. MS 332, ser. 2, box 143, folder 10 ("Volume 1—Production 1993"), Special Collections and Archives, University Library, University of California, Santa Cruz.

32 Harvey, "Embalming the Dead," 94.

33 From an entry included as part of the Dick Latvala Papers, MS 333, box 1, folder 5 ("1973 Entries"), Special Collections and Archives, University Library, University of California, Santa Cruz.

34 From an interview with Norman included in Getz and Dwork, *Deadhead's Taping Compendium*, 3:5–6. Bassist Phil Lesh also participated in the *Dick's Picks* project for a short time. After being informed that his exceedingly high standards and tendency to veto proposed recordings were delaying the release of new volumes in the series, Lesh agreed to step back from the project.

35 Getz and Dwork, *Deadhead's Taping Compendium*, 3:6.

36 Getz and Dwork, *Deadhead's Taping Compendium*, 3:6.

37 Dwork, "DDN Interviews Dick Latvala," 13.

38 Dwork, "DDN Interviews Dick Latvala," 11.

39 Dwork, "DDN Interviews Dick Latvala," 12.

40 Peter Richardson examines the early community around the WELL (the Whole Earth 'Lectronic Link) in *No Simple Highway*, 264–67. See also Shenk and Silberman, *Skeleton Key*, 312–14.

41 The following references are drawn from Dennis McNally's press release for *Dick's Picks, Volume Five* available at Grateful Dead Records: Business Records. MS 332, ser. 2, box 143, folder 14 ("Volume 5–1996"), Special Collections and Archives, University Library, University of California, Santa Cruz.

42 Dwork, "DDN Interviews Dick Latvala," 11.

43 Dwork, "DDN Interviews Dick Latvala," 11–12.

44 Dwork, "DDN Interviews Dick Latvala," 12.

45 Dwork, "Keeper of the Flame," 21.

46 Dwork, "Keeper of the Flame," 21 (emphasis in original).

47 Dwork, "Keeper of the Flame," 23.
48 Dwork, "Keeper of the Flame," 21.
49 Dwork, "Keeper of the Flame," 22.
50 Dwork, "Keeper of the Flame," 21.
51 Dwork, "Keeper of the Flame," 21.
52 Dwork, "Keeper of the Flame," 21.
53 Dwork, "Keeper of the Flame," 22.
54 Dwork, "Keeper of the Flame," 21.
55 Dwork, "Keeper of the Flame," 21.

CHAPTER 6

1 Foege, "Funeral for a Friend," 24.
2 Foege, "Funeral for a Friend," 24.
3 Foege, "Funeral for a Friend," 28.
4 Notes relating to "Grateful Dead Productions, Inc." dated August 14, 1995. Grateful Dead Records: Business Records. MS 332, ser. 2, box 138, folder 2 ("Business: Meeting Minutes, 1995"), Special Collections and Archives, University Library, University of California, Santa Cruz (emphases in original). All subsequent citations are to this source.
5 Minutes from a shareholders meeting dated August 14, 1995. Grateful Dead Records: Business Records. MS 332, ser. 2, box 138, folder 2 ("Business: Meeting Minutes, 1995"), Special Collections and Archives, University Library, University of California, Santa Cruz. All subsequent citations are to this source.
6 In 2000, the Dead also began to release archival video footage as part of a series called *View from the Vault*. Between 2000 and 2003, the Dead (in conjunction with Monterey Video) released four volumes as part of the series, each featuring multidisc DVDs documenting select concerts from the late 1980s and 1990s.
7 Minutes from a band meeting dated August 14, 1995. Grateful Dead Records: Business Records. MS 332, ser. 2, box 138, folder 2 ("Business: Meeting Minutes, 1995"), Special Collections and Archives, University Library, University of California, Santa Cruz. All subsequent citations are to this source.
8 Meriwether, "The Dead Play Egypt," 132.
9 Harvey, "Embalming the Dead," 89.
10 McNally, *Long Strange Trip*, 385.
11 Shenk and Silberman, *Skeleton Key*, 280.
12 The essay is reprinted in Benjamin, *Illuminations*, 1.
13 Benjamin, *Illuminations*, 2.
14 Benjamin, *Illuminations*, 2–3.
15 Benjamin, *Illuminations*, 10.
16 Turkle, *Evocative Objects*, 5.
17 Turkle, *Evocative Objects*, 5.
18 Stewart, *On Longing*, ix.

19   Roy, *Media, Materiality and Memory*, 2.

20   Roy, *Media, Materiality and Memory*, 7.

21   Barlow, "Selling Wine Without Bottles," 11.

22   From the "About" page of the EFF, accessed September 20, 2022, https://www.eff.org/about.

23   Barlow, "Selling Wine Without Bottles," 9.

24   Barlow, "Selling Wine Without Bottles," 10.

25   Barlow, "Selling Wine Without Bottles," 10.

26   Barlow, "Selling Wine Without Bottles," 8.

27   Barlow, "Selling Wine Without Bottles," 21.

28   Barlow, "Selling Wine Without Bottles," 21.

29   Barlow, "Selling Wine Without Bottles," 22.

30   From a forum post by Matthew Vernon, "Brief History of the GDIAP Project to Hopefully Clarify Some Misunderstandings," Internet Archive, November 30, 2005, https://archive.org/post/49431/briefhistory-of-%20the-gdiap-project-to-hopefully-clarify-some-misunderstandings. All subsequent citations are to this source.
       The site's emphasis on "lossless" file types (notably .shn) reflects longstanding concerns among traders and collectors regarding the sound quality, format, and lineage of recordings. For more on file types and online sharing practices, see Harvey, "Embalming the Dead," 160ff.

31   Burnett, "Colliding Norms," 698.

32   The posting can be found at "Grateful Dead Concert Recordings on the Internet Archive," Internet Archive, November 30, 2005, https://archive.org/post/47634/grateful-dead-concert-recordings-on-the-internet-archive.

33   On the response of fans, see Burnett, "Colliding Norms." See also Berg, "On the Removal of Download Access to Grateful Dead Soundboards."

34   Burnett, "Colliding Norms," 699.

35   Pareles, "The Dead's Gamble," B13.

36   See the interview with Jerry Garcia and Bob Weir on *The David Letterman Show* from April 13, 1982, accessed April 4, 2023, https://www.youtube.com/watch?v=4skH27r5dLc.

37   Pareles, "The Dead's Gamble," B13.

38   Pareles, "The Dead's Gamble," B13.

39   Pareles, "The Dead's Gamble," B7.

40   Pareles, "The Dead's Gamble," B13.

41   Light, "A Resurrection, of Sorts, for the Grateful Dead," C2.

42   For more on the band's concerts in Egypt in September 1978, see Getz and Dwork, *Deadhead's Taping Compendium*, 2:247–50. See also the discussion in McNally, *Long Strange Trip*, 508ff.

43   Meriwether, "The Dead Play Egypt," 127.

44   Meriwether, "The Dead Play Egypt," 126.

45   Meriwether, "The Dead Play Egypt," 127.

46   Meriwether, "The Dead Play Egypt," 130.

47   Meriwether, "The Dead Play Egypt," 131.

48 Meriwether, "The Dead Play Egypt," 131–32.

49 Meriwether, "The Dead Play Egypt," 131.

50 From the announcement "Holy S#%*! It's the Complete Europe '72 Box! On Over 60 Discs!," Dead.net, January 19, 2011, https://www.dead.net/features /europe-72/holy-s-it%E2%80%99s-complete-europe-%E2%80%9972-box-over -60-discs.

51 The rerelease was called *Europe '72: The Complete Recordings—All Music Edition*. GDP and Rhino also released each of the twenty-two concerts separately as multidisc sets.

52 Stewart, *On Longing*, 140.

53 David Lemieux quoted in Paumgarten, "Deadhead," 51.

54 Knopper, "Every Tape Tells a Story," 64.

55 Goodman, "Jerry Garcia," 73.

56 Goodman, "Jerry Garcia," 73.

57 From the minutes to the band meeting on August 14 cited above. All emphases in original.

58 David Browne, "Inside Grateful Dead's 'Truckin' Virtual Reality Experience," *Rolling Stone*, April 20, 2016, https://www.rollingstone.com/movies/movie -news/inside-grateful-deads-truckin-virtual-reality-experience-51073/.

CONCLUSION

1 From the press release "Recordings by Donna Summer, Prince and Dolly Parton Named to the National Recording Registry: Additions Mark 10th Anniversary of Registry," Library of Congress, May 24, 2012, https://www.loc.gov /item/prn-12-107/.

2 From a description included on the preorder page for the *May 1977* box set. See "Pre-order Grateful Dead–May 1977: GET SHOWN THE LIGHT and CORNELL 5/8/77," Rhino, February 16, 2017, https://www.rhino.com/article /pre-order-grateful-dead-may-1977-get-shown-the-light-and-cornell-5877.

3 Nicholas G. Meriwether, "The Road to Ithaca: Five Days in May," liner notes included with Grateful Dead, *May 1977: Get Shown the Light*, 18.

4 Meriwether, "Road to Ithaca," 42.

5 From Dick Latvala's notebook entry for May 8, 1977, Dick Latvala Papers, MS 333, ser. 1, box 1, folder 9 ("Dick Latvala Collection: Notebooks 1977, Feb.– June Entries"), Special Collections and Archives, University Library, University of California, Santa Cruz. This entry can be viewed at "Documenting the Dead: The Dick Latvala Collection," Dead.net, May 14, 2015, https://www. dead.net/features/blog/documenting-dead-dick-latvala-collection.

6 Dwork, "Seek and Ye Shall Find," 6.

7 David Lemieux, "Get Back Where You Belong," liner notes included with Grateful Dead, *May 1977: Get Shown the Light*, 6.

8 Dwork, "Keeper of the Flame," 22.

9 Lemieux, "Get Back Where You Belong," 6.

10 Lemieux, "Get Back Where You Belong," 7.

11   Interested readers may wish to see Jamie Howarth and Patrick J. Wolfe, "Correction of Wow and Flutter Effects in Analog Tape Transfers," Plangent Processes, accessed September 20, 2022, https://www.plangentprocesses.com /_files/ugd/2aa449_58e0c825b6f74ebdbb65ecd1390c2067.pdf.

12   "Pre-order Grateful Dead–May 1977."

13   Goldstein, "Flourishing Underground," 34.

14   Kaye, "[Review] *Live Dead*, the Grateful Dead," 44.

15   From a letter published in *Dead Relix* 2, no. 5 (September–October 1975): 1.

16   Dwork, "Seek and Ye Shall Find," 6.

17   From Hal Neely's liner notes to James Brown, *The James Brown Show* [*Live at the Apollo*].

18   Ulanov, "[Review] BG: 1938," 29.

19   "7,000 of 25,000 Theater Musicians Held Jobless," 1.

20   Johnson, "To the Editor of the Scientific American," 304. All subsequent citations are to this source.

21   "A Wonderful Invention," 304. All subsequent citations are to this source.

Bibliography

Althusser, Louis. *Lenin and Philosophy and Other Essays*. New York: Monthly Review Press, 2001.

Altman, Rick, ed. *Sound Theory Sound Practice*. New York: Routledge, 1992.

Anderson, Tim. "'Buried under the Fecundity of His Own Creations': Reconsidering the Recording Bans of the American Federation of Musicians, 1942–1944 and 1948." *American Music* 22, no. 2 (Summer 2004): 231–69.

Archetti, Enzo. "In the Popular Vein." *American Record Guide*, March 17, 1951, 253–54.

Auslander, Philip. "Live from Cyberspace: Or, I Was Sitting at My Computer This Guy Appeared He Thought I Was a Bot." *PAJ: A Journal of Performance and Art* 24, no. 1 (January 2002): 16–21.

Auslander, Philip. *Liveness: Performance in a Mediatized Culture*. 2nd ed. London: Routledge, 2008.

Bangs, Lester. "[Review] *Get Yer Ya-Ya's Out*, the Rolling Stones, London (NPS-5)." *Rolling Stone*, November 12, 1970, 32.

Barlow, John Perry. "Selling Wine Without Bottles: The Economy of Mind on the Global Net." In "The Past and Future of the Internet: A Symposium for John Perry Barlow," edited by James Boyle. Special symposium issue, *Duke Law and Technology Review* 18 (August 18, 2019): 8–31.

Benjamin, Walter. *Illuminations*. Translated by Harry Zohn. Edited by Hannah Arendt. Boston: Mariner Books, 2019.

Benjamin, Walter. *The Work of Art in the Age of Its Technological Reproducibility and Other Writings on Media*. Edited by Michael W. Jennings, Brigid Doherty, and Thomas Y. Levin. Cambridge, MA: Belknap Press of Harvard University Press, 2008.

Berg, Jeremy. "On the Removal of Download Access to Grateful Dead Soundboards from the Live Music Archive." *Popular Music and Society* 36, no. 2 (2013): 175–93.

Bessman, Jim. "Dead's Popularity Nudges Arista's Home Vid Launch." *Billboard*, October 3, 1987, 49–50.

black shadow. "[Review] *Live/Dead* (Grateful Dead) on Warner Bros.–Seven Arts." *San Francisco Good Times* 2, no. 49 (December 18, 1969): 14.

Boone, Graeme M. "Tonal and Expressive Ambiguity in 'Dark Star.'" In *Understanding Rock*, edited by John Covach and Graeme M. Boone, 171–210. New York: Oxford University Press, 1997.

Boyle, James, ed. "The Past and Future of the Internet: A Symposium for John Perry Barlow." Special symposium issue, *Duke Law and Technology Review* 18 (August 18, 2019).

Brendel, Alfred. *Music Sounded Out: Essays, Lectures, Interviews, Afterthoughts.* New York: Farrar, Straus and Giroux, 1991.

Brown, Lee B. "Phonography, Rock Records, and the Ontology of Recorded Music." *Journal of Aesthetics and Art Criticism* 58, no. 4 (Autumn 2000): 361–72.

Brown, Toni A. "Dan Healy, from the Vaults to the Pyramids: An Interview—Part 1." *Relix*, August 1991, 17–20.

Brown, Toni, Lee Abraham, and Ed Munson, eds. *Relix, the Book: The Grateful Dead Experience.* New York: Backbeat Books, 2009.

Browne, David. "Inside Grateful Dead's 'Truckin' Virtual Reality Experience." *Rolling Stone*, April 20, 2016. https://www.rollingstone.com/movies/movie-news/inside-grateful-deads-truckin-virtual-reality-experience-51073.

Burnett, Gary. "Colliding Norms, Community, and the Place of Online Information: The Case of archive.org." *Library Trends* 57, no. 4 (Spring 2009): 694–710.

Butler, Jan. "Clash of the Timbres: Recording Authenticity in the California Rock Scene, 1966–1968." In *The Relentless Pursuit of Tone: Timbre in Popular Music*, edited by Robert Fink, Melinda Latour, and Zachary Wallmark, 279–99. New York: Oxford University Press, 2018.

Carr, James Revell. "Black Muddy River: The Grateful Dead in the Continuum of American Folk Music." In *All Graceful Instruments: The Contexts of the Grateful Dead Phenomenon*, edited by Nicholas Meriwether, 117–55. Newcastle-upon-Tyne: Cambridge Scholars Press, 2007.

Cavicchi, Daniel. *Tramps Like Us: Music and Meaning among Springsteen Fans.* New York: Oxford University Press, 1998.

Christgau, Robert. "The Grateful Dead Are Rising Again." *New York Times*, July 27, 1969, D22.

Conners, Peter. *Cornell '77: The Music, the Myth, and the Magnificence of the Grateful Dead's Concert at Barton Hall.* Ithaca, NY: Cornell University Press, 2017.

Constanten, Tom. *Between Rock and Hard Places: A Musical Autobiodyssey.* Eugene, OR: Hulogosi, 1992.

Covach, John, and Graeme M. Boone, eds. *Understanding Rock.* New York: Oxford University Press, 1997.

Crowe, Cameron. "The Grateful Dead Flee Big Business." *Circus*, October 1973, 24–27.

Cummings, Alex Sayf. *Democracy of Sound.* New York: Oxford University Press, 2013.

Darling, Cary. "Music Monitor." *Billboard*, August 29, 1981, 30.

Davies, Stephen. *Musical Works and Performances: A Philosophical Exploration.* New York: Oxford University Press, 2001.

Davis, Clive, with Anthony DeCurtis. *The Soundtrack of My Life.* New York: Simon and Schuster, 2013.

Davis, Clive, with James Willwerth. *Clive: Inside the Record Business.* New York: Ballantine Books, 1974.

"Dead Is Alive." *Billboard*, July 25, 1987, 23–24.

Dewar, Cameron. "Music as Written: Boston." *Billboard*, June 22, 1963, 18.

Dodd, David G., and Diana Spaulding, eds. *The Grateful Dead Reader.* Oxford: Oxford University Press, 2000.

Dwork, John. "DDN Interviews Dick Latvala: Dead Tape Vault Archivist." *Dupree's Diamond News* 27 (Winter 1994): 10–17.

Dwork, John. "Keeper of the Flame: An Interview with Dick Latvala." *Dupree's Diamond News* 34 (Summer 1996): 18–32.

Dwork, John. "Seek and Ye Shall Find." *Dupree's Diamond News* 7 (June 1987): 6.

Eisenberg, Evan. *The Recording Angel: Music, Records and Culture from Aristotle to Zappa.* 2nd ed. New Haven, CT: Yale University Press, 2005.

Feuer, Jane. "The Concept of Live Television: Ontology as Ideology." In *Regarding Television*, edited by E. Ann Kaplan, 12–22. Frederick, MD: University Publications of America, 1983.

Fields, Karen E., and Barbara J. Fields. *Racecraft: The Soul of Inequality in American Life.* London: Verso, 2014.

Fink, Robert, Melinda Latour, and Zachary Wallmark, eds. *The Relentless Pursuit of Tone: Timbre in Popular Music.* New York: Oxford University Press, 2018.

Flick, Larry. "Arista Execs Rise for the Dead." *Billboard*, December 2, 1989, 26, 29.

Flory, Andrew. "Liveness and the Grateful Dead." *American Music* 37, no. 2 (Summer 2019): 123–45.

Foege, Alec. "Funeral for a Friend." *Rolling Stone*, September 21, 1995, 23–24, 26, 28.

Fong-Torres, Ben. "Not-So-Good Old Dead Records." *Rolling Stone*, October 28, 1971, 12.

Freeman, Kim. "Outa' the Box." *Billboard*, July 18, 1987, 10.

Garcia, Jerry, Charles Reich, and Jann Wenner. *Garcia: A Signpost to New Space.* Cambridge: Da Capo Press, 2003.

Gendron, Bernard. "Moldy Figs and Modernists: Jazz at War (1942–1946)." *Discourse* 15, no. 3 (Spring 1993): 130–57.

George-Warren, Holly, ed. *Garcia: By the Editors of Rolling Stone.* Boston: Little, Brown, 1995.

Getz, Michael M., and John R. Dwork. *The Deadhead's Taping Compendium: An In-Depth Guide to the Music of the Grateful Dead on Tape, Vol. 1, 1959-1974.* New York: Henry Holt, 1998.

Getz, Michael M., and John R. Dwork. *The Deadhead's Taping Compendium: An In-Depth Guide to the Music of the Grateful Dead on Tape, Vol. 2, 1975–1985.* New York: Henry Holt, 1999.

Getz, Michael M., and John R. Dwork. *The Deadhead's Taping Compendium: An In-Depth Guide to the Music of the Grateful Dead on Tape, Vol. 3, 1986–1995.* New York: Henry Holt, 2000.

Gilmore, Mikal. "The New Dawn of the Grateful Dead." *Rolling Stone,* July 16–July 30, 1987, 46–50, 55, 146–48.

Gleason, Ralph J. "Dead Like Live Thunder." *San Francisco Chronicle,* March 19, 1967, 31.

Gleason, Ralph J. *The Jefferson Airplane and the San Francisco Sound.* New York: Ballantine Books, 1969.

Gleason, Ralph J. "[Review] 'Live/Dead' (Warner Bros. 1830)." *San Francisco Examiner,* December 14, 1969, 63.

Goehr, Lydia. *The Imaginary Museum of Musical Works.* New York: Oxford University Press, 1992.

Goldstein, Richard. "Albumin." *Village Voice,* April 13, 1967, 19.

Goldstein, Richard. "The Flourishing Underground." *Village Voice,* March 2, 1967, 5, 7, 34.

Goodman, Fred. "Jerry Garcia: The Rolling Stone Interview." *Rolling Stone,* November 30, 1989, 66–68, 73–74, 118.

Gracyk, Theodore. *Rhythm and Noise: An Aesthetics of Rock.* Durham, NC: Duke University Press, 1996.

"The Grateful Dead, *Anthem of the Sun.*" Advertisement. *Crawdaddy* 19 (October 1968): 4.

"Grateful Dead, *In the Dark.*" Advertisement. *Billboard,* July 4, 1987, 12–13.

Greenfield, Robert. *Bear: The Life and Times of Augustus Owsley Stanley III.* New York: St. Martin's Press, 2016.

Grein, Paul. "'La Bamba' Gives Valens His 1st No. 1 Hit; Def Leppard's 'Hysteria' Album in Top 10." *Billboard,* August 29, 1987, 6.

Grein, Paul. "On Charts, It's Summer of Love Again; Suzanne Vega's Standing Solid in Top 20." *Billboard,* July 25, 1987, 6.

Grein, Paul. "Whitney, Barry Share Multiplatinum: Platinum Bow for the Dead in Sept." *Billboard,* October 10, 1987, 6, 98.

Groenke, Randy, and Mike Cramer. "One Afternoon, Long Ago . . . : A Previously Unpublished Interview with Jerry Garcia, 1967." *Golden Road* 7 (Summer 1985): 24–28.

Harvey, Katie A. "Embalming the Dead: Taping, Trading, and Collecting the Aura of the Grateful Dead." Master's thesis, Tufts University, 2009.

Heylin, Clinton. *Bootleg! The Rise and Fall of the Secret Recording Industry.* London: Omnibus Books, 2003.

Holt, Joseph. "Crowned Anarchy: Songs, Segues, and the Golden Road to Unlimited Devotion." In *Reading the Grateful Dead: A Critical Survey,* edited by Nicholas G. Meriwether, 139–45. Lanham, MD: Scarecrow Press, 2012.

"An Interview with Joseph N. Weber, 'Will Machine-Made Music Displace Real Music in Our Theaters?'" In *Music, Sound, and Technology in America: A Documentary History of Early Phonograph, Cinema, and Radio,* edited by Timothy D.

Taylor, Mark Katz, and Tony Grajeda, 226–29. Durham, NC: Duke University Press, 2012.

"Is Art to Have a Tyrant?" Advertisement. *Atlanta Constitution*, September 8, 1930, 3.

"Is the Robot Fooling You?" Advertisement. *Atlanta Constitution*, May 12, 1930, 2.

Jackson, Blair. *Grateful Dead Gear*. San Francisco: Backbeat Books, 2006.

Jackson, Blair. "Record Review: *Steal Your Face*, by the Grateful Dead (Grateful Dead Records) and *We've Got a Live One Here*, by Commander Cody and His Lost Planet Airmen (Warner Brothers)." *BAM*, August 1976, 5.

Jarnow, Jesse. *Heads: A Biography of Psychedelic America*. New York: Da Capo Press, 2016.

Johnson, Edward H. "To the Editor of the Scientific American." *Scientific American*, November 17, 1877, 304.

Kaler, Michael. "How the Grateful Dead Learned to Jam." *Grateful Dead Studies* 1 (2013/2014): 11–32.

Kaplan, E. Ann, ed. *Regarding Television*. Frederick, MD: University Publications of America, 1983.

Katzenjammer, Basho. "Grateful Dead Pig Backlash." *East Village Other*, October 6, 1971, 15.

Kaye, Lenny. "[Review] Grateful Dead, *Grateful Dead*, Warners 2WS-1935." *Rolling Stone*, November 11, 1971, 55–56.

Kaye, Lenny. "[Review] *Live Dead*, the Grateful Dead (Warners, 1830)." *Rolling Stone*, February 7, 1970, 44.

Keightley, Keir. "Live Album." In *Continuum Encyclopedia of Popular Music of the World*. Vol. 1, *Media, Industry, Society*, edited by John Shepherd, Paul Oliver, Peter Wicke, David Horn, and Dave Laing, 620. London: Continuum, 2003.

Kelley, Robin D. G. "Without a Song: New York Musicians Strike Out against Technology." In *Three Strikes: Miners, Musicians, Salesgirls, and the Fighting Spirit of Labor's Last Century*, edited by Howard Zinn, Dana Frank, and Robin D. G. Kelley, 121–55. Boston: Beacon Press, 2001.

Kippel, Les. "The History of Taping through the Eyes of One Deadhead." In *Relix, the Book: The Grateful Dead Experience*, edited by Toni Brown, Lee Abraham, and Ed Munson, 121–22. New York: Backbeat Books, 2009.

Knoll, Steve. "Majors Face 'Pressing' Problem." *Variety*, February 18, 1981, 1, 96.

Knopper, Steve. "Every Tape Tells a Story." *Billboard*, March 18, 2017, 64.

Kopp, George. "Grateful Dead in Concert Due on RCA Videodisk." *Billboard*, October 18, 1980, 56.

Kraft, James P. *Stage to Studio: Musicians and the Sound Revolution, 1890–1950*. Baltimore: John Hopkins University Press, 1996.

Kreutzmann, Bill, with Benjy Eisen. *Deal: My Three Decades of Drumming, Dreams, and Drugs with the Grateful Dead*. New York: St. Martin's Griffin, 2015.

Leigh, Tony. "Live Sound of the Grateful Dead." *KRLA Beat*, January 27, 1968, 19.

Lesh, Phil. *Searching for the Sound: My Life with the Grateful Dead*. New York: Little, Brown, 2005.

Levin, Michael. "Mix Reviews the Goodman Carnegie LP." *Downbeat*, January 12, 1951, 14–15.

Light, Alan. "A Resurrection, of Sorts, for the Grateful Dead." *New York Times*, July 10, 2006, C2.

Loren, Richard, with Stephen Abney. *High Notes: A Rock Memoir*. Damariscotta, ME: East Pond Publishing, 2014.

Lydon, Michael. "An Evening with the Grateful Dead." *Rolling Stone*, September 20, 1970, 22–23.

Lydon, Michael. "The Grateful Dead." *Rolling Stone*, August 23, 1969, 15–19, 22–24.

Malvinni, David. *Grateful Dead and the Art of Rock Improvisation*. Lanham, MD: Scarecrow Press, 2013.

Marcus, Greil. "The Bootleg LP's." *Rolling Stone*, February 7, 1970, 37–38.

Marshall, Lee. "For and against the Record Industry: An Introduction to Bootleg Collectors and Tape Traders." *Popular Music* 22, no. 1 (January 2003): 57–72.

Mayfield, Geoff. "Over the Counter: Dead Zone." *Billboard*, May 18, 1991, 93.

McDonough, Jack. "The Dead Are Anything But." *Billboard*, June 21, 1986, 22, 25.

McNally, Dennis. *A Long Strange Trip: The Inside History of the Grateful Dead*. New York: Broadway Books, 2002.

Meriwether, Nicholas, ed. *All Graceful Instruments: The Contexts of the Grateful Dead Phenomenon*. Newcastle-upon-Tyne: Cambridge Scholars Press, 2007.

Meriwether, Nicholas G. "The Dead Play Egypt, Thirty Years Later: Myth, Memory, and Marketing." In *Reading the Grateful Dead: A Critical Survey*, edited by Nicholas G. Meriwether, 122–35. London: Scarecrow Press, 2012.

Meriwether, Nicholas G., ed. *Reading the Grateful Dead: A Critical Survey*. Lanham, MD: Scarecrow Press, 2012.

Middleton, Richard. *Studying Popular Music*. Milton Keynes: Open University Press, 1990.

Miller, Jim. "[Review] *Anthem of the Sun*, the Grateful Dead (Warner Brothers WS 1749)." *Rolling Stone*, September 28, 1968, 28.

Morris, Chris. "CDs Sail Past LPs in $ Volume." *Billboard*, July 4, 1987, 1, 84.

Morton, John Fass. *Backstory in Blue: Ellington at Newport '56*. New Brunswick, NJ: Rutgers University Press, 2008.

Muhlberg, Dylan. "Grateful Web Interview with Len Dell'Amico." Grateful Web, August 11, 2018. https://www.gratefulweb.com/articles/grateful-web-interview -len-dellamico.

"Music? A Picture No *Robot* Can Paint!" Advertisement. *Chicago Daily Tribune*, August 4, 1930, 18.

"My Next Imita-a-ashun." Advertisement. *Austin Statesman*, October 13, 1930, 3.

Nash, Michael. "Grateful Tapers: An Informal History of Recording the Dead." *Audio* (January 1988): 54–63.

Neumann, Mark, and Timothy A. Simpson. "Smuggled Sound: Bootleg Recording and the Pursuit of Popular Memory." *Symbolic Interaction* 20, no. 4 (1997): 319–41.

O'Donnell, Shaugn. "American Chaos: Charles Ives and the Grateful Dead." In *The Grateful Dead in Concert: Essays in Improvisation*, edited by Jim Tuedio and Stan Spector, 58–70. Jefferson, NC: McFarland, 2010.

"O Fairest Flower! No Sooner Blown but Blasted!" Advertisement. *New York Times*, November 10, 1930, 16.

Olsson, Ulf. *Listening for the Secret: The Grateful Dead and the Politics of Improvisation*. Oakland: University of California Press, 2017.

Palmer, Landon. "The Portable Recording Studio: Documentary Filmmaking and Live Album Recording, 1967–1969." *Journal of the International Association for the Study of Popular Music* 6, no. 2 (2016): 49–69.

Pareles, Jon. "The Dead's Gamble: Free Music for Sale." *New York Times*, December 3, 2005, B7, B13.

Paumgarten, Nick. "Deadhead: Annals of Obsession." *New Yorker*, November 26, 2012, 40–48, 50–55.

Perry, Charles. "Alembic: Sound Wizards to the Grateful Dead." Audio supplement, *Rolling Stone*, September 27, 1973, 49–50.

Perry, Charles. "A New Life for the Dead." *Rolling Stone*, November 22, 1973, 48–52, 54, 56, 58.

Peters, John Durham. "Helmholtz, Edison, and Sound History." In *Memory Bytes: History, Technology, and Digital Culture*, edited by Lauren Rabinovitz and Abraham Geil, 177–98. Durham, NC: Duke University Press, 2004.

"Pop Spotlight: *The James Brown Show* (King 826)." *Billboard*, June 8, 1963, 25.

Porcello, Thomas. "Speaking of Sound: Language and the Professionalization of Sound-Recording Engineers." *Social Studies of Science* 34, no. 5 (October 2004): 733–58.

Rabinovitz, Lauren, and Abraham Geil, eds. *Memory Bytes: History, Technology, and Digital Culture*. Durham, NC: Duke University Press, 2004.

Reeder, Nicholas. "The Co-evolution of Improvised Rock and Live Sound: The Grateful Dead, Phish, and Jambands." PhD diss., Brown University, 2014.

Reich, Charles, and Jann Wenner. "Jerry Garcia: The Rolling Stone Interview (Part Two)." *Rolling Stone*, February 3, 1972, 28–36.

Research Company of America. *The National Crisis for Live Music and Musicians: A Nationwide Survey and Analysis of the 20% "Cabaret Tax" and Its Depressive Effects on Employment, Federal Revenues and Music Culture*. New York: American Federation of Musicians, 1955.

Ressner, Jeffrey. "Stellar Slate of LPs Set for Release in '83 First Quarter." *Cashbox*, December 25, 1982, 9, 20.

Richardson, Peter. *No Simple Highway: A Cultural History of the Grateful Dead*. New York: St. Martin's Griffin, 2015.

"The Robot as an Entertainer." Advertisement. *Daily Boston Globe*, October 28, 1929, 5.

"The Robot Sings of Love." Advertisement. *Atlanta Constitution*, August 19, 1930, 3.

Rosen, Charley. "Mr. 'Tapes' of Brooklyn: He Rules the Grateful Dead Tape Empire." *Rolling Stone*, October 11, 1973, 22.

Roy, Elodie A. *Media, Materiality and Memory*. London: Routledge, 2020.

Sanden, Paul. *Liveness in Modern Music: Musicians, Technology, and the Perception of Performance*. New York: Routledge, 2013.

Schuyten, Peter J. "RCA Videodisks Due in 1981." *New York Times*, December 7, 1979, D1, D6.

Scott, John W., Stu Nixon, and Mike Dolgushkin. *Deadbase 50: Celebrating 50 Years of the Grateful Dead*. San Francisco: Watermark Press and Pacific Standard Print, 2015.

Sculatti, Gene. "San Francisco Bay Rock." *Crawdaddy* 6 (November 1966): 24–26.

"The Serenade Mechanistic." Advertisement. *Washington Post*, December 1, 1930, 11.

Seachrist, Steven. "*Europe '72*: Notes on Song Selections and Overdubs for the Original Album and Volume 2." *Grateful Dead Guide*, January 31, 2014. http:// deadessays.blogspot.com/2014/01/the-europe-72-overdubs-guest-post.html.

"7,000 of 25,000 Theater Musicians Held Jobless." *Film Daily*, October 28, 1929, 1, 3.

Shenk, David, and Steve Silberman. *Skeleton Key: A Dictionary for Deadheads*. New York: Doubleday, 1994.

Shepherd, John, Paul Oliver, Peter Wicke, David Horn, and Dave Laing, eds. *Continuum Encyclopedia of Popular Music of the World*. Vol. 1, *Media, Industry, Society*. London: Continuum, 2003.

Smith, Bernard B. "What's Petrillo Up To?" *Harper's Magazine*, December 1, 1942, 90–96.

Snyder-Scumpy, Patrick. "[Review] *Europe '72*: Grateful Dead Warner Bros. (3WX 2668)." *Crawdaddy* 21 (February 1973): 73–74.

"The Sound Ideas of Dan Healy." *Golden Road*, Winter 1985, 8–13.

Sousa, John Philip. "The Menace of Mechanical Music." In *Music, Sound, and Technology in America: A Documentary History of Early Phonograph, Cinema, and Radio*, edited by Timothy D. Taylor, Mark Katz, and Tony Grajeda, 113–22. Durham, NC: Duke University Press, 2012.

Sterne, Jonathan. *The Audible Past: Cultural Origins of Sound Reproduction*. Durham, NC: Duke University Press, 2003.

Stewart, Susan. *On Longing: Narratives of the Miniature, the Gigantic, the Souvenir, the Collection*. Durham, NC: Duke University Press, 1993.

Stratton, Jon. "Capitalism and Romantic Ideology in the Record Business." *Popular Music* 3 (1983): 143–56.

"Survivors: Grateful Fans Camp Out for Tickets." *Newsweek*, September 23, 1980, 9.

Tackley, Catherine. *Benny Goodman's Famous 1938 Carnegie Hall Jazz Concert*. Oxford: Oxford University Press, 2012.

Taylor, Timothy D., Mark Katz, and Tony Grajeda, eds. *Music, Sound, and Technology in America: A Documentary History of Early Phonograph, Cinema, and Radio*. Durham, NC: Duke University Press, 2012.

Théberge, Paul. "The 'Sound' of Music: Technological Rationalization and the Production of Popular Music." *New Formations* 8 (Summer 1989): 99–111.

Thornton, Sarah. *Club Cultures: Music, Media, and Subcultural Capital*. Hanover, NH: Wesleyan University Press, 1996.

Tuedio, Jim, and Stan Spector, eds. *The Grateful Dead in Concert: Essays on Live Improvisation*. Jefferson, NC: McFarland, 2010.

Turkle, Sherry, ed. *Evocative Objects: Things We Think With*. Cambridge, MA: MIT Press, 2007.

Ulanov, Barry. "[Review] BG: 1938." *Metronome*, February 1951, 29.

Wadsley, Pat. "Video Possibilities Are Mulled in 'Exploring Other Areas' Panel." *Billboard*, October 17, 1981, 33, 38.

Walters, Charley. "[Review] *Steal Your Face*, Grateful Dead, Grateful Dead Records, GD-LA620-J2/GD-104." *Rolling Stone*, August 26, 1976, 60.

Warfield, Patrick. "John Philip Sousa and 'The Menace of Mechanical Music.'" *Journal of the Society for American Music* 3, no. 4 (2009): 431–63.

Weber, Joseph N. "Canned Music—Is It Taking the Romance from Our Lives?" In *Music, Sound, and Technology in America: A Documentary History of Early Phonograph, Cinema, and Radio*, edited by Timothy D. Taylor, Mark Katz, and Tony Grajeda, 123–26. Durham, NC: Duke University Press, 2012.

Williams, Charles. "Mr. Petrillo's Hopeless War." *The Nation*, October 3, 1942, 291–93.

Williams, Paul. "The Golden Road: A Report on San Francisco." *Crawdaddy* 10 (July–August 1967): 5–14.

Williams, Richard. "[Review] Grateful Dead: 'Live Dead' (Warner Bros.)." *Melody Maker*, March 14, 1970, 28.

Wolfe, Tom. *The Electric Kool-Aid Acid Test*. New York: Farrar, Straus and Giroux, 1968.

"A Wonderful Invention—Speech Capable of Indefinite Repetition from Automatic Records." *Scientific American*, November 17, 1877, 304.

Wood, Brent. "The Musical Imagination of Phil Lesh: The Grateful Dead's Difference Engine." *Popular Musicology Online*, no. 4 (2009). http://www.popular-musicology-online.com/issues/04/wood-01.html.

Wurtzler, Steve. "'She Sang Live, But the Microphone Was Turned Off': The Live, the Recorded, and the Subject of Representation." In *Sound Theory Sound Practice*, edited by Rick Altman, 87–103. New York: Routledge, 1992.

Young, Charles M. "The Awakening of the Dead." *Rolling Stone*, June 16, 1977, 11–13.

Zak, Albin J., III. *I Don't Sound Like Nobody: Remaking Music in 1950s America*. Ann Arbor: University of Michigan Press, 2010.

Zak, Albin J., III. *The Poetics of Rock: Cutting Tracks, Making Records*. Berkeley: University of California Press, 2001.

Zimmerman, Nadya. "Consuming Nature: The Grateful Dead's Performance of an Anti-commercial Counterculture." *American Music* 24, no. 2 (Summer 2006): 194–216.

Zinn, Howard, Dana Frank, and Robin D. G. Kelley, eds. *Three Strikes: Miners, Musicians, Salesgirls, and the Fighting Spirit of Labor's Last Century*. Boston: Beacon Press, 2001.

Zwerling, Andy. "[Review] *Workingman's Dead*, Grateful Dead (Warner Bros. WS 1869)." *Rolling Stone*, July 23, 1970, 32.

SELECT DISCOGRAPHY

(Refer to the index for a complete list of recordings that appear in the text.)
Brown, James. *The James Brown Show* [*"Live" at the Apollo*]. King LP 826, 1963. LP.

Ellington, Duke. *Ellington at Newport*. Columbia CL-934, 1956. LP.

Grateful Dead. *Anthem of the Sun: 50th Anniversary Deluxe Edition*. Rhino Records R2-564265, 2018. CD.

Grateful Dead. *Dick's Picks, Volume One (Tampa Florida 12/19/73)*. GDCD 40182 Grateful Dead Records, 1993. CD.

Grateful Dead. *Dick's Picks, Volume Three (Pembroke Pines, Florida 5/22/77)*. GDCD 4021 Grateful Dead Records, 1995. CD.

Grateful Dead. *Europe '72*. 3 WX 2668 Warner Bros. Records, 1972. LP.

Grateful Dead. *Grateful Dead*. 2WS 1935 Warner Bros. Records, 1971. LP.

Grateful Dead. *Live/Dead*. 2WS 1830 Warner Bros. Records, 1969. LP.

Grateful Dead. *May 1977: Get Shown the Light*. Grateful Dead Records/Rhino Records R2 557479, 2017. CD.

Grateful Dead. *One from the Vault*. GDCD 40132 Grateful Dead Records, 1991. CD

Grateful Dead. *Reckoning*. R2 73282 Rhino, 2006. CD.

Grateful Dead. *Two from the Vault*. GDCD-41062 Grateful Dead Records, 1992. CD.

Grateful Dead. *Vintage Dead*. SUN-5001 Sunflower, 1970. LP.

VIDEOGRAPHY

Marre, Jeremy, director. *The Grateful Dead: Anthem to Beauty*. Eagle Vision EREDV014, 1998. DVD.

Index